HANDBOOK OF PATIENT EDUCATION

Ann Haggard, RN, MS, PhD
Huntington Memorial Hospital
Pasadena, California

AN ASPEN PUBLICATION®
Aspen Publishers, Inc.
1989
Rockville, Maryland
Royal Tunbridge Wells

Library of Congress Cataloging-in-Publication D.

Haggard, A.
Handbook of patient education
Bibliography:
Includes ind.
1. Patient education. I. Tit
R727.4.H33   1989   615.5'07   88-79
ISBN: 0-8342-004.

Editorial Services: Susan Bedfor.

Library of Congress Catalog Card Number: 88-790
ISBN: 0-8342-0041-

Printed in the United States of Americ

1 2 3 4 5

To all patient educators, who labor so hard and so well.

Table of Contents

About the Author

Preface

Patient education is a unique branch on the tree of knowledge. In no other field does the educator have such a direct impact on the lives of students; it is an endeavor that can be both rewarding and frustrating. This book was designed to provide you, the patient educator, with information to make your job easier. Whether you teach in a hospital, an outpatient facility, or a home health agency or are an independent practitioner, the tools and ideas are here to help you.

The longer one works in patient education, the more tips and teaching techniques one learns. As you read through this collection of "things that have worked for me and for others," mesh the information with your own experience. I hope that the book not only will give you information but, more important, will act as a stimulant for your own imagination and creativity.

Since this book is intended as a tool for both experienced educators and those just starting out, for coordinators of established programs, and for staff nurses working at the bedside, I have tried to gather a wide range of both theoretical and practical information.

Chapter 1 introduces the whole concept of patient education, including its professional and fiscal implications. A discussion of who should teach explores the roles and responsibilities of physicians, nurses, and allied health professionals, including potential conflicts. The idea of discharge planning is introduced, since discharge planning and patient education are inextricably entwined.

Chapter 2 discusses the principles of adult learning, including the problems that can result from treating adults like children. The issue of responsibility is raised, since clients must take responsibility for their own learning—the nurse can provide only the facts they need to carry out that responsibility. If we try to take over that burden we may be hindering rather than helping our patients.

Chapter 3 explores needs assessment techniques, learning styles and their impact on learning, and the influences that cultural differences can have on patient education.

Chapter 4 examines the role of motivation in learning from the standpoint of both intrinsic patient motivation and the nurse's capacity to touch motivational wellsprings within the patient.

Chapter 5 defines the planning process: writing goals and objectives, obtaining patient agreement, and developing and implementing the plan. This process includes the importance of communicating the plan to others and meshing the patient education plan with overall discharge planning.

Chapter 6 looks at the role of the family in patient education. Gaining the support of family members for home care, teaching the family, helping with problem solving, and linking patient and family with community resources are vital parts of a patient educator's job.

Chapter 7 analyzes the tools of patient education. The discussion covers composing and using written materials, preparing displays, and creating and using audiovisual resources.

Chapter 8 covers teaching techniques for both one-on-one and group instruction. Special approaches for both older patients and patients with reading problems are also considered.

Chapter 9 discusses patient education in outpatient settings—surgicenters, clinics, physicians' offices, emergency departments, and the home.

Chapter 10 focuses on the importance of adequate documentation of educational efforts. Different charting systems such as problem-oriented charting and nursing diagnostic approaches are adapted to patient education needs.

Chapter 11 looks at evaluation techniques, both to determine the effectiveness of patient learning and to assess the effectiveness of the program, including instructor performance and quality assurance measures.

Chapter 12 concludes the book by discussing patient education and professional nursing practice, including career ladder concepts, bioethical considerations, future trends, and new opportunities.

You will notice that the issue of reimbursement comes up over and over again throughout the book. We can no longer rest on our laurels where patient education is concerned. These days we must be concerned with cost recovery issues as well as issues of quality and patient support. Yet the final issue is the patient—and all of your patients are counting on you to give them the information that they need in order to live the best lives they can.

Good luck!

Ann Haggard

1

Introduction

What is the most important thing that you can do for your patients? That is a tough question when you think about all of the vital tasks you perform. But if the patient's long-range outcomes and life style are considered, the most important single action of a caregiver is preparation for patient self-care. If our patients cannot maintain or improve their health status once they are on their own, all of the sophisticated surgery, medicine, treatments, and therapy will have been wasted.

Despite the importance of patient self-care, some caregivers do not value patient teaching. Since it always has the lowest priority, teaching self-care may be done hastily or not at all. Caregivers who follow this philosophy not only block patients from achieving their potential but ultimately shortchange both their own careers and the hospitals that employ them. How can this happen to dedicated, caring professionals?

PROBLEMS IN PATIENT EDUCATION

Teaching patients what they need to know in order to care optimally for themselves has been a nursing priority for many years. Most nurses had an instinctive realization that providing knowledge about self-care was a necessary component of the nursing process. As health care grew in sophistication, two things happened: research proved that patient education did indeed help patients and their families, and new technology and patterns in patient care pulled nurses away from the bedside.

Now it is often difficult for nurses to take the time necessary for effective patient education. Tight staffing, ever-increasing paperwork, and the multitude of new responsibilities and new technology put terrible pressures on the staff. When not everything can be done and priorities must be set, education is often one of the

1

first things to go. The ultimate outcome of this understandable but misguided choice is that patients go home with no idea of what to do when they get there, resulting in more frequent admissions and longer hospital stays.

One of the aims of this book is to provide nurses with strategies for teaching patients in time-effective ways. Adapt these to your practice. Once patient education is incorporated into the care of every patient, every time, it becomes a habit.

KEY TO PATIENT COMPLIANCE

Costs of Noncompliance

One of the stated aims of most patient education programs is improved patient compliance with prescribed regimens. The general mean rate of noncompliance in all illnesses in the United States is about 33 percent.[1] That statistic is appalling enough, but it combines all illnesses, major and minor. With the more serious disorders that require profound revisions in life style, the noncompliance rate is probably much higher.

Diabetes leaps to almost every nurse's mind when serious diseases requiring extensive patient education are discussed. Every American has one chance in five of developing this disease.[2] A 1982 study revealed that 80 percent of patients made errors in insulin administration, 75 percent failed to comply with diet requirements, 50 percent demonstrated poor foot care, and 95 percent performed incorrect urine testing.[3] Yet another study found that 50 percent of diabetic patients were administering incorrect insulin dosages.[4] In research conducted in a diabetic children's summer camp—a much more controlled situation than the home setting—the diet plan was broken by 61 percent of the children.[5]

This evidence of noncompliance becomes even more ominous in light of the complications caused by poor control of blood sugar levels. Diabetes is the third leading cause of death in the United States, with a thousand people dying of the disease each day. Associated complications and risks for diabetics include the following: blindness, twenty-five times that for the general population; renal disease, seventeen times; gangrene, five times; and heart attack and stroke, two times. Diabetes accounts for 50–70 percent of all nontraumatic amputations in the country. Both the prevalence and incidence of diabetes have increased steadily, with 1650 new cases of diabetes diagnosed every day. Kilo states, "Because of the genetic factor, the incidence of diabetes will double every 15 years, so that by the year 2010 there should be some 40 million diabetics in the United States alone."[6]

These sobering statistics indicate a national problem of growing seriousness—and chilling implications for health care. As the number of diabetics grows, how will care be delivered? And who will pay for it? The economic toll of diabetes in the United States is currently about ten billion dollars a year.[7] Projected future costs based on increasing numbers of patients predict a national burden of appalling size.

What of the human costs of noncompliance? Statistics recited about blindness and gangrene isolate us from the personal suffering caused by a disease process out of control, ravaging the lives of patient and family. When you talk with a lonely elderly woman whose joy and consolation have always been reading, and hear her expression of grief over being unable to read even large print, then the costs become vividly real. How did the health care system fail her? How can we assist these patients—and all of the others who need information and self-care skills—to learn about their illnesses and the care that only they can give?

Impact of Education on Compliance

The entire concept of patient education postulates that education leads to increased compliance with the medical regimen. This may be too simplistic an approach: education does not always cause learning, and compliance may not always be the correct response. These issues are discussed in more depth in Chapter 4, but most health care professionals will accept the idea that compliance with ordered diet and medication regimens is a goal of patient education.

Compliance should lead to such positive results as better disease control, fewer complications, decreased admissions, and shorter hospital stays. These things are measurable. Research is being done to discover the impact of patient education on both compliance and the desired results of compliance. In one study, groups of diabetic patients were given intensive three-day courses on diabetes care. During the six-week follow-up period, significant declines in both fasting blood sugar and glycosylated hemoglobin levels were seen.[8] As encouraging as these results sound, further study is necessary to determine the long-term effects of such courses and whether such lengthy sessions are required.

An outpatient diabetes education program in North Dakota cut the number of days participants spent in the hospital by 78 percent, resulting in substantial savings for third-party payers. Blue Cross of North Dakota was so impressed that it agreed to cover the costs of the patients' tuition.[9]

In Maine, an audit of 898 hospital charts of diabetic patients indicated that 16.5 percent of admissions were probably caused by lack of self-management skills and that 19.9 percent were readmitted within the year for similar complications. A model patient education program was offered in twenty-five hospitals and six health centers throughout the state. A 12-month follow-up for the 461 patients who completed the course found that there were 33 percent fewer hospitalizations in the year following education than in the previous year. Using average length of stay data, cost savings were estimated to be $203,791. The cost of educating the 461 patients was $69,150, resulting in an estimated net savings of $135,641.[10]

Two issues arise at this point, one intangible and the other very tangible indeed.

First, what unstated human benefits result from the more measurable ones? Behind the statistics on decreased length of stay and fewer complications lies a wealth of personal positives. Each day not spent in the hospital may be a day spent with loved ones. Improvements in disease control and preventing or minimizing complications result in a better quality of life for patient and family. These emotional benefits may be hard to measure, but they are very real to the people involved—and perhaps are more important than the results amenable to statistical analysis.

The second issue involves money. No more vital or realistic measure exists in today's health care environment. If educators can prove that their efforts result in cash savings for their employers, the future of patient education is assured.

IMPLICATIONS FOR FISCAL HEALTH

Most people involved in patient education have taken the position that the activities are valuable in and of themselves. Education is a good thing: therefore it should be done. Unfortunately, that axiom is not enough any more. In our cost-conscious, cost-contained, prospectively paid environment, administrators are casting a coldly pragmatic gaze on every program. It is not enough to be good any more. It is not even enough to *do* good—you must be able to prove that your efforts in some way benefit the institution.

Look for the financial positives in patient education. If it costs money to do it, how does it correspondingly bring in money? Few patient education programs make a profit, so the stress is not on reimbursement but on cost savings and cost recovery. Cost savings result when hospital stays are shortened or the utilization of services decreases. Cost recovery occurs when someone, third-party payer or the patient, pays a fee for services.

The cost/benefit of patient education intervention was evaluated in a study of pediatric patients with the same diagnosis and initial treatment. Two groups of patients, one receiving education and one not, were followed for utilization of health care services resulting from noncompliant behavior. The incidence of complications was much lower in the group that had received education, resulting in cost savings of seven to one compared with the other group.[11]

In another example, a randomized, prospective trial of self-care educational activities was carried out by the Rhode Island Group Health Association. The health education implements consisted of a newsletter, self-care packages on health problems of the elderly, resource books, and a telephone information system. The experimental group visited the Plan 15.2 percent less frequently than did the control group. Cost savings were estimated at two dollars saved in medical expenses for every dollar spent on educational activities.[12]

If you have not attempted such studies of cost effectiveness, seriously consider doing so. Be able to prove that your teaching activities with patients actually save money for the organization by shortening hospital stays, preventing complications, or increasing patient satisfaction. This last benefit is an issue of growing importance. As hospitals grow more competitive, patient and visitor satisfaction that leads to return utilization of services becomes crucial. Since consumers want and need information and self-care training, this is an avenue that should not be neglected in your search for benefits.

Besides focusing on cost savings and patient satisfaction, do not forget cost recovery. Explore methods of reimbursement. While the law does not specifically identify patient education programs as covered services, according to *Medicare and Medicaid Guide*, reimbursement may be made under Medicare for programs "furnished by providers of services to the extent that the programs are appropriate, integral parts in the rendition of covered services which are reasonable and necessary for the treatment of the individual's illness or injury."[13] For example, educational activities by nurses to prepare patients for discharge are reimbursable as part of covered routine nursing care.

Outpatient education has an even better chance of being reimbursed. In some states Blue Cross/Blue Shield has been allowing payment of outpatient diabetic education if it follows guidelines set by accepted associations (such as the Association of Diabetic Educators). The most telling point for third-party payers is still the projected (and proven) cost savings of the education. If you can demonstrate that your learners take better care of themselves and experience fewer hospitalizations, reimbursement becomes much easier to obtain.

Another approach to outpatient cost recovery involves direct payment by the patient. Some people shy away from this alternative, believing that it is somehow wrong to charge patients directly. But why should it be? If outpatient education is a valuable service, if patients benefit from it, they should be willing to pay for it, and most patients are willing. If third-party payment is hard to arrange in your area (and the difficulty varies with locale), set up a fee-for-service arrangement, perhaps with sliding-scale charges dependent on ability to pay. Not only will this demonstrate cost recovery to the powers that be, it may cause patients to value the information even more. Human nature often concludes that something free cannot be worth much, and even a token fee places automatic value on the commodity.

PROFESSIONAL NURSING PRACTICE AND PATIENT EDUCATION

To this point the discussion has centered on pragmatic issues such as patient compliance, decreased incidence of complications, and money, but another area deserves serious consideration: the importance of patient education to professional nursing practice. Teaching patients and their families has been recognized as an integral part of nursing by such authorities as the American Nurses Association, the Association of Diabetes Educators, and the Board of Registered Nursing in most states. But until everyone in the profession internalizes the importance of patient education, it joins professional autonomy and nationwide standards and preparation as unfulfilled dreams.

Only by working together as responsible professionals can nurses establish their own area of practice, interdependent with but distinct from those of physicians, respiratory therapists, physical therapists, social workers, and all of the other professions in health care. Educating patients and their families should be an important part of nursing's responsibilities. Who else is in such an ideal position to present information, follow up on instructions, observe patient actions, and give feedback and reinforcement?

These actions are vital to preparing patients for effective self-care and necessary life style changes, yet in many hospitals and clinics education is "catch as catch can." No integrated plans exist for routine education of the institution's clients. Hospitals, particularly, often fail to provide these services—a direct violation of the standards of the Joint Commission on Accreditation of Healthcare Organizations (Joint Commission).

The Joint Commission's parent, the American Hospital Association, states:

> The hospital has a responsibility to provide patient education services as an integral part of high-quality, cost-effective care. Patient education services should enable patients and their families and friends, when appropriate, to make informed decisions about their health; to manage their illnesses; and to implement followup care at home. Effective and efficient patient education services require planning and coordination, and responsibility for such planning and coordination should be assigned. The hospital should also provide the necessary staff and financial resources.[14]

Most nurses would agree the last sentence is perhaps the most important. In order to carry out the directives in the first part of the statement, someone must have time available actually to provide services. Who should that someone be?

Patient Education Coordinator or Nurse at the Bedside?

Who should perform the education required for patients to function effectively at home? Traditionally this has been done by the staff nurses caring for the patients, as part of their regular care. Recently, however, many hospitals have created the position of patient education coordinator. The person in this position has the responsibility for creating the hospital's patient education program, sharing it with the staff, and in many cases even providing education to the patients.

For hospitals trying to decide whether to use a patient education coordinator or to keep the responsibility for patient education at the staff nurse level, an analysis of the pros and cons of such a position might prove helpful (see Table 1-1). Not only do the positives outweigh the negatives, most of the negatives can be overcome with a little effort. When a patient education coordinator is hired, the role must be clearly defined and communicated to all of the staff. This role and the role of the staff nurse deserve a closer look.

Role of the Patient Education Coordinator

Since there are no nationally accepted standards for the role of patient education coordinator, each institution must develop its own. The Michigan Society for Healthcare Education and Training and the Society for Public Health Education— Great Lakes Chapter combined to develop recommended competencies for patient education coordinators:

- policy development
- management competencies
- coordination of institution-wide patient education services
- consultation
- training and continuing education
- program development for target populations
- evaluation of patient education services
- generic knowledge and skills[15]

Table 1-1 Analysis of Patient Education Coordinator Position

Benefits	Drawbacks
• One person is responsible for all of the education of patients (when all are responsible, no one is)	• Staff nurses may decide that they have no responsibility for teaching patients
• The coordinator can keep up with new developments in the field	• Teaching may not be done when the coordinator is ill or on vacation
• The coordinator can provide workshops and inservices for the staff	• A hiring mistake could have serious impact on the quality of patient education in the institution
• New materials and audiovisual software can be screened, purchased, and developed by the coordinator	
• Required documentation and records can be centralized	
• Individual patients and the program can be evaluated in a centralized, organized way	
• The coordinator can be hired with specialized skills in education	

Notice that nowhere in the list is "all teaching for all patients" stated. No one person can possibly meet the educational needs of a hospital full of patients. Enlisting the help of the staff and making clear the need for bedside teaching and reinforcement are a coordinator's most critical responsibilities.

Although the nature of the coordinator's role requires political skills as well as teaching skills, it is important for the coordinator to model excellent bedside teaching for the staff. Besides setting hospitalwide policy, composing forms, keeping records, serving on committees, and all of the other tasks required of such a position, the coordinator must find time actually to teach patients. To delegate this task totally removes the coordinator from the ultimate purpose of the role and can cause a fatal loss of credibility with the staff. For most educators this is not a problem, but some institutions committed to excellence in patient teaching have a coordinator supervising a number of instructors. It is not enough to audit the instructors occasionally; the coordinator must teach a few patients, coping with all of the triumphs and problems along the way, or risk losing touch with the very essence of patient education.

Role of the Staff Nurse

The single most important person in patient education is the patient. The next most important person is the nurse caring for that patient. No one else has the opportunity to see the progress being made, day by day, hour by hour. No one else can spot problems so quickly, give feedback, reinforce learning, and evaluate the patient's ability actually to give self-care.

When staff nurses abdicate the patient teaching role because "We have a patient educator now," no one suffers more than the patient. Lack of adequate follow-up and reinforcement dictates a less than optimum outcome, and that shortchanges patients and may even shorten lives.

Beyond the implications for patient care, what does such an abdication do to the nurse's professional image? Studies have shown that patients typically do not perceive nurses as teachers.[16] This perception probably exists because nurses do not often teach. Again the issue of time constraints arises: "I don't have *time* to teach patients." "I can barely get my work done, let alone find time for teaching." But teaching is part of a professional nurse's work, perhaps one of the most important parts. Only someone with a thorough grounding in theory and scientific fact can teach well (although other skills are needed). Who else but the professional nurse has the knowledge and expertise required to teach patients adequately?

Anyone who has seen patients desperately asking the person who cleans the room about their surgery or about the intravenous fluids they are receiving can tell that more information is needed by almost every patient. To seek actively the role of patient educator may be the most needed step a nurse can take. That it is a difficult step makes it no less needed.

Reconciling Patient Educator and Bedside Nurse

How can the patient education coordinator help staff nurses feel comfortable with teaching patients? When a patient education program begins, responsibilities should be worked out first. Do not let things "just happen." Roles should be planned and communicated to everyone involved right at the outset. Who will assess patient needs initially? Should it be the patient educator, who will then make the teaching plan and enlist the staff's help in implementing it? Or should it be the bedside nurse, who then calls in the patient educator for consultation? Each institution must decide these issues individually, since many factors influence the decisions. For instance, if the organization uses primary care, the primary nurse might be the logical person to assess needs and devise a teaching plan. Figure 1-1 shows a sample role analysis.

These activities are examined in detail in later chapters, for both the patient education coordinator and the staff nurse, but first another role in patient education needs to be analyzed.

PHYSICIANS AND PATIENT EDUCATION

By the very nature of their role as primary caregivers, physicians should be leaders in providing patient education. Unfortunately, that does not always prove to be

Figure 1-1 Roles and Responsibilities for Patient Teaching

Patient Education Coordinator | Staff Nurses

Visit patient in response to staff request ◄——— Identify problems requiring education

Assess learning needs and barriers ◄——► Consult with educator on teaching plan

Devise and record teaching plan

Communicate plan to all concerned

Initiate teaching activities and provide ——► Assess patient learning, correct
learning materials   misunderstandings, reinforce learning

Document teaching done and patient reactions to teaching

Communicate progress

Encourage patient to demonstrate skills ——► Encourage patient to carry out self-
care activities in daily care

Evaluate patient education activities and results

the case. During a survey by the American Hospital Association, 42 percent of the hospitals questioned cited medical staff attitudes as a hindrance to the development of patient education programs.[17]

In private discussions with patient education coordinators, the subject invariably turns to how this program or that film or this block of content was stalled by a physician or group of physicians. Most hospitals require that anything that concerns consumer education be approved by a committee of physicians. Although some argue that this allows one profession to dictate another profession's practice, the reality is that physicians will continue to have this power in most institutions. So the question is not whether physicians control content but how people can work together to ensure the best possible patient education program.

Problems generally arise when physicians block educational activities that others perceive as needed and beneficial. Boyd found that this conflict occurs as a result of three primary factors: (1) physicians' beliefs about the physician-patient relationship, (2) nurses' beliefs about independent nursing functions, and (3) poor interprofessional communication.[18] The need to be "gatekeepers of information" probably arises from physicians' concerns about interference in the care of their patients. What if the information contradicts something the physician told the patient? Worse, what if the patient challenges the treatment plan or threatens legal action? These concerns may seem to border on paranoia—except that all of them have happened.

Education provides the learner with information—information that may be used positively or negatively depending on one's viewpoint and goals. When education involves diagnosis, treatment, and prognosis—areas that physicians regard as exclusively theirs—conflicts often arise. The only way to prevent or resolve such conflicts is to include the medical staff in the patient education program from the beginning.

Soliciting physician input is not always easy. With their time at a premium, most physicians do not care to spend hours sitting on committees. But do not use their reluctance to get involved as an excuse not to try. Deliberately "forgetting" to develop physician rapport and approval for the program or any part of its content will backfire. When the medical staff discovers that it has been outflanked, the counterattack it launches can cripple or even eliminate the entire program. Military metaphors are appropriate in this case, for such conflicts can escalate quickly to total war.

Kriewall and Trier suggest three strategies for facilitating physician cooperation and support:

1. easy access to patient education
2. physician endorsement
3. high program visibility[19]

Easy Access to Patient Education

How easy is it for physicians to gain access to the program? Can they simply write an order for inpatients to receive the teaching they need, or must special forms be filled out or separate calls made? The easier the access, the more likely physicians are to use the program. But no matter how accessible, if the content of the educational program is suspect many physicians will be reluctant to order it for their patients.

Obtaining Physician Endorsement

Whether through medical committees, section meetings, or letters, patient educators must solicit physician support and endorsement for the program. The medical staff must be confident that the information provided to its patients is accurate and appropriate and will not contradict its treatment plans. Boyd states,

> Physicians should be assured that they will be the first health care professionals to give information to the patient about the diagnosis, treatment plan, and prognosis. Nurses' teaching should focus on helping the patient to understand and cope with the diagnosis, to comprehend and adhere to the treatment plan, and to understand and meet future health care needs.[20]

Some patient educators may feel that this circumscription limits the scope of their practice, as well as limiting the information available to the patient. If so, it is a necessary limitation. Physicians order education for their patients just as they do drugs and diagnostic tests. This makes the medical staff the gatekeeper of the process. The only way to assure that patients get the information they need is to negotiate with physicians about content and presentation.

In meetings with representatives of the medical staff (some hospital educators attend section meetings—obstetrics/gynecology, surgery, and anesthesia, for example), educators may present their programs for physician input and endorsement. A word of caution, however: never go to these meetings unprepared and ask the physicians to develop the content. Not only will the process drag on forever but the doctors will not be able to agree, and the ensuing arguments may result in nothing's being approved. Always have the program completed just the way you want it—in writing—ready to present. Nine times out of ten the group will endorse it unchanged. The tenth time some individual physician may object, usually to a minor detail. At that juncture, decide whether the point is important enough to discuss and negotiate, or whether it is better simply to eliminate the offending detail.

Once the physician group endorses your program, patient education can usually proceed without interference.

Program Visibility

Keep patient education at the forefront of hospital activities. Sometimes it is tempting to keep a low profile in the hope that no one will notice you, allowing your activities to flow along as you like. Unfortunately, low profiles often lead to notice when you least want it—at budget time. Is patient education an unnecessary frill that should be eliminated when funds are scarce? Without constant efforts at maintaining visibility, the answer is all too often yes.

Your staunchest allies will be the physicians—if you have shown that your activities make a difference to their patients. This validation requires constant interaction with key members of the medical staff. Face to face and by telephone, talk to them about patient problems and progress. Become known as a resource they can come to when their patients need help. If the need requires another health care professional's expertise, do not put it back on the physician. Volunteer to contact the necessary person: "I'll talk to the social worker and ask her to see Mrs. X."

Showing actual improvement in a patient's condition through your teaching is the single most impressive thing that you can do to become visible. Chapter 11 discusses evaluation of patient education—a necessary step to demonstrate program effectiveness. If the patient educator obtains (and publicizes) proof that teaching activities make a difference to patients, supporters will multiply.

Another important aspect of program visibility involves expansion of services. It is often tempting to rest on your laurels, especially if you have a superior program. But too often hospital educators offer excellent teaching for diabetic patients or for patients needing cardiac rehabilitation, and nothing for any other patients. Expand program support by expanding the customer base. What other patient education needs are out there? Attend quality assurance meetings, talk to staff members, study patient questionnaire results. Most important, ask the physicians.

Exhibit 1-1 is an example of a survey sent to members of the medical staff to elicit input on needed areas for patient education. The use of results from a survey such as this can give educators new ideas and new directions for their efforts. Constant expansion of services leads to more work, admittedly, but it may also lead to approval for additional staff and resources when the program proves its worth.

DISCHARGE PLANNING—THE OVERALL CONCEPT

Discharge planning is a handy concept to us when planning a patient education program—handy because most hospitals have some kind of discharge planning already in place. But exactly what is discharge planning, and how does it fit together with patient education?

What Is Discharge Planning?

Discharge planning is commonly seen as the actions taken by hospital staff to ensure that patients can care for themselves after discharge from the acute care facility. This may be done through educating patients and families, arranging home care with an outside agency, or placing patients in a long-term or intermediate care facility. Discharge planning may be handled by a separate department staffed by discharge planning specialists, by the social services department, or by the nursing staff.

Exhibit 1-1 Patient Education Questionnaire for Physicians

Dear Dr.   :

Would you please look over this questionnaire and let us know if having patient education programs (similar to the Diabetes Program) available would be helpful to you and your patients? Thank you for your help.

[   ] COPD patients
[   ] Patients on antihypertensive medicines
[   ] Patients on home ventilators
[   ] Patients requiring home wound care
[   ] Patients with AIDS
[   ] Patients with cirrhosis/hepatitis/other liver disorders
[   ] Chronic renal patients
[   ] Patients with orthopedic problems (please list specific problems):

Other suggestions: _____
_____
_____
_____
_____

PLEASE DROP THE COMPLETED FORM OFF AT ANY ADULT CARE STATION. A SPECIAL BOX WILL BE PROVIDED THERE. THANKS AGAIN!

Almost every hospital in the United States has some kind of discharge planning mechanism in place. Unfortunately, some consist of lip service and red tape rather than actual help for the patients. If discharge planning is considered accomplished when the discharge form is completed, the patient probably is receiving little actual benefit.

What Discharge Planning Can Be

The truly excellent discharge planning programs have several characteristics in common.

- They are patient-oriented.
- They begin at admission, not near discharge.
- A discharge plan is drawn for every patient in the hospital, not just for selected categories.
- Responsibilities are clearly spelled out, communicated, and enforced.
- Discharge planning is clearly documented.
- Patient education is an integral part of the program.

Patient-Oriented. If a discharge planning program focuses on staff convenience, medical records requirements, or any other nonpatient concern, it is not doing its job. A major cause of this problem is an emphasis on process rather than end result. Mezzanotte thinks that, by basing discharge planning on *outcome criteria* (what patients demonstrate that they can do) rather than on *process criteria* (what you tell the patient), you can better prepare patients to continue care after discharge.[21] This patient-centered approach guides everyone's efforts toward the skills, knowledge, and support needed for patients to maintain or improve their condition after discharge. Exhibit 1-2 is an example of a discharge planning work sheet that is process-oriented; note the emphasis on staff activities rather than on patient accomplishment. Exhibit 1-3 shows a patient-oriented plan that focuses on patient/family concerns and accomplishments.

Beginning the Plan on Admission. For a plan to be carried out in an organized way, with appropriate resources, problems must be identified on admission and throughout the hospital stay. Waiting until the day before discharge (or worse, the day of discharge) to initiate discharge planning and needed patient education is a negligent act and can prove actively harmful to patients.

Plans for All Patients. Some hospitals require discharge planning only for certain categories of patients: diabetics, ostomy patients, or amputees, for example. This approach is a disservice to patients and their families. Patient need is not al-

Exhibit 1-2 Process-Oriented Discharge Planning Work Sheet

DISCHARGE SUMMARY   PATIENT:

Date: Time: Diagnosis:

VALUABLES:

FOLLOW-UP APPOINTMENTS:

DISPOSITION:
    Accompanied by:
    Discharged by:
( ) Wheelchair   ( ) Stretcher   ( ) Ambulatory   ( ) Other

EXPIRATION:
    Pronounced by: Time:
    Postmortem care:
    Disposition of valuables:

EDUCATION PERFORMED:
    Date   Subject

Signature of nurse performing discharge: _____

ways dictated by diagnosis. A frail, elderly patient who lives alone may need a great deal of help after the simplest hospitalization. Even young patients with seemingly strong support systems may develop problems that require education or outside help. Constant vigilance toward problem identification is vital.

Responsibilities Enforced. Leave nothing to chance. Discharge planning needs to be carefully spelled out in written procedures, taught to all staff through in-services and orientation, and followed up by hospital managers. Exhibit 1-4 is a procedure used in one hospital. Note that responsibilities are clearly defined, including time frames and required documentation.

Exhibit 1-3 Patient-Oriented Discharge Planning Work Sheet

DISCHARGE SUMMARY		
Name: Date:	Diagnosis: Time:	
Problems identified during hospitalization:	Interventions:	Results:
Patient/family objectives after discharge: Objective:		Time line:
Follow-up required: Type:	Date:	By whom:

Documentation. Whether discharge planning is documented in the narrative notes; on a special form; or on progress notes in the form of subjective, objective, assessment and plans (SOAP) charting, it must be completely documented. Quite aside from the importance of communicating progress to other members of the health care team, documentation of discharge planning provides legal protection for hospital staff and physicians. Blaes found that legal claims are based on contentions that:

1. The patient was dismissed before he or she should have been, in violation of standards of care, contrary to accepted hospital practice, and motivated by purely economic reasons to stay within DRG [diagnosis-related groups] limits; and
2. The physicians and nurses involved did not properly inform, counsel, and educate the patient or family with respect to effective home care, follow-up, administration of drugs, use of medical supplies, and subjective or objective symptoms developed which indicate complications or an unfavorable clinical response.[22]

Obviously, documentation of staff actions and patient response is critical in avoiding lawsuits. As with any charting, the rule is: If it isn't written, it didn't happen.

Exhibit 1-4 Discharge Planning Procedure

DISCHARGE PLANNING PROCEDURE:

BY WHOM: R.N. responsible for patient.

PURPOSE: Complete all preparations and arrangements for optimal home care prior to discharge.

PROCEDURE:

1. Every patient will be assessed on admission for the discharge planning needs. Document needs on the admission assessment form in area provided. Document on the patient care plan the identified discharge planning objectives.
2. Consult with the Patient Education Coordinator about teaching plan, implementation, and evaluation.
3. Refer patients who may need placement in an extended care facility to the Social Services Department.
4. Document completed teaching, special arrangements, and patient reactions to the progress notes.
5. Record each completed objective on the patient care plan and in the progress note as accomplished.
6. Coordinate discharge planning efforts with other disciplines, using informal conferences and the patient care plan.
7. Request that a formal multidisciplinary discharge planning conference be scheduled whenever indicated because of complexity or problems or special concerns.
8. Document completed parts of the plan at time of discharge on Discharge Summary, and add objectives and time line for post-discharge activities for patient and family. Include any formal follow-up required.

Patient Education and Discharge Planning. The preceding discussion should make it clear that patient education is inextricably entwined with discharge planning. The whole process of assessment, problem identification, problem solving, resource allocation, and evaluation describes discharge planning, patient education, and the practice of nursing itself. Preparing patients to care for themselves and attain/maintain an optimal life is the very essence of patient education. As the methods of effective patient education unfold throughout the rest of the book, never lose sight of this ultimate goal.

NOTES

1. Charles Kilo, *Educating the Diabetic Patient* (New York: Science & Medicine Publishers, 1982), p. 30.

2. Ibid., p. 9.

3. Sharon A. Brown, "An Assessment of the Knowledge Base of the Insulin-Dependent Diabetic Adult," *Journal of Community Health Nursing* 4, no. 1 (January 1987): 11.

4. Kilo, *Educating the Diabetic Patient*, p. 30.

5. Ibid.

6. Ibid., p. 9.

7. Ibid.

8. C.J. Smith et al., "The Effect of an Intensive Education Programme on the Glycaemic Control of Type I Diabetic Patients," *South African Medical Journal* 7 (February 7, 1987): 164.

9. Barbara Hughes, "Diabetes Management: The Time Is Right for Tight Glucose Control," *Nursing87* 17, no. 5 (May 1987): 64.

10. Centers for Disease Control, "Impact of Diabetes Outpatient Education Program—Maine," *Morbidity and Mortality Weekly Report* 31 (1982): 307.

11. Sister Judith Ann Karam, Steven M. Sundre, and George L. Smith, "A Cost/Benefit Analysis of Patient Education," *Hospital and Health Services Administration* 31, no. 4 (July/August 1986): 82.

12. "Medicare Study Finds Health Education Benefits," *Patient Education Newsletter* 6, no. 5 (October 1983): 7.

13. *Medicare and Medicaid Guide* (Washington, D.C.: U.S. Government Printing Office, 1986), p. 9023.

14. *Policy and Statement: The Hospital's Responsibility for Patient Education Services* (Chicago: American Hospital Association, 1982), p. 1.

15. Barbara Young, "Proposed Competencies for Patient Education Coordinators," *Patient Education Newsletter* 7, no. 1 (February 1984): 1–2.

16. Linda Corkadel and ReNel McGlashan, "A Practical Approach to Patient Teaching," *Journal of Continuing Education in Nursing* 14, no. 1 (January 1983): 13.

17. Ibid., p. 12.

18. Marilyn Boyd, "Patient Education: Whose Territory Is It?," *Patient Education Newsletter* 7, no. 6 (December 1984): 1.

19. Beth Kriewall and Kathryn Trier, "Consultation Corner," *Patient Education Newsletter* 7, no. 1 (February 1984): 8.

20. Boyd, "Patient Education," p. 2.

21. Jane E. Mezzanotte, "A Checklist for Better Discharge Planning," *Nursing87* 17, no. 10 (October 1987): 55.

22. Stephen Blaes, "Patient Education Protects from Malpractice Claims," *Patient Education Newsletter* 7, no. 6 (December 1984): 9.

2

Teaching Adults

ADULT LEARNING: AN ACTIVE PROCESS

Learning can be defined as the addition of new knowledge and skills that result in mental activity and behavior change.[1] With that definition as a base, the stress is on the learner, not on the teacher. Unless our teaching activities stimulate patients to take active part in learning the information, very little may occur.

This chapter stresses the principles of adult learning as formulated by Malcolm Forbes and others, but all learners, regardless of age, may benefit from application of these principles. The focus is on *active* learning. Passive learning occurs when the instructor spends most of the teaching time conveying information that learners are expected to internalize without active participation. Active learning happens when learners invest time and effort in acquiring new knowledge and skills. It is a self-directed activity, beneficial only when learners see it as relevant and helpful.[2]

PRINCIPLES OF ADULT LEARNING

The most important concept to keep in mind when teaching adults is practicality. Adult learners generally tackle learning projects because they want the information to solve real-life problems. This pragmatism is as true in health care as anywhere else. Constant attention should be given to how the information will be used by the learner. Do not assume that the application is obvious—it may not be to the patient. You will need to stress the uses that the facts can be put to, not the facts themselves.

Too often instructors focus on content rather than on what the learner needs to accomplish, on facts to be imparted rather than goals. Make what you teach relevant. Keep the patient at the center of all learning activities, and the information

19

automatically becomes practical and useful. Adult learners also have a great deal of experience to draw from when learning new skills. By incorporating their own past experience into learning, you again increase relevance.

Other precepts of adult education include the following:

- Encourage the learners to play an active role in managing their own learning.
- Provide examples that show the material in real settings.
- Make sure that the learners see value in spending time in learning and absorbing new information.
- Provide ample opportunity for practice and feedback so that learners can improve their skills and competence.[3]

Problems and Opportunities

Using the adult learning principles as a basis for patient education activities keeps the focus where it belongs: on the patient. It also makes the patient education process more complicated. Patient education is blessedly simple if all that you do is go into the patient's room and impart facts. It is also ineffective. Using adult learning principles both increases effectiveness and requires difficult decisions.

Problem. The most serious problem arising from the use of the adult learning approach is that of time. Involving learners in planning, implementation, and evaluation of patient education activities consumes precious time. It seems much more efficient to use a set speech for all diabetics, another for all ostomy patients, and so on. But patient educators' goals should involve not how much information they can cram into their patients, but what their patients can do when they leave the hospital.

Zander has stated that the product of nursing is not nursing care but rather the individual set of outcomes for each patient.[4] With that statement as a guide, the product of patient education is not teaching but learning: the individual achievement of patient-centered goals and objectives. If time is not allowed to involve learners in the process from start to finish, little of benefit to the patient will actually be achieved.

Opportunity. When you flip this problem into an opportunity, the time limits inherent in patient care settings can actually work for you. When patients only receive information rather than become involved in the learning process, how much time is wasted in repeating facts the patient already knows or in teaching skills that the patient sees no use for and will never use? Both errors cause patients to lose interest because of impatience or boredom, and the knowledge they *can* use gets lost in the shuffle. This is inefficiency at its worst.

How much better to use the time exploring patient needs, setting realistic goals, and teaching patients only what they need in order to function effectively outside the hospital. The learner's involvement all through the process ensures that the content will be internalized, and that patients will be able to apply it to real situations.

Problem. One of the adult learning principles recommended is to encourage learners to play an active role in managing their own learning. This sounds both positive and noble. But suppose that the learner decides that he or she wants no part of your plan—that learning is not a priority? This happens in patient education more often than most of us would like to admit. Following adult education principles then becomes hard to justify: if something is not taught, this patient will be discharged knowing nothing about self-care. More often than not the patient educator involved will plunge grimly forward, determined to teach the patient anyway. But teaching is not learning. A resistant learner is probably not learning, no matter how hard the educator tries to impart information.

Opportunity. Encouraging learners to manage their own learning can actually make patient education more effective and efficient. This tactic requires the educator to turn control over to the patient, not an easy task for most of us. Health care professionals, particularly nurses, tend to like structure and to impose it on their work routines and on patients. When patients are consciously given control over goal setting and scheduling of learning, their decisions may not be perceived as positive by health care providers, but those decisions ultimately may prove best. Allowing patients to work through whatever is blocking learning enables them to absorb and use the information when they finally receive it. This takes not only patience on the part of the patient educator but also the ability to arrange learning opportunities on an outpatient basis. Since our ultimate goal is to produce patients who can improve or maintain their health through effective self-care, using the ability of adult learners to plan their own learning can prove to be a tremendous advantage in the final evaluation.

Problem. Making sure that learners see value in spending time in learning and absorbing new information implies that the educator values these activities. The instant reaction to this is "Of *course* I value the time spent in learning new information," but a problem arises in some settings that contradicts that instinctive declaration. When they teach the elderly, some patient educators have the attitude that their activities are of little use because older patients have lost the ability to learn new information. Teaching sessions then become exercises in futility, with the educator simply going through the motions. Expectations that the learner will fail to absorb the facts being covered becomes a self-fulfilling prophecy. Any educator who has ever read a chart and noted "age 75" with a sinking heart is guilty of this unreasoning prejudice.

Opportunity. Luckily for all of us (since the alternative to aging is unattractive), the mind does not suddenly grind to a halt at age 65. On the contrary, the great majority of older people function at an intellectual level that compares favorably with that of the young. Their greater experience enables them to link learning with life events and to organize it into practice. The key to tapping into this potential involves instructor attitudes and actions.

Rendon et al. found that elderly people within institutions generally functioned far below their capacity. However, their function level rose dramatically when they were exposed to greater opportunities for involvement or learning, when expectation levels were increased, and when they received more attention.[5] Developing an educator attitude that elderly patients can and will learn is the first and most important step toward achievement of the goal.

The finding that older people seem to be affected disproportionately by task meaningfulness is linked directly to patient education.[6] Relate every fact to what patients will be doing; show them what the tasks that you teach mean in relation to their everyday life. The use of overlearning and frequent rest periods will also help older learners to absorb needed information readily. In the following chapters, special techniques for helping older learners are discussed wherever appropriate.

Individual versus Group Learning

Adult learning principles may be used effectively to impart information to one person, two persons, or a group. It is necessary to stress this fact because some educators who religiously use adult learning principles when teaching one-on-one abandon them when faced with a group. Their argument is that a group is too diverse in interests and experiences to allow for much sharing or interaction, but it is that very diversity that provides unique opportunities for learning.

Table 2-1 illustrates the advantages and disadvantages of individual versus group learning in patient education. Each approach offers benefits for patients and each has drawbacks. A judicious mix of both approaches might be the wisest course, depending on patient needs and instructor resources.

Initial assessment and planning of learning might be done individually, with some common information and demonstrations done in a group setting. Return demonstrations, feedback, and further practice might be more beneficial if done individually. Coping with problems and emotional reactions to an illness, however, might be fostered if shared with a group of fellow sufferers rather than with an instructor who has never had the problems and can only imagine the emotional reactions.

Whether you use the individual or the group approach or a mixture of both, embroider adult learning principles throughout your teaching. Only in this way can you assure that the patients and family members with whom you deal will see the value of what you offer.

Table 2-1 Advantages and Disadvantages of Individual and Group Learning

Type of Learning	Advantages	Disadvantages
One-on-one (educator with one learner)	• More individual attention • Educator can tailor learning exactly to the learner's needs and desires • Each point can be related to the learner's own life • Ample time can be allowed for practice and feedback	• Inefficient use of instructor time • Leads to much repetition and instructor burnout • Limited experiences to draw on to illustrate points • Lack of other learners puts total burden of observed performance and testing on one learner
Group (educator with many learners)	• Effective use of instructor time • Many real-life experiences to share and to illustrate learning points • Nonthreatening to some learners (safety in numbers) • Learners can support each other and share common feelings	• Not as much individual attention from instructor • Group may be hard to control—too talkative, argumentative, or hostile • One member may try to dominate discussions; strong instructor control needed • Some learners may be shy with a group, unwilling to share feelings or ask questions

RESPONSIBILITY FOR LEARNING

Instilling Accountability for Learning

Many adults carry heavy emotional baggage from their school days. If the schools they attended followed the model most commonly seen, little responsibility was placed on the students. Information was spoon-fed to them by lecturing teachers; few practical applications of the information were presented; and a warm, breathing body was all that was required. At test time they crammed, memorizing what they thought the teacher would ask; after the test the information was forgotten even faster than it was memorized. Note that the word *memorized* is used rather than the word *learned*, for very little learning took place.

Some educators believe that these past experiences will not affect learning as an adult. They reason that the information being offered relates directly to real life and has obvious benefits for the person being taught: this is true. But problems sometimes arise not from the learner's failure to perceive value in the information but from the assumption that the instructor is responsible for the outcomes. This assumption is particularly damaging when the instructor shares it. Once and for all: the learner is responsible not only for learning the information but for making the life changes necessary to cope with illness or to achieve wellness. The patient educator can serve only as a facilitator, offering the service needed by the patient—in this case, information.

If many adults think that the instructor carries the responsibility for causing learning, how can educators instill accountability in the patient, where it belongs and must stay? One way is to make clear at the outset of any educational relationship the roles expected of each participant. You may need to say bluntly, "I can offer you all of the information and equipment you need, but it's up to you to use it, to help yourself to health."

Throughout your teaching, stress the applications the patient must make, the actions the patient must take. Elicit patient input on what will be done at home, what problems may arise, how he or she will cope with those problems (or call for help if needed). Our patients are adults. It is up to us to treat them as adults. They deserve the respect that adult learning principles imply.

The Nurse's Role As Facilitator

How can we support our patients through this difficult transition from invalid to independent self-caregiver, from dependent listener to adult learner? Nurses are uniquely suited to facilitate adult learning and independent functioning because nursing is concerned with health rather than illness. Illness and pathology are medical concerns; nursing focuses on the whole person and how to assist that person to the highest level of wellness that can be achieved. Educating people to care for themselves fits comfortably into that philosophy.

Every interaction with every patient should be viewed as an opportunity to facilitate learning. For patient educators this thought is second nature, but nurses at the bedside also need to keep it in mind. Explore the needs revealed by patient questions and comments. Be aware of the education plan and what progress the patient is making. Reinforce not only acquisition of knowledge but performance and attitude change as well.

The following chapters analyze the activities of patient education: needs assessment, motivating learners, planning, involving the family, developing patient education tools, teaching, and documenting and evaluating effectiveness. As you gain access to new ideas and techniques, you will be acting as an adult learner, taking responsibility for your own knowledge acquisition and applications. Share that achievement with your patients and help them to experience the thrill of true adult learning.

NOTES

1. Lynda Juall Carpenito and T. Audean Duespohl, *A Guide For Effective Clinical Instruction* (Wakefield, Mass.: Nursing Resources, 1981), p. 45.

2. Ibid.

3. Lawrence Holpp, "Technical Training for Nontechnical Learners," *Training and Development Journal* 41, no. 10 (October 1987): 55.

4. K. Zander, "Second Generation Primary Nursing: A New Agenda," *Journal of Nursing Administration* (March 1985): 18.

5. Diane C. Rendon et al., "The Right To Know, the Right To Be Taught," *Journal of Gerontological Nursing* 12, no. 12 (December 1986): 35.

6. Ibid.

3

Assessing Learning Styles and Needs

One of the things stressed most often in courses about teaching others is assessment. Over and over we hear about the importance of assessing needs before attempting to teach people anything. Needs assessment prevents needless repetition of already known material, increases learning, saves time, and increases rapport between learner and instructor. Yet needs assessment is one of the most neglected skills in patient education.

Although patient assessment receives lip service from nurses, little actual assessment is done to determine learning needs. How often have you seen every diabetic given exactly the same materials and pretty much the same speech? Or every new mother taught the same things about infant care or breast-feeding?

In one study, a significant difference was found between the problems that patients identified for themselves and the diagnoses identified for them by their nurses. In twelve of the twenty-one areas there were *no* shared perceptions by any of the nurse-patient pairs. A comparison of the numbers of problems agreed upon with the numbers of problems disagreed upon by nurse-patient pairs resulted in congruence scores that, when compared with a possible 100 percent agreement level, showed a mean nurse-patient agreement level of only 19.53 percent.[1]

It is certainly quicker and easier to operate from assumptions about what patients need, but if we fail to determine their actual needs, our efforts not only are doomed to fail, they may actually do more harm than good. How frustrating for the patients to be told things they already know—or do not care whether they ever know. How frustrating for the nurses to spend time teaching information that will not be absorbed or used by their patients.

One patient stated, "Nurses only see the surface things. They never ask about the things underneath, and those are the *real* problems."[2] How can we tap into those "things underneath"—the needs that must be explored if we are to help our patients? Bartlett believes that patient needs assessment is vital both to involve the consumer and to provide a patient orientation rather than a provider orientation.[3] Conducting this kind of assessment involves exploring three areas:

1. learning needs (what the patient needs to learn)
2. learning styles (how the patient needs to learn)
3. readiness to learn (when the patient needs to learn)

NEEDS ASSESSMENT METHODS

Assessing learning needs is not just the process of discovering what to teach—it gives one a chance to learn whether instruction is necessary at all. Not every patient perceives a need for education. One woman who had been a diabetic for years became irate when the patient educator entered the room. She cared for herself well and was in the hospital for something entirely unrelated to the diabetes. The automatic assumption that she needed instruction because she was diabetic insulted her abilities, and the educator could only agree with her. She did not need the educator's services and instruction should not have been ordered.

Table 3-1 lists the methods of patient learning needs assessment. The most reliable results are obtained by using several methods together, rather than relying on just one. However assessment is done, recognize that the process will be time-consuming. One expert on nutritional counseling for diabetics recommends that 55–65 percent of the caregiver's total time with the patient be spent in assessing learning needs.[4] This time is well spent, since the caregiver is pinpointing exactly what must be learned, or deciding whether instruction is even necessary or appropriate at this time.

Interviewing Patient and Family

The interview is perhaps the most common form of patient needs assessment; it enables the caregiver to ask the patient or other informant questions directly to elicit learning needs. Once the initial socializing is over, tell the patient that you need to ask a number of questions, and why this is necessary. Before the patient invests time and effort providing answers, he or she deserves to know how the information will be used. This also helps you to focus on questions that are really necessary. If the answer will not be used, do not ask the question. For instance, some admission forms require the nurse to ask patients what their sleep schedule is, how many pillows they use, and whether they like the window open or closed—this despite the fact that patients are awakened at a set time, no extra pillows are available, and the windows do not open. This kind of questioning not only is a waste of time, but it sets up patient expectations that go unfulfilled.

Since it is the *patient's* view of the illness and possible goals that we wish to

Table 3-1 Methods of Patient Learning Needs Assessment

Method	Advantages	Disadvantages
Interviewing patient and family	• Promotes nurse-patient interaction and rapport • Enables nurse to focus on specific needs and follow-up on spoken clues • Can explore feelings and values	• Provider-directed • May be hard to interpret patient statements correctly • Time-consuming with a talkative patient • Occasionally perceived as threatening ("too many questions")
Questionnaires and forms	• Time-efficient for nurse • Can be written to elicit specific information • Patients have time to think about answers	• Impersonal • May be misinterpreted • May need to interview to clarify answers
Charts and records	• Organized information • Professional observations and judgments	• Relies on other people's interpretations of patient behavior • Time-consuming to extract data
Written tests	• Quickly discovers knowledge • Can be written to stimulate problem solving and recall	• Some people are poor test-takers • Perceived negatively by many people
Observation	• Patient actually performs skills/activities • Nurse can make own interpretation of observations	• Time-consuming • Patient may feel uncomfortable being watched

elicit, questions should be directed with that view constantly in mind. Redman suggests the following examples:

• What do you think caused your problem?
• Why do you think it started when it did?
• What do you think your illness does to you? How does it work?
• How severe is your illness? Will it have a long or short course?
• What kind of treatment do you think you should receive?
• What are the most important results you hope to receive from this?
• What are the chief problems your illness has caused for you?
• What do you fear most about your illness?[5]

Note that these questions are feeling-based as well as fact-based. The replies should provide valuable clues to motivating the patient to learn.

As the patient answers your questions, be alert for clues about not only learning needs but concerns that the patient may have. Powers states that a major goal during learning needs assessment is gathering information about patients' strengths, beliefs, and motivations that will serve as leverage later in motivating them to make changes.[6] Explore further if some chance comment or nonverbal reaction hints at uncertainty, conflict, or unexpected problems.

One critical function of the interviewer is to remain nonjudgmental. If the information collected upsets some cherished belief or value, it is all too easy to judge adversely the person who gave you that information. This attitude may form at an unconscious level and must always be guarded against. For instance, a patient who makes a negative comment about the care given at your hospital or who disparages a respected physician may provoke equally negative reactions from staff members. Even patient fears can trigger these reactions. One educator expressed contempt for patients who feared giving themselves injections, terming them "cowards who should be thinking about more important things." Condemning patients for expressed feelings or apprehensions is both unproductive and unprofessional.

During the interview, notes should be taken so that important information is not forgotten. Important details may be jotted down quickly, either on a blank sheet or on a structured interview sheet with topics listed as a guide for the interview (see Exhibit 3-1). This generally is not a chart form but serves as a work sheet for the patient educator. Once the data have been processed by the interviewer, a more concise compilation of learning needs and other findings results. Important information gleaned from the interview then may be recorded on the chart at the interviewer's convenience.

Questionnaires and Forms

Eliciting written responses to questions about learning needs is a widely used approach to needs assessment, particularly in outpatient settings. In a health maintenance organization, Bartlett obtained a behavioral diagnosis for nonadherence to antihypertensive routine by asking ten patients to agree or disagree with a list of fourteen reasons why "people might not take their pills."[7] Questionnaires may be either general, for use with almost any patient (Exhibit 3-2), or specific to a single disease or problem (Exhibit 3-3). Check-off responses are easier to collate, but open-ended questions generally elicit more information. No matter which approach is used, a section for "questions about your condition" or "other comments/ questions" should always be included to encourage patients to share additional information.

Exhibit 3-1 Structured Interview Guide

PATIENT LEARNING NEEDS GUIDE

Name:

Age:

Diagnosis:

Patient's definition of illness: _____

_____

_____

Patient's understanding of treatment plan: _____

_____

_____

Questions about condition: _____

_____

_____

Patient's goals: _____

_____

_____

Home conditions: _____

_____

Family resources: _____

_____

Learns best by: _____

_____

Learning needs identified: _____

_____

_____

_____

Exhibit 3-2 Questionnaire about General Learning Needs

We are here to answer your questions and to help you learn what you need to know about managing your illness at home. Please answer the following questions to let us know your needs.

Name:
Your illness is:
How long have you had this illness?
What problems has it caused you?

What will you need to do to care for yourself at home?

What questions or concerns do you have?

Do you have someone at home to help you? If so, who?

Please check off your favorite method of learning (check as many as you want):
Reading _____   Lecture _____   Films _____   Group discussion _____
Problem solving _____   Demonstration _____   Individual practice _____
Other:

Once the responses from the questionnaire have been collated, examine them for patterns revealing patient learning needs. Do some of the comments link to other responses? Is anything left glaringly unsaid? Questionnaire responses usually should be followed with an interview directed at the problem areas identified.

Charts and Records

The patient's medical records hold many clues to learning needs, but ferreting them out can be a problem. Nuggets of important information can be buried amidst a clutter of useless data. Luckily, this source is usually organized into sections, some of which may be skipped. What parts should be read? The physician's progress notes are the most likely source of useful information on the patient's condition, future treatment plan, and prognosis. Ancillary department sections can provide clues to home problems identified by social workers, dietary counseling by dietitians, and so forth. Discharge planning forms are an obvious source of learning needs if they are properly filled out.

Where do the nurses' notes fit into all of this information? Unfortunately, in many hospitals the nurses' narrative notes contain a plethora of entries such as "Family at bedside," "Patient watching TV," "Resting comfortably," and the ever-

Exhibit 3-3 Questionnaire on Learning Needs for a Diabetic Patient

---

Please check off as many of the items as you like. Thank you for helping us to help you.

I would like to know more about:

_____ Insulin administration
_____ Blood sugar monitoring and measurement
_____ Menu planning
_____ Skin care/care of the feet
_____ What causes diabetes
_____ Effects of diabetes on vision
_____ Controlling diabetes through diet
_____ Exercise: benefits and problems
_____ Planning your social life
_____ Alcohol and diabetes
_____ What to do when you're ill

Other things I'd like to know: _____
_____
_____
_____
_____
_____
_____

---

popular "No complaints." Sifting through inane entries for significant information is frustrating and time-consuming. As more organizations switch to problem-oriented approaches to charting such as nursing diagnosis or subjective, objective, assessment and plans (SOAP) charting, nursing documentation will become more helpful in pinpointing patient needs.

Written Tests

Tobin, Yoder-Wise, and Hull list two reasons for using written tests as a basis for identifying learning needs: (1) to determine whether or not the person has the knowledge and skills necessary for participating in a specific learning experience and (2) to determine what the participant already knows about the subject.[8] Since patient education sessions are usually tailored to the individual patient, the first reason seems inapplicable. But is it? Might it not be helpful to discover the patient's reading skills, ability to comprehend written material, and general level of knowledge before attempting to teach?

Determining what learners already know about the subject, whether that subject is diabetes, myocardial infarction, childbirth, or whatever, is obviously valuable. The whole purpose of needs assessment is to prevent repetition of already known material while ensuring that needed information is presented. A written test can determine areas of knowledge as well as deficits quickly and efficiently. Exhibit 3-4 shows an excerpt from a test designed to identify learning needs. Note that it elicits attitudes as well as knowledge.

A key determinant of success in using tests for learning needs assessment lies in presentation. Since many people perceive tests as threatening, educators must make a point of presenting the test as a tool for helping both patient and instructor discover where needs lie. "I have a test I'd like you to take" is guaranteed to freeze the patient into anxiety-laden self-consciousness. A better approach would be: "I think we're getting a good idea of what needs to be discussed. I have a questionnaire I'd like you to go over that will help me pinpoint exact areas I need to cover. Would you take a few minutes to fill it out?"

Keep in mind that tests can also be used to determine success. Administering a test as a part of learning needs assessment followed by a similar test at the end of

Exhibit 3-4 Portion of a Pretest for Determining Learning Needs

---

QUESTIONNAIRE ABOUT HEART PROBLEMS

1. All of the following can cause heart disease. Which one does the American Heart Association say is the greatest contributor to heart disease?
   a. Too much fat in the blood
   b. Lack of exercise
   c. Cigarette smoking
   d. Stress

2. What happens in a heart attack?
   a. One of the blood vessels of the heart is blocked, causing part of the heart muscle to be injured.
   b. After many episodes of chest pain, the pain finally becomes too great and causes the heart to stop.
   c. The heart becomes strained from overuse and is too damaged to keep beating properly.

3. After a heart attack the person who had it will:
   a. Have to become a semi-invalid
   b. Need to follow a diet and exercise program, and resume a normal life
   c. Do the same things as always, since nothing can be done to affect chances for recovery

4. Which of the following foods is highest in sodium?
   a. Cheddar cheese (one serving)
   b. Potato chips (one serving)
   c. Bacon (two strips)
   d. They all have approximately the same amount

teaching is an evaluation tool that deserves careful consideration. This pretest/ post-test cycle is discussed in more detail in Chapter 11, as are some skills involved in actually writing test questions.

Observation

Actually observing patients performing skills is perhaps the best way of assessing what teaching is needed. Are the steps performed in the correct order? How well does the patient handle equipment? Are sensory deficits causing problems? Are procedures demonstrated correctly? Where does the patient seem uncertain? What mistakes are made?

Observation can be supplemented with questions to patients to elicit reasons for their actions. Discussing the rationale behind skills helps patients to link what they are doing with why it is important to do it. Alternatively, you may ask the patient to explain what is being done rather than ask questions while the skills are being performed.

Although observing performance is a valuable tool, great care must be taken not to intimidate patients. It can be nerve-wracking to have someone watch you do something. Even a familiar task becomes difficult when an observer is present; a new or unfamiliar task can seem insurmountable. The presence of an observer, however, can affect performance positively as well as negatively: the patient may strive harder to accomplish the task when being observed. Combining observation with encouraging feedback and positive reinforcement will help to make the experience less threatening.

CHECKPOINTS ON NEEDS ASSESSMENT

There are other sources for determining patient learning needs—sources that relate to patients only indirectly. Educators need to check periodically with nurses, physicians, hospital committees, discharge planners, social workers, dietitians, and anyone else who might have insight into patient needs. These key people often note problems while providing care to patients.

Most hospitals have a Patient Education Committee that serves in an advisory role for patient educators. Valuable input obviously can be obtained from this group, but other committees in the hospital also provide helpful information, particularly those involved in quality assurance, risk management, and discharge planning. Arrange to have minutes sent to you, and keep in contact with key members. The Joint Commission on Accreditation of Healthcare Organizations (Joint Commission) is placing more and more emphasis on documented responses to problems identified by such committees. The patient educator can assist in meeting

Joint Commission requirements as well as better meeting patient needs.

As you obtain input from various staff members and physicians, keep in mind that conflicting information may result. Your key source of data must always be the patient. Bartlett conducted a needs assessment for prenatal classes at an urban health center and found that topics and priorities selected by the staff were markedly different from those selected by patients. The patient needs assessment was the crucial factor that resulted in a well-attended and enthusiastic series of prenatal classes.[9]

IMPACT OF LEARNING STYLES ON PATIENT EDUCATION

Part of learning assessment involves identifying the best ways in which patients learn. Learning style is defined as "the manner in which an individual perceives and processes information in learning situations."[10] To impart information effectively to patients, educators should assess each person's preference for receiving information.

Learning style models incorporate learning theory, individual development, and personality types. Perhaps the best known model is the Kolb Learning Style Inventory, which describes four different approaches to learning:

1. Converger: Likes a single correct solution to a problem. Enjoys dealing with things rather than people.
2. Diverger: Likes situations that call for generation of ideas. Interested in people.
3. Assimilator: Likes to create theoretical models. Less interested in people; more concerned with abstract concepts.
4. Accommodator: Likes doing things such as carrying out plans and experiments. Relies heavily on other people for information rather than on own analytic ability.[11]

Although it is hardly practical to administer a learning styles test to each patient, once you are familiar with the characteristics of the styles, it is often easy to guess the learning preferences of patients. A few simple questions will help: "Do you find reading handouts helpful?" "Would you prefer to examine this first, or would you rather have me explain it?" Asking patients to describe how they learn best will provide helpful hints for planning learning experiences.

Exhibit 3-5 lists some approaches that might help patients to learn, based on the learning style they prefer. Using a variety of approaches is vital. Do not get locked into learning strategies that work for you—an easy trap to fall into. Garity discovered that nurses and other health care professionals have a preference for learning *and teaching* through concrete and teacher-structured learning experiences.[12]

Exhibit 3-5 Approaches to Learning Based on Learning Style

CONVERGER WILL PREFER:	DIVERGER WILL PREFER:
Reading handouts Diagrams Demonstrations/return demonstrations	Discussions Group work Individual problem solving Brainstorming
ASSIMILATOR WILL PREFER:	ACCOMMODATOR WILL PREFER:
Studying theory of disease process Planning self-care in detail Diagrams Diary recordings	Demonstrations/return demonstrations Written directions/procedures Question-and-answer sessions Lecture

If the educator is a converger, for instance, he or she will be attracted to converger-style approaches and may tend to rely on lectures and diagrams during teaching. This will work well for some patients, but will prove ineffective for others. As the different teaching strategies are discussed in Chapter 7, remember to develop a number of different techniques to use so that you can vary approaches to suit patient needs.

ASSESSING READINESS TO LEARN

Until now we have been concerned with identifying patients' learning needs—what the patient needs to know. But readiness to learn significantly affects patient teaching. No matter how sound the information, how needed by the patient, or how well taught it is, if the patient is not ready to learn, the information will not be absorbed. Dealing with problems in this area may be the single most frustrating aspect of the patient educator's job.

Redman has stated what may be the best philosophy in this regard—that every patient is ready to learn something. It is up to the provider of care to find out what. [13] Before making a detailed teaching plan it behooves the educator to explore this area thoroughly. You need not be limited to teaching only the information the patient is ready to learn, but you definitely should *start* there.

One approach to determining readiness to learn is to take careful note of the questions patients ask about their illnesses. Some typical ones are:

- What is my condition?
- What causes it?
- What can be done about it?

- What can I do?
- What about home remedies?
- Can any groups help me? [14]

What do your patients ask you? Questions indicate the patient's areas of immediate concern. Addressing these concerns first shows respect for the patient, whether the order of information fits the pattern you would choose or not.

Sometimes caregivers express concern and puzzlement over patients' *lack* of readiness to learn. Despite apparent great need, the patient expresses no interest in the information offered. We have all encountered patients who actively resist teaching. "I don't want to hear that," or "Thank you, but I'm just not interested," are typical statements made by these resistant patients. Since patient educators by definition value learning activities, they find this resistance incomprehensible.

Anderson reminds us that patients act to minimize the threat of illness and to maximize safety and well-being. If conduct appears irrational or counterproductive, it is because that particular behavior is associated with enhancing a patient's survival according to the unique meaning that the illness has for the individual.[15] Discovering that meaning is an important part of needs assessment.

Talking with the patient usually will elicit this information, *if* the interviewer remains sensitive to both verbal and nonverbal clues dropped by the patient. One vital quality for the educator is empathy, the ability to understand what other people are feeling—to "walk a mile in their shoes." Unfortunately, empathy is a quality often sadly lacking among caregivers. Research indicates that nurses score lower on measures of empathy than most other occupational groups; one study reported that 71 percent of the nurses studied showed no evidence of empathy.[16] This apparent lack of empathy may be a protective mechanism. Imagine the emotional devastation in store for nurses who empathize with every patient all the time. Perhaps nursing education should develop ways of teaching "selective empathy," helping nurses to find ways to empathize with patients without suffering themselves.

Since patient educators must use empathy as a tool for determining readiness to learn, they must develop this ability. One way of doing this involves imagining how you would feel under the same circumstances. Then search for patient clues indicating whether the feelings are similar. Once feelings are tentatively identified, probe to check your assessment: "I'd be feeling frustrated and a little angry right now if I were you. Is that how you feel?" or "You don't seem interested in this information—is there something else you'd like to talk about?"

Information about readiness to learn will prove invaluable in motivating the patient to learn (see Chapter 4) and in planning the sequence of information and teaching approaches (see Chapter 5). Besides determining what should be tackled first and when learning should begin, the actions you take to elicit this information help to establish a caring attitude and positive rapport between patient and educator.

With the time pressures we all work under, it is sometimes tempting to skip an assessment of readiness to learn. An attitude of "The heck with it—they need this and they're going to get it" may prevail. This attitude is not only patronizing to the patient but also counterproductive. Since an important part of learning about an illness is creating or changing the personal meaning of having that disorder, and changes in meaning are usually related to changes in behavior, an important educational principle emerges: "Educators don't cause learning; patients cause learning."[17] When we fail to keep this in mind we are also likely to fail our patients.

CULTURAL INFLUENCES AND THEIR IMPACT ON LEARNING

Ethnic background has been shown to influence peoples' concepts of disease and illness in the following ways:

- Varying degrees of knowledge exist about biomedical categories of disease.
- Symptoms are classified into illness categories in different ways—culture-specific syndromes such as *susto* among Mexican-Americans.
- Different concepts about the causes of disease exist, such as hot-cold theories among Hispanics.[18]

All of these factors obviously can influence learning. Another culture-specific influence on patient behavior is more subtle but perhaps just as important—patient attitudes about illness and acceptable reactions to it. As an example, people of British background tend to view illness as something to be "toughed out." Their reaction to teaching is likely to be polite, reserved, and intellectual rather than emotional. Since they tend to view recovery and self-care as matters of willpower, they may or may not value the information given to them. Most significant in terms of nursing care and patient education, these patients will not readily share their feelings, fears, doubts, or sorrows. Anger will generally be suppressed, grieving will be done in private, and trust will not easily be given to a stranger. Their affect will be one of calm acceptance of teaching, which encourages educators to believe that they are communicating effectively. This may or may not be true. Multiply these potential problems by the myriad of cultural groups one encounters, and the scope of cultural influences becomes apparent.

Assessing Cultural Differences

Discovering the cultural factors that could affect your approach to teaching the patient is not easy. If the patient happens to fall into your cultural group, you will probably pick up emotional cues without too much effort. But different cultural backgrounds not only create different attitudes and reactions to illness, they even cause patients to express themselves differently. As discussed earlier, such things as affect, nonverbal reactions, and use of unfamiliar words or expressions may be

difficult to interpret.
Harwood suggests questioning patients of different cultural groups to elicit their own models of illness. Such questions include:

- What do you think has caused your problem?
- Why do you think it started when it did?
- What do you think your sickness does to you? How does it work?
- How bad do you think your illness is? Do you think it will be better soon?
- What kind of treatment would you like to have?
- What are the most important results you hope to get from treatment?
- What are the chief problems your illness has caused you?
- What do you fear most about your illness?[19]

Select the questions most helpful for your particular patient. The answers can serve as a starting point for a discussion of what this illness means to the patient. If the educator maintains an open and accepting manner, useful information will result. This point cannot be overstressed, because it is all too easy to fall into the "answer trap." For example, a patient is sharing cultural beliefs about illness and treatment, going into the therapeutic virtues of spiced tea, or pepper, or hot mustard poultices. If the caregiver immediately interrupts with a discourse of why this is not true or how it has no scientific basis, trust is lost. Such an approach shows no respect for the patient's cultural background and no ability to incorporate past knowledge into new learning—violations of adult learning principles.

Remaining Sensitive to Cultural Influences

The patient educator's role is to serve as a cultural bridge, spanning the gulf between the patient's world and the medical one (see Figure 3-1). Patients are generally influenced by (1) the general society; (2) their specific cultural group; and (3) their particular family's beliefs, values, and attitudes. But few patients are familiar with the health care value system. To most people, entering a hospital, outpatient facility, or even a physician's office is a venture into a strange and alien environment.

It pays to remember that we work in our own culture—not a geographic or ethnic one, but a vocational one. When viewed that way, it becomes clear that *every* patient needs help in adjusting to cultural differences. As you talk with patients about their beliefs about illness and treatment, build on that knowledge base rather than try to tear it down or change it. A little imagination will show you ways to incorporate patient cultural beliefs into your teaching. For instance, if the patient expresses the folk belief that "low blood" (anemia) can be cured by eating something red or

Figure 3-1 Cultural Influences on the Patient and the Role of the Nurse

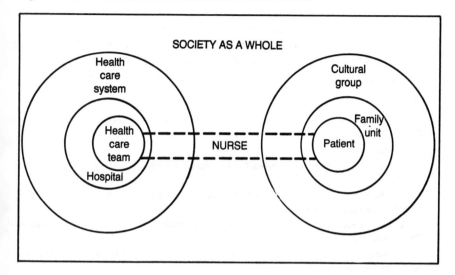

by eating yeast, rather than give a scientific recitation of facts about the causes and cures of anemia, the educator might choose to encourage the patient to select foods rich in iron that are red (organ meats, for example) and suggest that the prescribed dietary supplements will make the yeast work better.

Most patients are not prepared to discard or drastically change their cultural beliefs. It is up to us to correct dangerous misinformation without trying to force patients to abandon dearly held values.

CAUTIONARY NOTE ABOUT LEARNING NEEDS ASSESSMENT

This chapter has discussed many different aspects of assessing patient learning needs. The more approaches you can incorporate into your practice, the more useful information you are likely to get. But it is important to remember that needs assessment activities will not elicit all of the information you want or need. Indeed, because we are dealing with people, with all of their emotions and defenses, some of the information obtained is likely to be wrong. Sifting through all of the patient data to identify learning needs requires sensitivity and intuition as well as scientific knowledge and logic.

The most important part of needs assessment lies in the rapport established between patient and nurse. If we can establish ourselves as helpers concerned with the patient, as credible resources, the patient is much more likely to perceive us as people to be believed and valued. In one study of post-mastectomy patients, only

42 percent of the women felt that their needs for information were met. Only 20 percent of the patients indicated that nurses were a significant source of information, while 37 percent found physicians to be a source of information.[20] This perception must be turned around. Nurses can help patients immeasurably once the correct starting point is discovered through learning needs assessment.

NOTES

1. Cynthia Roberts, "Identifying the Real Patient Problems," *Nursing Clinics of North America* 17, no.3 (September 1982): 484–5.

2. Ibid., p. 489.

3. Edward E. Bartlett, "Consultation Corner," *Patient Education Newsletter* 5, no. 1 (February 1982): 5.

4. J.W. Pichert, S.L. Hanson, and C.A. Pechmann, "Modifying Dietitians' Use of Patient Time," *Diabetes Education* 10 (1984): 43.

5. Barbara Klug Redman, *Issues and Concepts in Patient Education* (New York: Appleton-Century-Crofts, 1981), p. 15.

6. Margaret A. Powers, *Handbook of Diabetes Nutritional Management* (Rockville, Md.: Aspen Publishers, Inc., 1987), p. 483.

7. Bartlett, "Consultation Corner," p. 5.

8. Helen M. Tobin, Pat S. Yoder-Wise, and Peggy K. Hull, *The Process of Staff Development: Components for Change*, 3rd ed. (St. Louis: C.V. Mosby Co., 1979), p. 108.

9. Bartlett, "Consultation Corner," p. 5.

10. Agnes G. Rezler and Victor Rezmovic, "The Learning Preference Inventory," *Journal of Allied Health* 10, no. 2 (February 1981): 28.

11. David A. Kolb, *Learning Styles Inventory* (Boston: McBer and Co., 1976), p. 7.

12. J. Garity, "Learning Styles Basics for Creative Teaching and Learning," *Nurse Educator* 10 (1985): 13.

13. Barbara Klug Redman, *The Process of Patient Education*, 5th ed. (St. Louis: C.V. Mosby Co., 1984), p.35.

14. Matthew Cahill, ed., *Patient Teaching* (Springhouse, Pa.: Nursing87 Books, 1987), pp. 84–85.

15. Robert M. Anderson, "The Personal Meaning of Having Diabetes: Implications for Patient Behavior and Education," *Diabetic Medicine* 3 (1986): 86.

16. Marlene Kramer and Claudia Schmalenberg, "The First Job: A Proving Ground," *Journal of Nursing Administration* 7, no. 1 (January 1977): 14.

17. Anderson, "The Personal Meaning," p. 87.

18. Redman, *The Process of Patient Education*, p. 32.

19. A. Harwood, ed., *Ethnicity and Medical Care* (Cambridge, Mass.: Harvard University Press, 1981), p. 48.

20. B. Bullough, "Nurses As Teachers and Support Persons for Breast Cancer Patients," *Cancer Nursing* 4 (1981): 221–5.

4
Motivation and Patient Learning

There is much discussion of "motivating the learner" in patient education. Caregivers often say, "He's just not motivated" or "This should motivate her to learn." They are half right. No one can "motivate" someone else to do anything. Motivation comes from within—a psychological force that moves the person toward some kind of action. Why then a whole chapter on motivation? Because educators can create an environment that encourages patients to motivate themselves. By making learning easy, by making information valuable, we can help learners *want* to learn.

OBSTACLES TO LEARNING

Many factors can affect motivation for patients. In Chapter 1 compliance was discussed as a major goal of patient education, and most studies of patient motivation have approached the issue in terms of motivating not only learning but actual compliance with therapeutic regimens. Falvo found that in many instances the caregiver's lack of understanding of compliance issues can itself be a factor in noncompliance.[1]

In one study of patients following a drug regimen, the following factors were found to influence compliance:

- number of drugs prescribed and frequency
- complicated regimens
- patient living alone or taking drugs unsupervised
- poor memory/confusion
- misconceptions about drugs

- poor eyesight
- poor manual dexterity, and containers that are difficult to open
- side effects[2]

These can be discussed under general headings of:

- severity of illness
- extent of changes needed
- environmental barriers
- sensory deficits
- psychological obstacles
- health care system

Severity of Illness

Most caregivers would probably assume that the more severe the illness, the more potential danger for the patient, the more the patient would be motivated to comply with ordered treatments. Research does not bear this out. Davis found that patients with less severe medical problems were actually more likely to follow medical advice than those with more severe illnesses.[3] This finding is probably related to anxiety. Any educator knows that some anxiety stimulates learning, but severe anxiety often overwhelms learners and makes learning difficult if not impossible. In the classroom this is often seen in "test anxiety," where good learners freeze up and fail written tests because their anxiety level surges beyond their ability to compensate.

While anxiety about illness is a difficult factor to manipulate, educators can perhaps alter the tone of explanations according to patient reactions. Patients with little or no anxiety probably will not be motivated to learn or to change their life styles. This lack of anxiety accounts for the poor success of advertisements and speeches on the importance of a sensible diet, exercise, and regulation of damaging habits such as smoking. Asymptomatic people may not be anxious enough to alter long-held habits. On the other hand, patients with overwhelming anxiety due to diagnoses of heart disease, diabetes, or cancer may be immobilized as far as learning goes. That would not be the time for scare tactics. Stressing aspects of care totally under the patient's control, offering help with care, presenting information about sources of support in the community—approaches such as these may be helpful in lessening patient anxiety to a more manageable level.

Extent of Changes Needed

The more changes that the patient must make (or the more complicated those changes), the less motivated the person will be to change. Research has found that the more treatments or drugs prescribed, the more adverse the effect on patient compliance. Compliance also decreases with the length of time it takes for the changes to be carried out.[4]

These factors should encourage educators to approach teaching cautiously, in a planned, organized way. If patients are simply hit with everything that they must do all at once—the infamous "day of discharge" teaching session—it is little wonder that they become overwhelmed and noncompliant. Revealing a small portion at a time, on a need to know basis, helps patients to absorb information without feeling that it is all too complicated to understand.

Environmental Barriers

When analyzing environmental barriers, caregivers generally think in terms of stairs in the home of a wheelchair-bound patient or lack of an adjustable bed. But examining environmental barriers to compliance—and to motivation for learning—requires a slightly different focus. Factors in the patient's home environment that may block learning and compliance include such things as family reinforcement of habits causing or contributing to illness, lack of help or support for a person living alone, perceived lack of time to perform exercises, dietary planning, or other ordered treatments, and lack of reinforcement when patients do comply.

Environmental barriers are hard to cope with because caregivers have little control over the patient's home conditions. Teaching should take these factors into consideration, preparing patients and family for problems that will arise. Perhaps the most important assistance you can give is to encourage patients to obtain community support through visiting nurses, community organizations, and/or self-help groups dealing with the specific illness or problem. Freudenberg found that educators achieve several results when they encourage patients to join such community groups.

- The likelihood of actually changing the conditions that caused the illness is increased.
- Involvement in community organizations can assist those with chronic illness to escape the isolation imposed by the disease.
- Increasing the amount of control a person has over the environment can itself be therapeutic. For example, animal, clinical, and epidemiological studies

suggest that the amount of control individuals have over their surroundings is directly related to blood pressure levels.[5]

Sensory Deficits

Problems with vision, hearing, touch, balance, or coordination directly affect a patient's ability and motivation to learn. Dealing with an illness requiring many life changes is difficult for anyone, but patients who must also cope with a sensory deficit have two strikes against them. These obstacles to learning are usually obvious and much more likely to be addressed by caregivers. During assessment, remain sensitive to sensory problems that patients sometimes disguise, such as hearing deficits. Many devices are manufactured to assist patients with these problems: magnifying syringes, special holders, phone amplifiers, and extenders for reaching dropped objects, for example. Educators must maintain current knowledge of such devices by receiving catalogs from companies supplying them.

Psychological Obstacles

When caregivers help patients learn how to care for themselves, one of the most important tasks is to construct a positive, helping relationship. Support is needed because of the many psychological sources of patient resistance to education and treatment. Some of these barriers include denial of illness, a struggle with caregivers for control, resentment over physicians' authority, unconscious aims to remain ill, and even masochistic wishes to punish the self through illness.[6]

Berg believes that compliance is largely a function of the nature of the physician-patient relationship, with the significant factors being the extent to which the relationship is characterized by support, negotiation, satisfaction, and mutual agreement.[7] If patients perceive caregivers as resource people who understand what they are going through and who are willing to help them to find their own way to cope with problems, psychological obstacles can be circumvented. Listen to patients without preconceptions about how they *should* feel about their illnesses, and recognize that they will resent their illnesses and the people who force them to cope with restrictions and changes. Be there to work with patients as they come to grips with the facts and become motivated to learn what they need.

Health Care System

Patients can be told about community resources. They can have appointments made for them in outpatient facilities or with community agencies. But sometimes he very follow-up mechanisms that we rely on to reinforce our teaching cause frustration and move patients to abandon needed regimens.

Freudenberg found the following factors to be significant problems in outpatient settings:

- inconvenient hours
- long waits for appointments
- long delays in seeing a physician
- practitioners with poor communication skills[8]

Caregivers in the system tend to shrug these things off as inevitable drawbacks. But are they inevitable results of the outpatient setting? Or are they the results of organizing the system to meet the convenience of caregivers rather than patients?

For example, in many health maintenance organizations, patients are required to see a physician acting as a gatekeeper before they can make an appointment with the specialist they need (surgeon, psychiatrist, dermatologist, or others). In some cases this is necessary to determine what kind of care is required. But if the patient knows what specialist is needed, this requirement simply adds one more obstacle, one more time-consuming, unnecessary step to the process. How many people decide that it is just too much trouble? Combine this obstacle with frustrations such as limited (or no) evening and weekend hours, excessive paperwork, and rushed, rude people providing reception and care, and the health care system becomes significantly demotivating.

Rather than accept these conditions, health care professionals should work to change them. Patients do not have the power to effect change. We do. If you work in an outpatient setting, look for ways to extend hours, simplify procedures, make care more accessible. In an inpatient setting, work with outpatient providers to make the same changes. Sharing your frustrations and patients' perceptions of the unresponsiveness may help; serving as a liaison between patients and outpatient facilities will help even more.

NONOBSTACLES AND COMPLIANCE

The preceding discussion detailing all of the obstacles to learning seems discouraging: how can anyone learn anything? On the other hand, factors that caregivers sometimes automatically assume to be obstacles really are not. Many people believe that patients who are uneducated or from a lower socioeconomic group are less likely to follow ordered regimens; research has not shown this to be true. Variables such as age, sex, socioeconomic level, and religion have been studied. These demographic variables have not been shown to be related consistently to patient noncompliance.[9]

Another issue to consider is the concept of compliance itself. Typically the literature stresses patient compliance as the be-all and end-all of education efforts. Certainly it is important, and we emphasize the value of compliance through all of the different aspects of patient education. But this emphasis can also lead to a punitive, disapproving attitude toward noncompliant patients. Noncompliance is discussed as though it were abnormal, almost aberrant behavior, yet experimental observation confirms that noncompliance is common and normal, a resilient response to the tyrannies of chronic illness.[10]

With this interpretation in mind, it makes sense for educators to maintain a realistic goal of helping patients to cope with their conditions in the most adaptive way rather than "making the patient compliant." If we consider that even health care professionals do not always follow recommended treatment, it seems a bit much to expect every patient to be totally compliant. In Chapter 5, where objectives are discussed, this issue comes up again. For now let us continue to look at compliance from the motivational point of view.

INFORMATION IS NOT ENOUGH

Health care professionals tend to be information-oriented—the disciplines are fact-based, analytical in nature. Because of this scientific background, caregivers often believe that if people are given the facts they will behave accordingly; therefore, the more that patients know about their conditions and treatments, the more compliant they will be—right? As any educator can testify, it is not that simple.

In one study, children were placed on a ten-day penicillin regimen to treat streptococcal infection. The children's families demonstrated a high level of knowledge regarding the diagnosis, treatment, and importance of carrying out the regimen. Yet researchers found that only 45 percent of the children were still receiving the penicillin by the third day. By the sixth day only 30 percent of the children were still receiving the medicine.[11] In another study, hypertensive patients' knowledge of their condition was found to be unrelated to taking medications correctly or to following dietary advice.[12] Dunn measured knowledge before, during, and after an educational program. Test scores increased by about 25 percent after the three-day program. However, an analysis of specific items revealed that 40 percent of the patients were picking up facts about diabetes, but they still failed to comprehend the underlying principles and therefore were not learning to anticipate and prevent avoidable negative consequences.[13]

These findings could be perceived as arguments against even having patient education programs. Yet any patient educator can recall numerous cases when patients have changed their approaches to illness, even changed their entire lives as a result of educational activities. The key difference may well involve how the information is imparted. Information is not enough. Facts are important, but individualizing your approach to each patient is vital.

PSYCHOLOGICAL COMPONENTS OF LEARNING

There are strong psychological implications in most motivational techniques. Whether educators are encouraging patients to discuss family problems, listening to an expression of angry feelings, or performing any of the other learning-related tasks of caregivers, coping with the psychological components of patient care is a major part of the job.

One way to analyze how patients view learning and compliance is through use of the Health Belief Model. The model is based on the hypothesis that behavior is motivated by the individual's perception of the value of success and the subjectively estimated probability of success.[14] It states that in order to take action to prevent illness or to comply with medical advice, the patient must believe that (1) he or she is susceptible to the disease; (2) the disease will have some serious impact; and (3) a certain action will be of benefit in reducing his or her susceptibility to the disease or its severity that will not lead to important barriers such as inconvenience, high cost, or pain. Demographic and sociopsychological "modifying factors" and caregiver-patient relationships may modify individual perceptions of susceptibility, severity, and the benefits and barriers of a health action. "Cues to action" may also be necessary to stimulate a person to take definite action. These cues may be internal or may come from external sources such as social group pressures, the work environment, or the media.[15]

Such a complex motivational model deserves close scrutiny from educators. The different factors (susceptibility, impact of the disease, benefits of action, minimizing drawbacks, and cues to action) can be manipulated by caregivers to move patients toward positive changes in self-care and life style.

MOTIVATIONAL STRATEGIES

What specific techniques can be used to increase patient motivation to learn and deliver self-care? Some general principles of motivation that have been found to be successful include the following:

- The environment may be used to focus the patient's attention on what is to be learned.
- Incentives motivate learning.
- Motivation is enhanced by the way in which the material to be learned is organized. In general, the best organization is that which makes the information meaningful to the person.
- Success is more motivating than failure.[16]

Environment

The environment of both the hospital and the home may be manipulated to encourage learning.

Hospital Environment

The key factor in the hospital environment is consistency. Too often patients receive different messages from physician, patient educator, bedside nurses, other caregivers, and family members. Figure 4-1 illustrates the contrast between conflicting information and a more consistent approach in enabling a patient to focus on needed information. It is the patient educator's responsibility to get everyone on the same wavelength.

Talk with the physician to make very clear the plans for the patient, both immediately and in the future. The teaching plan will be developed on the basis of this dialogue. The objectives, the steps for reaching those objectives, and the necessary follow-up and reinforcement then must be communicated to everyone involved, and commitment to the plan must be elicited.

Other changes in the hospital environment that support patient motivation include providing needed equipment and supplies; altering care schedules as necessary to allow adequate practice of techniques; and encouraging easy access to resources such as pamphlets, books, articles, and other library materials used for further study. These arrangements sound basic, but how often has patient education been compromised because the blood glucose monitoring equipment the patient will be using at home is unavailable in the hospital, or rigid adherence to a schedule blocks the patient and family from practicing a skill together? Nursing has the power to set necessary environmental modifications.

Home Environment

Changing the home environment to support learning and compliance to ordered regimens must of necessity be the responsibility of patients and families, but educators provide the information and the impetus needed to make productive changes. Through the assessment you have discovered what the patient's home is like. After analyzing what is needed, you are the one who can provide the necessary equipment, teaching, and encouragement.

For example, a diabetic patient has had a stroke. Preparing this patient for discharge will include instruction not only about the routine arrangements for a stroke patient, such as moving sleeping arrangements onto the first floor of a two-story home and any changes in the activities of daily living—an effective way to dress oneself, for instance—but also about any changes necessary to manage the diabetic condition. Providing an apparatus enabling the patient to draw up and administer insulin one-handed would be a minor environmental change that could

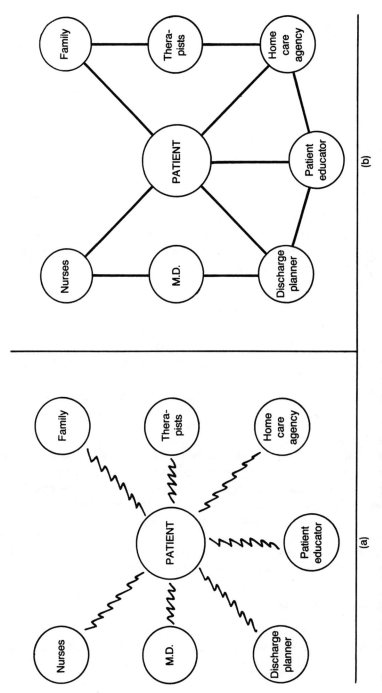

Figure 4-1 Conflicting Messages versus Consistent Approach to Teaching Patients. (a) Patient is pulled in different directions by conflicting messages. (b) Consistent approach supports patient through learning self-care.

have a major impact on the patient's independence. Helping the patient to work out a way to perform blood glucose monitoring with one hand or, if that proves impossible, teaching a family member to do it would again help to motivate the patient to comply with treatment.

Another example involves a post-myocardial infarction patient. What environmental changes need to take place at home to accommodate recovery and cardiac rehabilitation? These interventions could range from advising the patient to obtain wheeled garbage cans, to assisting the patient in planning home exercise and diet, to arranging for a MedicAlert bracelet.

Incentives

Since incentives motivate learning, how can you build them into patient teaching? One way is to focus on the inherent benefits patients derive from following the ordered regimens. In other words, rather than emphasize the risks of *not* complying, stress the good things that will happen if the patient *does* comply. These include

- an increased sense of control over the condition and life itself
- the ability to alter a schedule or diet or treatment based on thorough understanding of what is taking place in the body
- a feeling of confidence about one's ability to cope with whatever changes occur or are required
- independence from other caregivers—the ability to live alone if desired

Many other benefits specific to the situation will occur to you if you try this exercise in positive thinking.

Small incentives can be built into the teaching process as you work with the learner. Verbal praise and recognition constitute one of the cheapest, most readily available, and yet underused incentives in the patient education arsenal. Telling a patient, "That was excellent!" or "You kept it really steady that time and timed it just right," gives both feedback and an incentive to learn more. Make the praise both truthful and as specific as you can make it—both come through as sincere and thoughtful. Sometimes incentives such as increased activities or extra privileges can be used, especially in long-term care or rehabilitative settings.

Organization of Material

Organization and planning of the teaching sessions are addressed in detail in Chapter 5. In this chapter we merely stress the importance of making the information meaningful to the individual. During the discussion of assessment it was mentioned that you should discover what the patient was curious about—what questions were particularly "hot." These topics need to be addressed first in order to motivate the patient to want to learn more. Typically in diabetes education, for example, we explain how the pancreas works, what diabetes is, what the symptoms are, and the purpose of treatment. But what the patient desperately may want to know is why he or she can no longer read regular-size print. Addressing this concern first will relieve anxiety and support the patient's motivation to learn more.

Success versus Failure

It seems obvious to state that success is more motivating than failure. There is a tendency to say, "Well, of course," and dismiss it. But how often are patients set up for failure by having an unmanageable amount of information thrown at them on the day of discharge? In trying to understand unfamiliar material without sufficient time to process it and apply it to daily living, the patient inevitably will suffer frustration, anxiety, and ultimate failure.

Arranging learning experiences to promote success includes careful planning: breaking the material into small, discrete parts; relating each part to the patient's life and needs; allowing ample time for discussion and questions; and pointing out the patient's accomplishments to both patient and family. Each success at learning and performing new tasks reinforces the patient's confidence and adds motivation to learn more.

Another strategy educators should use involves their own attitudes toward patient achievement. Research has shown that patients respond well to evidence that the instructor believes they can and will succeed.[17] This means that the educator who thinks, "This patient won't be able to do this," for whatever reason (too old, too young, too debilitated) has just created a self-fulfilling prophecy. Even though the expectation is not verbalized to the patient, it comes through in many different ways. Expression, body language, tone of voice, eye contact, even the way in which the material is taught and reinforced—these subtle reactions and dozens more carry a clear message to the patient: You cannot do this. The educator probably is not even aware that this is happening. To combat this negativism, consciously force yourself to develop a positive attitude about every patient, even if you have to use such basic strategies as repeating, "This patient will learn this and will do well." Use praise lavishly, for your own attitude as well as the patient's.

MOTIVATION AND NURSE-PATIENT INTERACTION

Throughout the discussion of motivation, one factor has come up again and again—the critical importance of communication between patient and nurse. From assessment through discharge and beyond, the psychological impact of really listening to the patient, of developing empathy, and of basing interventions on that empathetic understanding cannot be overemphasized.

In working with diabetics, Dunn found that teaching facts and principles is not as important as the need to change attitudes and feelings about diabetes, since these are the changes that determine subsequent behavior and metabolic improvement. Evidence indicates that the most powerful determinant of attitude change in diabetics remains simple human interaction.[18]

Numerous studies have suggested that the caregiver's impersonality and lack of cognitive and emotional communication, as well as the brevity of the encounter, have a negative effect on compliance. Such variables as the patient's feeling that the caregiver understands the complaint, explains the diagnosis and cause of illness, and exhibits warmth to the patient have been found to increase compliance. Although an explanation of the disease and treatment alone does not increase patient compliance, it does have a positive influence when delivered in a personalized, warm, and understanding manner.[19]

Even in such a simple learning situation as teaching about take-home medications, interaction plays an important part. In one study, there was no significant difference in knowledge between patients given a handout on their medications and those with both the handout and a discussion of the information by a staff member. However, when compliance was studied, handouts alone did not positively affect compliance, but discussion of the handouts by a staff member caused a significant increase in compliance.[20]

One method recommended for increasing the effectiveness of nurse-patient interactions is mirroring. Mirroring involves the conscious imitation of the patient's posture, movements, rhythms, and other nonverbal behavior. It causes the caregiver to match the patient in a profound way that forms a bond of contact and trust. Powers recommends mirroring for very brief periods—perhaps a minute at a time—at the beginning of each interaction. By simply observing whether or not you and the patient are mirroring one another you can tell whether you are in rapport. Once practiced it is not unusual to find that you can establish rapport with persons with whom you might previously have predicted having a poor relationship. Be sure to employ mirroring unobtrusively so that the patient is unaware that you are doing it.[21]

NURSING'S ROLE IN MOTIVATION

Nurses have a unique role to play in motivating patients to succeed in learning and post-discharge care. Nursing is the one discipline that is always with the patient. This constancy enables nursing personnel to remain in touch with patients' reactions to such things as dressing changes, injections, ostomy bag applications, and other required treatments. Does the patient ask questions about what you are doing? Is your explanation accepted? Does the patient display fear, revulsion, or other negative reactions? Such insights are invaluable in planning education and motivation strategies.

Nurses also have a greater opportunity to establish and maintain a close rapport with patients than do more transient caregivers. This does not always happen, of course, but often there is more of a "we're in this together" feeling between nurse and patient as a result of the frequent contacts and intimately helping relationship. This feeling can be used to create a motivational climate that enables patients to learn what they need to know.

Health education researchers have found that patients are motivated to learn or to comply with treatment only when they believe that it is in their best interest.[22] Trust developed between patient and nurse over the length of the hospitalization fosters the patient's belief that the nurse has his or her best interests at heart. This belief lends credence to the nurse's teaching.

Even in short-term settings, nurses can make a tremendous difference in the success of efforts toward self-care. In a study of pediatric patients in an acute care clinic, compliance was increased by employing a nurse as a family health management specialist. The nurse's function was to interview the family, focusing on their concerns, discussing their treatment plan, and altering the plan to meet the patient's specific needs. As a result of these motivational activities, patient compliance increased.[23]

In another study, a nurse interviewed patients immediately after they had interacted with their physician in order to clarify the physician's recommendations to the patient and to alter the treatment regimen according to patient needs. When patients were asked what aspect of the visit had the most influence in increasing compliance, most stated that it was having someone take the time to talk with them, answer their questions, and consider their concerns.[24]

Taking the time to talk with patients is really the bottom line in nursing. The technical tasks of nursing are important, but how many of them could be done by trained technicians? It is in interactions with patients—ferreting out concerns and misunderstandings, clarifying their knowledge about their care and problems— that nurses make their greatest contribution to patient care.

NOTES

1. Donna R. Falvo, *Effective Patient Education* (Rockville, Md.: Aspen Publishers, Inc., 1985), p. 18.

2. Susan Bradshaw, "Treating Yourself," *Nursing Times 83*, no. 3 (February 11, 1987): 40.

3. M.S. Davis, "Physiologic, Psychological, and Demographic Factors in Patient Compliance with Doctor's Orders," *Medical Care* 6, no. 2 (1968): 115–22.

4. Falvo, *Effective Patient Education*, p. 51.

5. Nicholas Freudenberg, "Addressing the Environmental Barriers of Patient Adherence," *Patient Education Newsletter* 7, no. 3 (June 1984): 9.

6. Melvin Berg, "Patient Education and the Physician-Patient Relationship," *Journal of Family Practice* 24, no. 2 (February 1987): 172.

7. Ibid., p. 171.

8. Freudenberg, "Addressing the Environmental Barriers," p. 10.

9. L.W. Green, D.M. Levine, and S. Deeds, "Clinical Trials of Health Education for Hypertensive Outpatients: Design and Baseline Data," *Preventive Medicine* 4 (1975): 417.

10. Stewart M. Dunn, "Reactions to Educational Techniques: Coping Strategies for Diabetes and Learning," *Diabetic Medicine* 3 (1986): 419.

11. A.B. Bergman and R. J. Werner, "Failure of Children To Receive Penicillin by Mouth," *New England Journal of Medicine* 268 (1963): 1334–8.

12. J.P. Kirscht and I.M. Rosenstock, "Patient Adherence to Antihypertensive Medical Regimens," *Journal of Community Health* 3 (1979): 115–24.

13. Dunn, "Reactions to Educational Techniques," p. 423.

14. Yu-Tzu Dai and Marci Catanzano, "Health Beliefs and Compliance with a Skin Care Regimen," *Rehabilitation Nursing* 12, no. 1 (January–February 1987): 13.

15. Klea D. Bertakis, "Educational Impact of a Family Practice Clinic Patient Medical Advisor Booklet," *Family Medicine* 18, no. 4 (July/August 1986): 211.

16. Barbara Klug Redman, *The Process of Patient Education*, 5th ed. (St. Louis: C.V. Mosby Co., 1984), pp. 46–47.

17. Margaret A. Powers, *Handbook of Diabetes Nutritional Management* (Rockville, Md.: Aspen Publishers, Inc., 1987), p. 480.

18. Dunn, "Reactions to Educational Techniques," p. 427.

19. Falvo, *Effective Patient Education*, p. 24.

20. Gary L. Robinson, Alan D. Gilbertson, and Lawrence Litwack, "The Effects of a Psychiatric Patient Education to Medication Program on Post-Discharge Compliance," *Psychiatric Quarterly* 58, no. 2 (Summer 1986–87): 117.

21. Powers, *Handbook of Diabetes Nutritional Management*, p. 482.

22. "How To Shorten Your Patient's Hospital Stay Safely," *NursingLife* (July–August 1986): 51.

23. D. Fink et al., "The Management Specialist in Effective Pediatric Ambulatory Care," *American Journal of Public Health* 59, no. 3 (1969): 527–33.

24. D. Talkington, "Maximizing Patient Compliance by Shaping Attitudes of Self-Directed Health Care," *Journal of Family Practice* 6, no. 3 (1978): 591–5.

5

Planning Patient Education

SETTING A PLAN FOR ACTION

Patient education activities have the potential for causing tremendous positive changes for patients; indeed, they can be literally life-saving. We owe it to our patients to make these activities as fruitful and well-organized as possible. If patient education is presented in lock step fashion, with exactly the same content taught in exactly the same way to every patient, the lack of regard for patient individuality inevitably will retard learning. Perhaps the only thing more damaging is the haphazard approach, where disorganized information is thrown at patients willy-nilly. The lack of logic, of connection, of *plan* leaves patients and their families frustrated and confused.

One of the most important functions of the educator is to create a plan for teaching each patient, a plan individualized to meet the patient's needs. The information gathered during assessment serves as the basis for the educator's plan. There are many approaches to planning for patient education. Heins, Wylie-Rosett, and Davis, for example, recommend a three-step approach to nutritional education for diabetics.

1. The newly diagnosed diabetic grasps the general principles of altering the diet—learning the effects of food on diabetes.
2. The patient receives formal, in-depth education—learning how to select and time the use of specific foods and how to plan meals.
3. The patient learns to factor life style changes—exercise, illness, or altered diabetes status—into the therapy.[1]

This approach of moving from the general to the specific is used by many educators.

Blalock, DeVellis, and Friedberg prefer a problem-solving approach with the following steps:

1. *Confirmation of the problem.* Verify that the patient perceives the illness as a problem. If not, the matter is not pursued.
2. *Identification of alternative strategies.* The patient is encouraged to generate a number of alternative strategies that might be used to solve the problem.
3. *Identification of potential inhibitors.* The patient is helped to identify factors that might interfere with the use of each of these strategies.
4. *Selection of the "best" strategy.* This analysis is based on two considerations: how easily the inhibitors may be eliminated and the availability of facilitators that may be used to counteract them.
5. *Development of an action plan.* An action plan outlines the steps to be carried out, the person responsible for each step, and the date by which each step should be completed.
6. *Follow-up.* Patients are checked to see how they are managing. If necessary, changes in the action plan can be negotiated.[2]

Both of these approaches offer benefits, but both share the same drawback: their very structures make them inflexible. Going from the general to the specific is a well-established principle of education—but it ignores the patient's interests and concerns. In the same way, the problem-solving approach is soundly based as a scientific, well-accepted method—until you run into a patient who cannot or will not cooperate with it. Extracting helpful elements from these and other approaches to planning and putting a unique twist on them to make the plan wholly patient-centered may be the most productive attack.

Figure 5-1 outlines the recommended approach to planning for patient education. Notice that the first step after assessment involves answering the questions that have the highest priority *for the patient*, regardless of how specific or how "out of order" those questions might be. Doing this first not only will lower patient anxiety but also will stimulate interest in other information you offer. It may also lead to other problems and concerns not identified during the initial assessment, which can then be incorporated into the plan.

The rest of the planning process involves a number of activities that need to be addressed separately. The remainder of the chapter discusses in detail each aspect of planning for patient education.

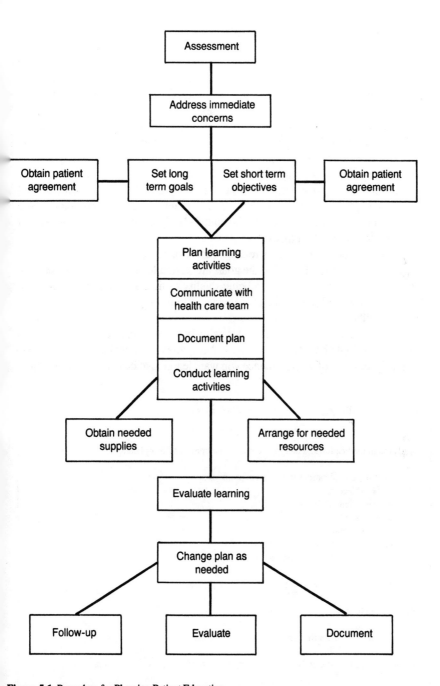

Figure 5-1 Procedure for Planning Patient Education

SETTING GOALS AND OBJECTIVES

Before a decision is made on content or how the teaching will be done or even who will do it, goals and objectives need to be set for the individual patient involved. Since the terms *goal* and *objective* sometimes can be confusingly interchanged, let us define them within the context of this discussion. A *goal* is an outcome—what is achieved; an improvement in patient health attitudes, knowledge, and behavior conducive to future health.[3] Goals are therefore more long-term in nature, focusing on "final" outcomes near the end of the teaching-learning process. Since we want to give the patient a successful experience, motivating further learning and compliance, it is vital that goals be achievable for that patient. Setting high-sounding but unrealistic goals such as "Patient will achieve complete blood glucose control" or "Patient will lose 80 pounds" only discourages patients as they encounter the inevitable setbacks.

Exhibit 5-1, for example, lists realistic, achievable goals for a patient with cirrhosis of the liver. Note that all of the goals are desirable outcomes for this patient, that if achieved they will lead to a better quality of life, a more positive outlook, and possibly even a longer life. These serve as long-range targets for patient and caregivers alike.

Objectives contrast with goals in terms of both time span and specificity. An *objective* is a single behavior for the patient to achieve. Mager describes an objective as a description of a performance you want learners to be able to exhibit before

Exhibit 5-1 Long-Range Goals for a Patient with Cirrhosis

---

1. Through medication and diet, prevent the development of complications.

2. Report any complications to physician promptly, i.e.:
   a. G.I. bleeding
   b. Persistent dizziness
   c. Persistent nausea
   d. Widespread bruising
   e. Confusion or disorientation
   f. Increase in abdominal girth

3. Totally abstain from any alcohol.

4. Maintain blood pressure below 150/90.

5. Maintain normal clotting time.

6. Involve immediate family in treatment plan to provide psychological support.

---

you consider them competent.[4] When setting objectives you must always think in terms of behavior that can be observed. For each objective, be sure that

1. there is an action verb describing what the patient will do (the patient will select . . .)
2. there is a description of what materials, equipment, or personnel should be used (using the daily menu, the patient will select . . .)
3. there is an unambiguous statement of the level of achievement expected or the criteria that will be used to judge that the objective has been successfully achieved (using the daily menu, the patient will select food for breakfast, lunch, and dinner to meet the requirements of a 1500-calorie American Diabetes Association diet)

Most objectives are very short-term in nature. An objective should be achievable by the end of a single teaching session or, at the longest, within a few days. These are small bites out of the larger, more global goals. Exhibit 5-2 shows a few of the objectives relating to the first goal of Exhibit 5-1. Note how much more specific the objectives are, each leading the patient one step closer to the overall, long-term goal.

The objectives for a complicated, chronic illness such as cirrhosis will not be

Exhibit 5-2 Specific Objectives Leading to a Goal

GOAL: Through medication and diet, prevent the development of complications.

OBJECTIVES (Partial List):

1. State the role of sodium in the development of ascites, high blood pressure, and congestive heart failure.
2. Given a list of foods, select those with a low sodium content.
3. Discuss why it is necessary to restrict protein.
4. Using the hospital menu, select meals for a day that will meet the restrictions of a 40-gram protein, 1-gram sodium diet while still meeting requirements for a balanced diet.
5. Given a list of ordered medications, write what each one is supposed to do for you.
6. State how you should take each medication (i.e., with food, after meals, before meals).
7. With the help of the instructor, draw up a daily chart of when the medications will be taken.
8. State what should be done if you accidentally forget to take a dose of medication.
9. State what should be done if you become ill and throw up a dose of medication.
10. Review the list of possible side effects of your medications with the instructor and state what you will do if one develops.

achieved in a few days, nor will they be achieved by the educator alone. A full team effort involving physician, nurses, social workers, therapists, family members, and outside agencies will be necessary to achieve both the objectives and the ultimate goals. For instance, a goal of achieving zero alcohol intake may be a long-term, difficult struggle for everyone involved. Yet that one goal can literally add years to the patient's life.

Luckily, most of our patients do not require such extensive teaching efforts. If the patient is going home with a simple surgical incision and some pain pills, the goals and objectives will be much easier to accomplish. Also, many disease processes will of necessity require patients suffering from them to have very similar goals. Diabetic patients, for example, will have the same goal of blood glucose control through diet and insulin administration. The specific objectives may be somewhat similar, but rarely identical. The individual patient's own knowledge base, abilities, and learning problems will dictate the objectives needed.

Should objectives always be written? Experienced patient educators may feel that their grasp of patient needs is so sophisticated that actually writing out objectives is superfluous. But how will anyone else know what objectives have been set? How will you evaluate and document success or failure? How will patients keep track of their progress? These considerations make it mandatory to write the objectives for every patient, on the care plan and medical record, with a copy for the patient.

Carefully thinking through objectives and putting them in written form helps to keep your thinking on target and learner-centered. Holpp found that when you ignore performance objectives in organizing your material you run the risk of getting lost in your content and forgetting the learner's stake in the process: to learn and apply your content information to real situations. Making benefit statements about objectives will make you think about why you are doing things and question your own motives.[5]

Benefit statements consist of analyzing just what accomplishing an objective will do for the patient. Once the objective has been achieved successfully, what positive result will be attained? Answering this question prevents setting goals and objectives because the patient "should" learn this, or because "we always teach _____ to these patients." It also fights a pervasive problem in patient education, that of the all-knowing, omnipotent caregiver who decides what should be taught without involving the patient in the process. Physicians often fall prey to this syndrome, but nurses are far from immune.

It is absolutely critical to make the patient a partner in creating goals and objectives. Involving patients at the very beginning enables them to "buy into" the plan. It also saves time and effort for the caregiver, since some content may be rejected by the patient as unimportant, inapplicable, or already known. Allowing the patient to have this kind of control goes against the grain for some caregivers, yet this acceptance or rejection of content *will* take place. The only question is will rejection happen openly, at the beginning of the planning process (where it may be open to negotiation), or covertly, during learning (when patient and caregiver alike may unconsciously conspire to ignore the fact that learning is not taking place)?

The key benefit of composing good goals and objectives is that it focuses attention on *learning*, not teaching. What is important is not what is taught, but what the patient comes away with when the process is over. The more specific you make the objectives, the more end-result-oriented they are, the easier it is for patients to visualize themselves actually doing the required actions.

As you work with the patient to compose goals and objectives, the entire planning process becomes easier. Focusing on what is to be accomplished not only enables you to time the teaching, it also provides clues to how the patient learns, what teaching techniques will work best, and how best to evaluate progress. Broadwell sums it up best by stating, "The most important single consideration in the teaching-learning process is the setting of objectives."[6]

DEVELOPING STEP-BY-STEP ACTION PLANS

Once goals and objectives are set and patient agreement is obtained, the next step is actually planning the sequence and timing of instruction. Falvo states that the purpose of the teaching plan is to help the health professional to develop clear, concise descriptions of planned teaching actions, and it should include:

- what type of information the patient should be given
- when the teaching will be done
- where the teaching should be done
- how the teaching will be done (through individual teaching sessions, group sessions, supplemental activities such as films or pamphlets, or a combination of activities)
- who will do the patient teaching[7]

Richert recommends the mnemonic DR. FIRM as a reminder of the components of a successful teaching plan:

Demonstrations, presentations, problem solving
Rehearsal of content by patients, evaluation of performance
Feedback and correctives given to patients
Independent practice of new learnings by patients on their own
Review and reassessment at periodic intervals
Motivation to persevere with new behaviors [8]

Selecting the information to be presented is easy—it essentially already was selected for you when you and the patient agreed on the goals and objectives. What you must do now is to find ways to get that information across in the clearest, easiest way. Assal believes that the role of the teacher is to create appropriate learning situations by choosing activities that will enable patients to acquire the necessary knowledge and skills for their treatment.[9] Considering the information that this patient must learn, what teaching strategies will be most successful, given this particular patient's needs and learning styles?

Perhaps the most critical part of the planning involves timing. Video recordings of classes for patients show that doctors, nurses, and dietitians tend to overload their patients with too much information without leaving sufficient time for what is being said to be correctly assimilated.[10] A number of short sessions (no longer than fifteen minutes at a time) is much more effective than one or two long sessions. Allow time for the patient to process and apply the information before offering more. And again, elicit feedback *from the patient* on the timing and speed of teaching. Frequent question-and-answer sessions coupled with return demonstrations serve as informal evaluation as well as checks on the viability of the plan.

As the plan is developed, put it into action steps. Each action step is an activity the patient will do to achieve an objective. These are learner-centered, not teacher-centered. They focus not on what you will do but on what actions the patient must take. Sample action steps might be: "Watch videotape 'Bathing Your Baby' at 3:00 P.M. Wednesday and complete the study sheet," or "Draw up and administer your own insulin Tuesday under the supervision of an R.N." Note that each action step describes not only what will be done but also the time line involved. No action steps should be open-ended. There should always be a deadline for the activity to be completed.

COMMUNICATING YOUR PLAN

A good rule of thumb about communicating your patient education plans is that there is no such thing as "enough" communication. Saturate people with information. Too many plans have been sabotaged because educators have taken communication for granted. These situations are usually indicated by comments such as, "Well, I wrote it on the care plan," or "Doesn't anyone read the chart?" The answer to the question is, of course, not always—just as people do not always read the care plan. Besides the documentation of your plan, it is imperative that you talk with the people involved, including the patient, the physician, direct care nurses, the charge nurse, the social worker, the dietitian—anyone who may be providing some aspect of the plan, following up its implementation, or evaluating its effectiveness.

Do not wait for people to approach you or to ask about something. Seek them out. Explain things in detail. Tell them exactly what you want them to do and what you will be doing. Show them where the plan is documented. Leave them notes. Leave them messages. Call them on the phone. Talk with them face to face. Communicating effectively is at least as much work as teaching, and it is *your* responsibility. If the patient educator does not bend over backwards to be sure that everyone knows what is planned for the patient, it will not be communicated.

Communication tools include the chart, the care plan, and forms created especially for patient education. But there is no substitute for person-to-person interaction. Only when you are actually talking with the people involved can you explain things in detail, answer questions, clarify a purpose, or clear up a misunderstanding. This means that more time is required—but that time is well spent if it ensures that everyone involved in the patient's care is on the same wavelength. Consider the time an investment in excellence.

DOCUMENTING YOUR PLAN

Once the plan is completed, it must be documented in the record. This may involve writing in several different places. Depending on the requirements of your hospital, the patient teaching plan may need to appear in the patient's chart, on the patient care plan, in the patient's room, and certainly in the educator's files. This duplication may be accomplished by laboriously writing the plan out several different times, but a more efficient method is to develop a single form that can be photocopied. The original goes on the chart. Copies are then attached to the care plan, given to the patient, and carried by the educator.

Exhibit 5-3 is an example of such a form. It can be filled out once, photocopied as many times as necessary, and then placed wherever needed. As each activity is completed by the patient, a check is made directly on the form in front of the appropriate item. The patient also checks off his or her copy, adding self-monitoring as reinforcement. At discharge the form can accompany the patient home, can be sent to a home care agency, or can be used by discharge planners to see exactly where the patient is in accomplishing the goals and objectives. At a glance they can see what has been done and what still needs doing.

Exhibit 5-4 illustrates an education plan filled out for a patient. Progress is being tracked as learning moves forward, and the patient has a handy way of actually seeing accomplishments. Some record needs to be kept of the actual teaching sessions themselves, but this is discussed in Chapter 10. At this point we are concerned with recording and tracking the plan itself.

Exhibit 5-3 Patient Education Plan

EDUCATION PLAN

Patient Name: _____

Room Number: _____ Age: _____

Physician: _____

✔ when   EDUCATION GOALS: _____
completed _____
_____
_____
_____
_____
_____

OBJECTIVES: (use back if more room needed)
_____
_____
_____
_____
_____
_____
_____

ACTION STEPS:
_____
_____
_____
_____
_____
_____
_____
_____
_____

For questions, please call _____ EXT. _____

BUILDING DISCHARGE PLANNING INTO YOUR OVERALL PLAN

Whether discharge planning is a unit responsibility where you work or whether it is run by a separate department, patient education is inextricably entwined with the entire discharge planning process. The focus of all of our activities must be

Exhibit 5-4 Completed Education Plan for Patient

EDUCATION PLAN

Patient Name: ___Jane Doe___

Room Number: ___101___   Age: ___35___

Physician: ___A. Physician, M.D.___

Check when EDUCATION GOALS: ✓ 1. Wounds healed cleanly,
completed   c̄ minimal scarring
    ✓   2. Pain controlled adequately.
          3. Normal gait regained.

OBJECTIVES: (use back if more room needed)
✓   1. Demonstrate proper wound care to nurse.
✓   2. Take off and apply splints correctly.
✓   3. State the actions, side effects, and
        correct method of taking pain med.
        4. Use the walker properly.
        5. Increase ambulation as ordered,
        until normal gait regained.

ACTION STEPS:
✓   1. Teach wound care. 2. Demonstrate
✓   wound care + have pt. return demonstration
✓   3. Demonstrate splint application + removal.
✓   4. Pt. returns demonstration.
✓   5. Have pt. read Package Insert for Synalgos.
✓   6. Review information + answer questions.
✓   7. Ask pt. questions to test recall of information.
        8. Demonstrate use of walker.
        9. Walk c̄ pt., correcting use of walker as needed.
        10. Review ambulation orders c̄ pt.; ✓ understanding

For questions, please call ___Ann___   EXT. ___5041___

---

preparing the patient for discharge. We are not teaching for teaching's sake, or because the information is "nice to know." We are imparting facts that the patient must know in order to improve or maintain wellness once he or she is out of the health care environment.

Keep in constant touch with the discharge planners. Be sure that they know what you are doing and that you know what they are doing. In some hospitals, these two functions take place completely separately from each other. You must make the effort to change "Never the twain shall meet" into "We're all in this together." Attend discharge planning meetings; invite the discharge planners to patient education meetings. Solicit their suggestions and advice. And get involved in home care follow-up—discovering what happens after discharge is the only really effective means of evaluating both patient education and discharge planning.

TIMING: WHEN DO YOU TEACH?

The rest of the patient education process—conducting learning activities, arranging for supplies and resources, evaluating learning—are covered in later chapters, but there is one more issue falling under planning that needs to be addressed: timing. When do you teach? We have stressed the importance of setting deadlines for accomplishment; that sort of time line is necessary to enable both teacher and learner to have a feeling of urgency and importance about learning. But timing is something more. It involves nursing judgment—knowing when to push and when to let up. This judgment must be made with the constant knowledge that time itself is limited.

Time Constraints: Reality versus Ideality

Ideally each patient would be allowed enough time to absorb new material completely before anything else was introduced. Numerous practice sessions with the educator would enable patients to feel completely comfortable and confident about their skills before discharge. In reality, of course, few patients can remain in the hospital long enough to become proficient in self-care. In outpatient settings the press of appointments forces rushed teaching sessions just as in acute care facilities. How can learning be paced?

Powers recommends aiming for a 75 percent success rate before implementing the next step in the plan. She states,

> The hard part is wanting to move the patient along faster; what is important, however, is that progress is made. Remember, no progress is possible when a patient completely dismisses an entire plan as unreasonable and unworkable. Early compromises pay off later.[11]

A 75 percent success rate seems workable—trying for perfection would be frustrating to learner and teacher alike.

Rather than try to cram information into a single session each day, schedule two, three, or even four shorter sessions instead. Enlisting staff and family for follow-up and reinforcement extends patient education beyond formal sessions. And communicating with home care agencies for long-term teaching and follow-up enables the education plan to be carried out at a more leisurely pace, giving more time for information processing and application when chronic illnesses are involved.

The Golden Moment

Nurses working at the bedside have a special opportunity to catch patients at "the golden moment"—that particular instant when the patient is most receptive to being taught. This may take place during a formal teaching session, but more frequently it occurs at odd times during the day, evening, or night. Perhaps during the bath the patient asks about skin care. Or while eating a meal the patient questions the significance of the restricted sodium notation on the menu. Or a family member asks about home care of the Broviac catheter while the nurse is changing a dressing.

Rather than say, "This will be explained during your teaching session tomorrow morning," or "The diabetic educator will teach you about that later," it is extremely important that the nurse on the scene at the time present the information. At this point the patient is ripe for teaching and really wants to learn whatever issue has arisen. To be put off is not only frustrating but ultimately demotivating.

Incorporate such teaching moments into your care. Rather than remain mute while you are performing treatments (or worse, boring the patient with personal gossip or reminiscences), explain what you are doing. Involve the patient in the procedure—holding something for you or handing you tape. When you go in during mealtimes, do not just ask how things are. Ask how the patient intends to follow the diet at home, or what questions there are about the food restrictions. In other words, think patient education!

Being familiar with the education plan for the patient enables you to use the time you spend with that patient to achieve learning objectives and to help prepare for a safe, effective discharge. The more carefully and completely education is planned, the more efficiently it can be implemented. A clearly communicated plan makes follow-up and evaluation quicker and easier, too. The remaining chapters deal with different aspects of, and influences on, the patient education plan.

NOTES

1. Joan M. Heins, Judith Wylie-Rosett, and Susan Green Davis, "The New Look in Diabetic Diets," *American Journal of Nursing* 87, no. 2 (February 1987): 198.

2. Susan J. Blalock, Brenda M. DeVellis, and Charlotte Friedberg, "Helping Patients Cope with Arthritis," *Patient Education Newsletter* 7, no. 6 (December 1984): 7–8.

3. Elsie Osinski, "Developing Patient Outcomes As a Quality Measure of Nursing Care," *Nursing Management* 18, no. 10 (October 1987): 28.

4. Robert F. Mager, *Preparing Instructional Objectives*, 2nd ed. (Belmont, Calif.: Fearon Publishers, 1975), p. 5.

5. Lawrence Holpp, "Technical Training for Nontechnical Learners," *Training and Development Journal* 41, no. 10 (October 1987): 55.

6. Martin M. Broadwell, *The Supervisor As an Instructor: A Guide For Classroom Training*, 2nd ed. (Reading, Mass.: Addison-Wesley Publishing Co., 1970), p. 47.

7. Donna R. Falvo, *Effective Patient Education* (Rockville, Md.: Aspen Publishers, Inc., 1985), p. 61.

8. J.W. Richert, *Effective Patient Teaching*, Module 3 (Pitman, N.J.: American Association of Diabetic Educators Continuing Education Self-Study Program, 1984).

9. J.P. Assal, "Self-Management of Diabetes: A Therapeutic Success but a Teaching Failure?" *Diabetic Medicine* 2, no. 5 (September 1985): 421.

10. Ibid.

11. Margaret A. Powers, *Handbook of Diabetes Nutritional Management* (Rockville, Md.: Aspen Publishers, Inc., 1987), p. 474.

6

The Role of the Family

THE FAMILY: HELP OR HINDRANCE?

Some health care professionals regard family members as adversaries at worst or obstacles at best when preparing patients for discharge. This attitude may be a carry-over from one approach to patient care, where the emphasis is on the person giving the care rather than on the person receiving it. If one looks at the nurse's job as a series of tasks that must be completed, then family members are indeed just so many hindrances to that job. They take time away from passing medications and giving treatments as they demand explanations or complain that their loved one is frightened or in pain. But of course from this point of view the *patients* are the biggest obstacles of all. They take even more of the nurse's time away from required tasks.

For the sake of the profession as well as the patients, let us hope that this task-oriented care philosophy is not widespread, despite environmental constraints in many settings that seem designed to encourage it. I believe that most nurses feel a deep commitment to their patients—that is why they went into nursing in the first place. A patient-oriented approach to nursing necessarily requires viewing the family as a prime force in the patient's life and as the educator's greatest ally in preparing the patient for discharge.

The patient's family is probably the single most significant determinant of success or failure for the education plan. By "family" we need to refer not just to the patient's blood relatives, but also to friends who serve in a support role. The hackneyed phrase "significant other" encompasses this group. If you work in an environment where only members of the immediate family are allowed to visit the patient and participate in care (critical care areas seem to be prime offenders), you should be working for change. Such a policy strips a significant number of patients

71

of the very people who will be helping them with self-care.

Social support can take three forms:

1. Tangible support occurs when someone provides money, skills, or other resources to help the patient achieve a specific goal.
2. Informational support is the provision of factual knowledge by someone for the purpose of influencing the patient's health behavior.
3. Empathy, encouragement, praise, positive reinforcement, and agreement combine to offer the patient emotional support.[1]

On first examination, tangible support would seem to be the most helpful, yet evidence suggests that the indirect role of family or friends as general providers of support is more important than any direct role they play in encouraging healthy behaviors and patient compliance. Patients who perceive that their families and friends are concerned and supportive appear to have better health outcomes than those who do not, regardless of whether or not members of their supportive networks are directly involved in encouraging them to adhere to the therapeutic regimen.[2]

This finding is important to keep in mind, particularly when contact (and thus teaching) with the family is limited. Ideally both patient and family can be informed fully about the plan of care, but if this proves impossible, a supportive family can help an informed patient comply with the treatment plan.

Cirincione studied diabetic children and found that how the family functions before the diagnosis of diabetes is perhaps the best indicator of how things will go later. The study indicated that a child's adherence to the diabetes regimen appeared to be predicted by the child's adjustment to the diabetes and by the child's self-esteem, competence, and ability to interact with peers and family.[3] Most of these factors are controlled by previous family socialization, so the influence of the family is underlined even more strongly.

GAINING FAMILY SUPPORT

Most families follow certain predictable stages when a loved one is ill:

Stage 1: *Denial.* Family members typically react with with shock and disbelief. This may lead to rationalizing away symptoms and resisting treatment. Clinging to unrealistic expectations is an offshoot of denial.

Stage 2: *Disorganization.* Out of denial comes a sense of disorganization. Family members may become demanding and irrational and give way to anger and blame directed at caregivers or each other.

Stage 3: *Anxiety*. Anxiety lasts until family members develop new ways to cope. They may be too overwhelmed to make any decisions confidently.

Stage 4: *Adjustment*. More information, more time, and new ways of coping with the reality of their situation help most families adjust to a loved one's illness.[4]

Assessing what stage individual family members are in is an important part of gaining family support. People struggling through Stages 1 and 2 will probably be unable to process information efficiently. Stage 3 is not a good time to offer difficult alternatives to patient and family. One of the most important interventions for an educator is assisting the family to a productive adjustment to the stresses of illness.

Family members need more than information to achieve this goal. They need a sympathetic ear, a caregiver who will listen to their fears and frustrations non-judgmentally. This is not the time to shrug off anxieties with some casual comment: "Oh, I wouldn't worry about that," or "There's no need to be afraid that he'll have another heart attack" (or "have an insulin reaction," or "not be able to walk," or whatever the fear may be). *Listen* to what they are saying. Be aware of the feelings underlying the words. Remember that tasks we take for granted, such as injections and dressing changes, can be terrifying to an unprepared neophyte.

This sort of active listening not only keys you in to what the family fears and feels, it also provides clues for what teaching will be necessary. Let the family know what a tremendous help they can be to the patient and how much their support will mean in working toward recovery. Enlist them in the war against noncompliance. Winning them over to the alliance of patient, physician, and nurse improves your chances of success 100 percent.

In return, your support for the family can be invaluable. The most helpful thing to offer immediately is a realistic orientation to the hospital world.[5] Family members (and patients) need to know the rules of this alien culture they are suddenly forced to join. What are their roles? What help can they expect? What recourse do they have? With whom should they lodge complaints? For that matter, what is a "reasonable" complaint? Few people want to be perceived as troublemakers, but they have a need to protect their loved ones. If they are told what problems and inconveniences are a natural and inevitable part of the hospital environment (such as a realistic waiting period for pain medication, for instance), they will know how to recognize a problem that needs their intervention.

The more help you can give to the family during early hospitalization the more likely they are to perceive you as a trustworthy source of information. When formal teaching begins, your goal of involving the family will be easier to achieve.

TEACHING FAMILY MEMBERS

Ideally, key family members will be present during patient teaching sessions, but in reality this rarely occurs. So many people work full-time that patient educators usually have to arrange family teaching sessions during evening and weekend hours. This flexibility is necessary to teach effectively the support people who will be caring for the patient at home. Requiring people to take time off from work leads to resentment and divided attention, neither of which is conducive to learning.

Whom Will You Teach?

One of the most important decisions involves which family members to teach. Should it be the spouse, a son or daughter, a friend? Sometimes this decision is made for you. The spouse may be physically unable to provide care, or all of the children may live far away. More often there will be a choice of possible caregivers. The temptation may be to teach as many different family members as possible. Resist it. Not only is it nearly impossible to coordinate instruction for three or four different people, but the more people involved, the more potential for misunderstandings.

More effective results are obtained by choosing one person, or at most two people, to support the patient in home care. The most appropriate person is the one who spends the most time with the patient. Sometimes this person will not want the job and will suggest someone else as the at-home caregiver. It is usually best to be guided by the family in this decision. Most family units have a person designated as "the responsible one," even if this terminology is never used. Typically this is the oldest daughter, but the designee may be male or female, young or old, in any birth order or relationship to the patient. There are some patients who prefer a friend to care for them, even if family members are available.

Assessment of the responsible person is as important as your original assessment of the patient. How does the designated caregiver feel about having to learn the information and provide support and care? Resentment or uncertainty must be dealt with before learning can begin. All of the learning needs assessments you made about the patient as to learning style preference, cognitive abilities, and current knowledge must be made for this person.

What Will You Teach?

The alternative caregiver needs the same information as the patient in order to provide support, feedback, and reinforcement once the patient embarks on self-care. In many cases, these family members need *more* information, particularly in cases where patients have sensory deficits or problems with memory or cognition. For instance, a daughter caring for an elderly parent who cannot remember to take medications on time will need to know not only the schedule of doses but also what the drugs are supposed to do, whether they can be taken with food, their possible side effects, what to do about a missed dose, and what to do if the patient vomits or cannot take the medicine because of illness. This information probably would be more than the patient could absorb or use.

A general breakdown of the information needed by family members includes:

- explanation of the diagnosis
- explanation of the prognosis
- goals of treatment
- overall plan of treatment
- specific procedures
- medication administration
- potential problems and how to react
- when to call the physician
- sources of help

The specific information required obviously depends on the individual patient involved. One special case involves parents of the child patient. Usually the mother is the selected caregiver, but it may be the father or both parents. Besides teaching the general categories of information listed above, educators must also teach parents ways to help their child manage hospitalization and treatment. The younger the child, the more dependent on parental support he or she will be. The goal in this case is to help the child learn to cope with the procedures and to develop skills in managing discomfort. Pridham, Adelson, and Hansen found that children between ages two and seven, because of their capacity for symbolic representation, imagination, and unrealistic notions of causality, are prone to a greater variety of fears than either younger or older children. These children are much more dependent on familiar adults than are older children.[6]

Since information from parents will be more readily accepted by children than the same information from a strange adult, teaching the parents to teach the child is the obvious strategy. Recommended instructions from educator to parent to child include:

- what will happen when
- what sensations are likely to be experienced
- what behavior is expected
- what can be done to tolerate or actively manage the procedure

These explanations should be given shortly before procedures occur.[7]

Caregivers supporting adult patients also have special needs. In many cases educators focus almost exclusively on performing procedures: "This is how you give an injection" or "Here's how to change the dressing." Certainly that is needed, but Feuer found that the greatest challenge for family caregivers is developing the confidence to do what is right for the patient. Teaching them not only the "what to do's" but also the "what to expects" is one of the best stress reducers.[8] Every family member (and every patient) fears the unexpected. What should things look like? And what do I do if they do not look that way? When should I get worried and when should I remain calm?

Helping patient and family to understand the normal variations in the recovery process enables them to understand that getting better is not always an easy or sequential process. For example, when teaching how to irrigate a catheter, the nurse can explain possible normal variations in the color of urine and how the rate of urine return may vary from day to day.[9] This sort of anticipatory teaching can prevent anxiety, uncertainty, and lack of confidence for family caregivers.

The importance of written instructions cannot be overemphasized. The "how-to's" of writing these are covered in Chapter 7, but two points deserve special attention here. First, the instructions should be very well organized and as simple as possible. Reams of closely printed pages will be confusing and may seem so overwhelming that the information may not even be read. Second, review the handouts with the family. Going over the written instructions provides the opportunity to answer questions and clear up misunderstandings. It also ensures that the written material has been read. This is especially important for very detailed information such as diets. Having something concrete to refer to at home can be quite literally a lifesaver.

HANDLING FAMILY PROBLEMS

Identifying potential (or actual) problems is an important and ongoing part of patient and family education. As problems are identified, strategies can be developed to cope with them *before* they cause active harm. Nurses are in a unique position to identify possible problems because they see the patient and family together more than do other caregivers.

In one instance, nurses caring for patients with cardiac disease noticed significant rises in the patients' blood pressures whenever the patients' wives showed unhappiness or apprehension during visits. When the nurses began discussing the patients' conditions, progress, diets, and medications with the wives before they saw their husbands, there were fewer sudden rises in blood pressure during the wives' visits, fewer phone calls from family members trying to contact the physician to check on a patient's condition, and less uneasiness on the part of the patients' wives when they came to visit.[10]

Many people are reluctant to express their fears and uncertainties, believing that to do so reflects badly on them or might delay the patient's discharge. Part of the problem identification involves "giving permission"—whether implicitly or explicitly—for family members to say that they are not sure they can do what is required of them. Even more difficult is the admission that they do not *want* to do it. When a chronic illness or a severely disabled patient requires the family to reorganize their lives completely, unspoken resentment is a natural development. This resentment eventually can affect care and patient compliance. Acknowledging these feelings as natural and expected encourages the family to talk about them and to work through ways to lessen stress. If home caregivers repress anger and resentment as undutiful or selfish, the feelings can fester and eventually become overwhelming.

We tend to forget the physical and psychological toll that providing care and support can take on family members. In the hospital, caregivers work their shifts and leave. Home caregivers cannot get away. Day and night they must cope with the problems inherent in the illness of a loved one. In one study of 600 women over 60 years of age, more than 50 percent had significant illnesses of their own that the researchers believe were exacerbated by the continued provision of physical care and emotional support to others.[11]

One useful intervention for family problems is a support group. Many hospitals offer these groups, usually facilitated by a psychologist or social worker. Home caregivers get together once a week in the evening to discuss what is going on at home and how they feel about it. One such group, aptly named "Help, I Can't Do It by Myself Anymore," has had large attendance and many testimonials from participants on how the support group helped them through the "most difficult period" of their lives.

Another extremely helpful resource for family caregivers is a respite program. Available in most large metropolitan areas, respite programs provide care for chronically ill patients so that the responsible family member(s) can get away from the intense demands of caregiving. The services offered by a respite program can range from providing an aide to stay in the home over the weekend to caring for the patient in a residential or special care facility for a week or more. Respite enables family caregivers to decompress from the incredible stress of dealing with twenty-four-hour responsibilities for care.

An important part of helping families to cope with patient care and compliance problems involves developing strategies to cope with problems that *might* occur as well as ones that already exist. Butterfield recommends promoting anticipatory problem solving by asking, "What could you do if this tube becomes twisted?" or "Who is available for you to call in the evening if you become concerned?" Helping patients and family to problem solve may prevent a panic episode at home when, for the first time, "It looked different than it did in the hospital." Research has found that patients who had received anticipatory problem solving on what to do if they missed a dose of medicine had significantly higher rates of compliance.[12]

Anticipatory problem solving should be done for all patients. We take for granted so many of the things that can happen at home, yet they can alarm home caregivers. How much drainage is normal? What should I do if part of the incision gapes open? If I'm sick and can't eat, should I stop taking my insulin? These are examples of questions that patients and family members might ask—or might not even think about until the situation arises and there is no one around to ask.

Cast your mind forward, and brainstorm what might happen in each case. Since you cannot possibly cover every possible contingency, select the problems most likely to occur, and guide the home caregivers through the problem-solving process. Do not take it for granted that the people you are teaching will know what to do or even what to observe. In one case the family member being taught was a registered nurse, and everyone assumed that she knew everything about diabetes. Teaching was perfunctory at best. The nurse involved worked in obstetrics and had not cared for diabetics since she graduated from nursing school. She said nothing to the patient educator because she felt as if she *should* know all of this. Although she eventually learned through self-study what was needed to care for her mother, on a follow-up interview with another educator she verbalized her frustration at receiving so little help.

The coolest health care professional can become unsure when a loved one is the patient. If a nurse can experience such fear and uncertainty, imagine the feelings of an inexperienced lay person. Patient educators must take the responsibility for guiding family caregivers through the minefield of home care; if we do not, who will?

COMMUNITY RESOURCES FOR THE FAMILY

Home caregivers need a supportive working environment just as do hospital staff members. Feuer points out that families need to know about the community services that are available, willing, and even eager to provide those extra services to lighten the load. Even more important, they need *access* and *instruction* through some helpful ombudsman.[13]

The patient educator can act as a bridge between patient/family and the most appropriate resources. Figure 6-1 illustrates this role in helping client and resource to connect. Most lay people know little about "what's out there" in their community, and without assistance either may not find the help that they need or may end up with something that is either inappropriate or much more expensive than need be.

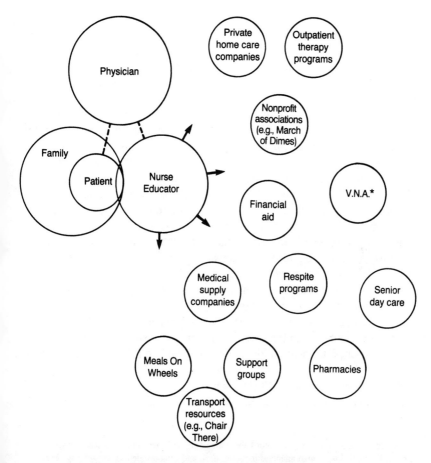

Figure 6-1 Patient Educator's Role As a Bridge to Community Resources

*Visiting Nurses' Association

Finding the Right Resources

Before you can help the family, obviously you must discover what community resources exist in your area. Figure 6-1 contains a sampling of agencies, associations, and groups available in most cities. Rural areas may not have access to as many organized resources, but they may have other sources of assistance not available in some cities, such as church aid societies, extended family groups, and social clubs that help certain cases through fund-raising activities.

Spend some time investigating what exists around you. Not only will it help your patients, it may someday prove invaluable for your own family. One source of information with which we are all familiar is the social services department. Hospital social workers are usually familiar with a spectrum of community resources in their roles as patient advocates and discharge planners. Make an appointment with a social worker and ask what resources he or she has used and how well they have worked out. If your hospital has a separate discharge planning section, speak to the discharge planners also. Take notes. Ask for evidence that the agencies they mention have helped patients and their families. Many discharge planning units are developing evaluation forms to assess the services offered by various community resources. Exhibit 6-1 is an example of such a form.

To get a patient's-eye view of the community, look through the yellow pages of the phone book. Notice how various agencies and companies advertise their services. Compare the statements about services provided, financial arrangements, and reliability with what you have learned from other sources. This information can furnish you with insights on questions the family members may ask and some of the concerns they may have.

Community newspapers are another source of information about available resources. Stories will be printed about community members involved in helping organizations or about victims of disease or accident being assisted by others in the area. Recent features from a single newspaper have revealed the existence of a group that teaches disabled children and adults how to ride and care for horses,

Exhibit 6-1 Community Resource Evaluation Form

EVALUATION

Please complete the following questions about the home care agency that has been serving you. This will help us know what agencies to recommend and what problems need solving. Thanks for your help!

1. How soon after referral were you contacted by the agency?

2. Was the initial contact person courteous and helpful?

3. Were you visited by a supervisor? If so, how often did he or she come and what did they do?

4. Were you satisfied with the care provided? If not, why?

5. Did you have problems getting service? If so, what was done about it by the agency?

6. Were you satisfied with the financial arrangements?

Please add any further comments and return the form in the enclosed envelope.

achieving many therapeutic benefits for the patients; a new summer camp for diabetic children; a club for elderly people that provides transport to social events, museums, plays, and other opportunities for socialization and stimulation; and a support group for caretakers of patients with Alzheimer's disease.

Do not forget patients and families themselves as a source of information about community resources. They may have discovered an organization, club, or source of financial aid that has escaped the attention of hospital people. Wherever you get the information—care provider, newspaper, telephone book, family member, or some other source—note the source. A simple card file works well: write the name, address, and phone number of the resource, as well as any special information about it that you want to be sure to remember. Refer to this file when recommending help for your patients. An alphabetical listing by condition name rather than by resource name may prove easier to reference. It is hard to remember the name of a particular group; it is much easier to look under "diabetes" or "ALS" (amyotrophic lateral sclerosis) to discover agencies specific to victims of these conditions.

Helping with Decisions

Besides providing information to the family, the educator may need to help them decide which resource to choose. This is not always an easy position to be in. One hesitates to urge family members to pick one agency over another, or one form of care over another. But if the family is trapped in one of the first three stages of adjustment mentioned earlier in the chapter, particularly the anxiety stage, they may be incapable of deciding on their own. Vacillating over decisions that must be made immediately because of financial or regulatory pressures can throw the family into a crisis state.

Present the information to patient and/or family. If they seemed locked in hopeless ambivalency after they have had a chance to think about it and discuss it, guide them through the decision-making process step by step:

1. Make a list of the pros and cons. What are the benefits and drawbacks attached to each alternative?
2. Discuss the appropriate family members' reactions to the alternatives. There may be emotional reasons affecting the decision that need to be brought out.
3. If the family still is unable to decide, suggest a trial of one choice. If after a fair period of time they find that it does not meet their needs, they can go to another resource.

Another factor to keep in mind concerns your own preferences and prejudices. Be aware of them so that you can consciously avoid affecting the decision with your own feelings. For instance, you may believe strongly that placing parents in a nursing home is wrong. But for the particular family you are counseling, nursing home placement may be the only viable choice. Do not force your own beliefs or values on them—let them make the best decision for their situation.

Before turning the family out on their own, be sure to check one more time that they understand the instructions. Answer any new questions. Feuer suggests checking that the home caregiver knows what *not* to do for the patient as well as what to do—a timely reminder of something that is easy to forget.[14] Some family members will be tempted to do everything for the patient unless reminded not to do so. Offer home caregivers your phone number so that they can call to clarify instructions or ask questions, and be sure that they have the phone numbers of any home care agencies or equipment suppliers. And have confidence that they can do it—that message will come through loud and clear.

NOTES

1. Alexis S. Budlong-Springer, "Enhancing Patients' Social Support Systems," *Patient Education Newsletter* 6, no. 6 (December 1983): 6.

2. Meredith Minkler, "Social Support and Health: Programmatic Implications," *Patient Education Newsletter* 5, no. 3 (June 1982): 32.

3. Sandra Cirincione, "Dealing with Diabetes: A Family Affair," *Countdown* IX, no. 2 (Spring 1988): 12.

4. Judy Bluhm, "Helping Families in Crisis Hold On," *Nursing87* 17, no. 10 (October 1987): 44–6.

5. Ibid., p. 46.

6. Karen F. Pridham, Freddi Adelson, and Marc F. Hansen, "Helping Children Deal with Procedures in a Clinic Setting: A Developmental Approach," *Journal of Pediatric Nursing* 2, no. 1 (February 1987): 13.

7. Ibid., p. 18.

8. Louis C. Feuer, "Discharge Planning: *Home* Caregivers Need Your Support, Too," *Nursing Management* 18, no. 4 (April 1987): 58.

9. Patricia Butterfield, "Nursing Interventions Aid Patient Transition from Hospital to Home," *Idaho R.N.* 10, no. 2 (March–April 1987): 13.

10. W.M. Wollert, "Achievement through Clinical Practice—A Practical Approach to Patient Care," in *Exploring Progress in Nursing Practice* (New York: American Nurses' Association, 1965), pp. 12–15.

11. Minkler, "Social Support and Health," p. 33.

12. Butterfield, "Nursing Intervention," p. 13.

13. Feuer, "Discharge Planning," p. 58.

14. Ibid., p. 59.

7

Developing Tools
for Patient Education

Most patient educators rely on audiovisual tools to support teaching efforts and emphasize key points. Audiovisual tools include written materials (handouts, books, pamphlets, instruction sheets), display materials (posters, bulletin board layouts), demonstration materials (models, equipment, mock-ups), and the various types of software (audiotape, slide/sound, film, slide, videotape, transparencies, and computer programs). Considering the wide range of materials available, it is important that educators know how to select the tools that will accomplish goals effectively and efficiently.

Some of the questions that need to be answered include: How effective are these tools in terms of retention of information? Do different tools have any impact on compliance? Should you purchase materials already prepared or make your own? How can you maximize the learning stimulated by the use of the various audiovisual tools?

GENERAL EFFECTIVENESS OF AUDIOVISUAL TOOLS

Bartlett discovered that both research and practitioner experience indicate:

- Instructional aids (such as pamphlets, models, slides, videotapes, and computers) are effective in increasing knowledge. However, no instructional aid has demonstrated a clear-cut advantage over another in promoting knowledge gain.
- Knowledge gain is not sufficient to assure patient adherence to the regimen.
- Instructional aids should *supplement*, not take the place of, personalized patient education efforts.[1]

These key findings have important implications for our practice. Since many different aids can influence learning positively, with no single aid proving most effective, a variety of learning materials is needed so that a tool may be selected to suit the individual patient. Keep in mind that flexibility is crucial. A rigid program that is the same for every patient will probably fail to reach the majority of learners. Here is where individual interaction makes the difference: working with the patient enables you to tailor instruction to fit patient needs.

Falvo stresses that educational materials should be used to supplement information the educator has given to the patient. Giving patients materials to take home provides a resource for reinforcement of information and clarification of facts.[2] Most patients will feel more confident with checklists, instruction sheets, and other resource materials they can refer to at home. Written materials stand in for patient educators when they cannot be there.

Written Materials

In these days of high-technology, slickly packaged audiovisual materials, some people tend to denigrate the simple handout. But in education as in art, simpler is often better. One hospital, believing that a new approach might be effective, conducted a market survey to determine whether written patient education materials should be supplemented with videotapes. Patients indicated that the current packet was satisfactory: only 1 percent said that they would purchase a videotape, and 90 percent said that the reading material helped with home care.[3]

Redman describes printed teaching material as "frozen language," selective in its description of reality, providing limited feedback, but constantly available. Print partially relaxes time requirements and is more efficient than oral language (except for those who have not learned to read well) because readers can control the speed at which they read and comprehend. Most people who can read efficiently prefer to acquire information by reading; it is ideal for understanding complex concepts and relationships.[4]

There are certainly many preprinted, mass-produced written materials that can be ordered for your patients. Every patient educator has probably used some prepackaged pamphlets, booklets, or posters, and yet every educator has also experienced frustration that specific patient needs are not addressed by available commercial literature. The use of a judicious mixture of purchased and self-composed material is the best strategy.

Composing Written Material

The advantages to writing your own material include the ability to:

- target the information to fit your facility's policies, procedures, and equipment
- build in answers to questions frequently asked by your patients
- highlight points especially important to the attending physicians on staff
- tailor written materials to reinforce specific oral instructions you normally give to patients
- clarify difficult concepts by using approaches that have worked for you

These advantages are undeniable; however, they will accrue only if the materials are well written and well laid-out. Too many tools composed by patient educators are too long, too detailed, and written at a level more appropriate for nuclear physicists than for the average lay person. Considering the many benefits of good written materials, how to put together effective handouts may be one of the most valuable skills a patient educator can learn.

Writing for Clarity and Completeness

As you sit down to compose patient education material, do not begin writing right away. You will save yourself time and trouble if you organize things first. Writing handouts, like teaching, begins with objectives. What is the patient to learn? What is this material supposed to accomplish? If these objectives are not already written, do them first. Once you have articulated the purpose of the handout, sketch an outline.

The outline enables you to organize the material before writing. Without this step, your writing will tend to wander, requiring extensive and time-consuming revisions and sometimes even a complete rewrite. Lay out the important points and the flow of information from one point to another before you actually try to put the material into words. Exhibit 7-1 is an outline for a handout to help patients administer medications to infants.

Use the outline to guide you through the actual writing. If the content is well-organized, putting it on paper will be an easier task, leaving you free to concentrate on making the information as understandable as possible. Research investigating patient communication has shown that most patients fail to remember what they are told and that the ratio of forgotten to remembered facts increases dramatically with the number of facts presented. For example, patients who are told four statements will forget only one; if given eight, however, they will forget four.[5] These facts underline the importance of composing clear, easy-to-read handouts to reinforce verbal instructions.

The almost overwhelming temptation when writing patient education materials is to load everything you can think of into the tool. Every fact, every precaution is written out in detail. This is a mistake. When faced with a long, wordy collection

Exhibit 7-1 Outline for a Handout on Administering Medication

---

OBJECTIVE: Administer medications orally to the infant once they have been drawn up.
(NOTE: How to draw up medications is shown in a separate handout.)

  I. Cautions about Safe Administration
     A. Preventing choking
     B. Importance of complete dosages

 II. Mixing with Formula
     A. Small amounts
     B. Total feeding—CAUTION

III. Medications Given a.c.

 IV. General Rules

  V. Missed Doses
     A. Vomited doses
     B. Forgotten doses

---

of pages, most people will either skim over it or not read it at all. To make your
materials appealing and readable, follow these guidelines:

- Choose the critical facts that patients *must* know, and make these the focus of
  the handout.
- Keep the terminology simple; the best way to accomplish this is to limit words
  to one or two syllables. This takes careful thought and creative writing, but it
  has a tremendous payoff.
- As much as possible, write the information in a logical, step-by-step fashion.
  Make it easy for the reader to follow instructions.
- Concentrate on *how to* rather than *why*. The reasons for doing things should
  be covered during oral instruction. Including rationales in the handouts
  lengthens materials unnecessarily.
- Make instructions active, using *you* rather than *the patient* or an unstated third
  person.
- KEEP IT SHORT!

Exhibit 7-2 shows a one-page handout based on the outline in Exhibit 7-1. Note
how the outline guides you through the content of the handout. Patients reading the
handout will not be confused by complex terminology or long rationales for action.
The instructions should guide them through the procedure with little room for
misunderstanding.

Exhibit 7-2 Handout on Administering Medication

GIVING THE MEDICINE

Any time you give medicine to your baby, remember that babies often have trouble swallowing. *Never* squirt medicine into the baby's mouth—this can cause choking. Follow the directions listed below to give the medicine safely.

IMPORTANT: The baby should receive the dose ordered by the doctor. Do not change the dose without checking with your doctor.

DIRECTIONS
1. Medicine can be mixed with a tablespoon or two of formula and given to the baby by bottle. Don't put the rest of the formula into the bottle until all the medicine is gone.
2. Don't add medicine to the whole feeding unless your baby takes all of the milk at every feeding.
3. If the medicine must be given on an empty stomach, mix it with with a few teaspoonfuls of water and give it to the baby by nipple.

BASIC RULES
- Shake liquid medicine hard before measuring.
- Read the label and instructions for all medicines.
- Never give medicine in the dark.

IF YOU MISS A DOSE
- If the baby vomits the medicine more than 20 minutes after giving it, do not repeat the dose.
- Give the medicine again if the baby vomits within 20 minutes of the dose, but only *once* again.
- Call the doctor if the baby vomits two doses in a row.

IMPORTANT: Do not try to make up for a missed dose by doubling or increasing the next dose. Give the ordered dose.

Testing for Readability

Studies have found that most people in the United States read on or below the eighth grade level. Yet a 1982 survey of patient education literature found that 92 percent of the material was written above the eighth grade level[6]; this is probably so because patient educators are highly educated people with a scientific background who are used to reading complex materials written at the college level or above. This can make it difficult to write simply.

There are many different ways to test for readability. Most involve time-consuming mathematical formulas. One of the simpler methods is the fog index, which anyone can calculate:

1. Select a 100-word passage of continuous sentences.
2. Count the number of sentences in the passage.
3. Divide the total number of words in the selection by the number of sentences.

This gives the average sentence length in words.

4. Count the words that are pronounced with three syllables or more in the passage. Exclude those that are capitalized, those that are combinations of short words (such as lifesaver), and three-syllable words formed by adding prefixes and suffixes (such as readjust and carrying). The total is the percentage of "hard" words in the selected passage.

5. Add the totals of steps 3 and 4 together and multiply by 0.4. This result is your fog index.

Most popular magazines have a fog index of about 6, meaning that a typical sixth grader can understand them with some difficulty. *Time* and *Newsweek* have fog indexes of about 10 (average tenth grader). The fog index of Exhibit 7-2 is 9.4, meaning that a typical high school freshman should be able to comprehend the directions. Yet if you give the handout to most sixth-graders, they will be able to understand it. Why is this? Because the two recurring, three-syllable words in the handout are *medicine* and *formula*—terms that are familiar to most English-speaking people. If we substitute the word *drug* for *medicine*, the fog index drops to 7.4. Substituting *milk* for *formula* as well drops it further to 6.2. So why not make the substitutions? Because *drug* is a word with negative connotations for many lay people, and someone might interpret *milk* to mean plain milk rather than the baby's formula that the directions intend.

This is the single greatest drawback to using readability formulas. They do not—cannot—take into account the meaning and intent of the words. *Medicine* and *formula* are commonly used, well-understood words, despite being pronounced with three syllables. The first word is nonthreatening and sounds far more therapeutic than its one-syllable synonym. The second word is more specific and accurate than its one-syllable counterpart. Write for understanding rather than by a hard and fast mathematical formula.

The second drawback to readability formulas is the time involved in calculation. The fog index is one of the simpler ones, but how many educators will take the time to calculate it for each handout and pamphlet they write? Yet some consideration of readability needs to be made. Exhibit 7-3 shows the same handout as in Exhibit 7-2, but it is written in a style often seen in patient education materials. Not only is the fog index 11.2, but the instructions are very hard to follow. Most lay people would need to read at the graduate-school level to comprehend a handout written like this.

When you prepare written material for patients and family, keep it simple. Do not write as if you were preparing a dissertation or composing an article for professional colleagues. Follow these rules:

1. Use simple terminology. Define any technical terms or abbreviations the first

Exhibit 7-3 Pedantic Style of Writing Handouts

ADMINISTERING THE MEDICATION

Medication administration to a neonate must be accomplished carefully, as difficulties with coordinating sucking and swallowing are often encountered. Although medication instructions sometimes instruct individuals to administer dosages through direct introduction of the liquid into the neonate's mouth, caution should be observed, as aspiration has occurred with this method. The physician has prescribed an exact dosage, so be certain that this dosage is administered with great accuracy. Readjusting the dosage without consulting the physician could result in serious difficulties for the neonate.

DIRECTIONS
1. The medication can be combined with 10 or 15 cc. of formula and administered by bottle. This should be administered separately from the balance of the feeding.
2. If the neonate is an excellent nippler, the medication can be added to the entire feeding. This can only be accomplished if the neonate typically ingests all the formula.
3. For medications that must be administered when the stomach is empty, the prescribed dosage can be combined with 10 or 15 cc. of water and administered by nipple.

Medications must be thoroughly mixed before administration. All the instructions on the container should be carefully studied. Administering medications without sufficient light to discern the label can lead to errors.

If a prescribed dosage is missed, serious problems can ensue. Often the medication administration can be disrupted when the neonate's digestive system becomes upset and emesis occurs. If the medication is vomited more than twenty minutes after the initial administration, it should not be readministered. If less than twenty minutes have ensued since initial administration, readminister the prescribed dosage. This readministration should not be repeated if vomiting reoccurs. If emesis disrupts administration of two regularly prescribed dosages, call the physician for instructions. If a dosage is forgotten, it should not be compensated for by administering a larger dosage at any time.

---

time you use them.
2. Limit severely the number of three-syllable words. If you can substitute a shorter word without losing the meaning, do so.
3. When you have finished writing the handout, ask several lay people to read it. Do not choose hospital professionals such as nurses or social workers; give it to family members or friends. Distribute it to at least one child in the eleven to thirteen age range. Get feedback from your test readers. Can they explain the information to you? Was anything unclear? What questions do they have?
4. Using that feedback, rewrite the material to make it more understandable. Remember, you know the information; the people you are writing for do not.

Layout and Appearance

What should the handout or pamphlet look like? Sometimes little thought is given to this, yet appearance can be vital in getting patients to read the material. A tool packed with crowded type, small margins, inadequate spacing, and long paragraphs looks daunting and difficult. Some patients will not even tackle reading material that looks too long or hard to read. Falvo states, "The general appearance of printed materials may be important in attracting patients' attention and motivating them to read the handout."[7]

The single most important step you can take to improve the appearance of your handouts is to allow plenty of white space. This does not mean just double-spacing between lines—leave generous margins, indent important points, separate out a key statement with extra spacing. Exhibit 7-4 shows a flier given out to parents

Exhibit 7-4 Handout for Parents

```
                              MEDICINE SHEET

MEDICINE: _____

_____ is receiving this beginning _____

REASON FOR GIVING THIS TO _____ : _____

_____

DOSAGE: _____


HOW OFTEN: _____

THINGS TO WATCH FOR: _____

_____

_____

_____

IF YOU HAVE QUESTIONS, PLEASE CALL _____

    Keep this medicine in a place away from children's reach!
```

when a child is receiving medicine. Note the use of spacing to make it appealing to the eye, the headings to make it easy to read, and the use of underlining to highlight important points. A nice individual touch is achieved by allowing space for the child's name to be inserted at a couple of points in the handout. One of the most helpful parts of this tool is the picture of the syringe. Besides writing down the amount of medicine to be given, the nurse colors in the dose on the syringe. This enables parents to check visually the amount of medicine being administered after they have drawn it up. Illustrations not only break up blocks of print in a handout, they can also vividly reinforce information.

Redman states that pictorial learning is superior to verbal learning for recognition and recall. However, when the subject matter is abstract, it is difficult to communicate with pictures. Pictures that vary in color, style, and approach have not been found to create differences in learning. People prefer color and motion, and realistic rather than abstract pictures, but preference may not be highly related to learning.[8] In most instances, simpler is better. Clear, concrete line drawings may have just as much impact on learning as more elaborate artwork or photographs. Use illustrations to highlight important points and to reinforce learning already covered in the text (as with the syringe in Exhibit 7-4).

Answering Questions When You Are Not There

The greatest virtue of written materials is that patients have something to refer to when health care providers are no longer with them to answer their questions. Design your tools with this in mind. Experience tells you the questions that concern most patients. Use this knowledge when writing content. In fact, a question-and-answer format can be extremely effective in catching the learner's attention. An example of this format is seen in Exhibit 7-5, which is part of a booklet for diabetic patients. Based on questions most often asked during teaching sessions, it provides answers that patients or family members may need at home, answers to questions either not asked during hospitalization or asked, answered, and then forgotten.

As new questions (or new information) come up, adjust the content of your written tools appropriately. Do not use the same handout year after year after year. In health care, nothing stays the same that long. Keep testing your new and rewritten material with real patients, not just your colleagues. Do the handouts provide useful information? Are they easy to read? What else needs to be included? What suggestions do the patients have to make the information more accessible?

Exhibit 7-5 Question-and-Answer Format for Handouts

QUESTION: What if I get sick and can't eat? Should I stop taking my insulin?

ANSWER: No, do not stop taking insulin. Your body needs it to work properly. If you are ill
for longer than two days and have not been able to eat, call your doctor and
follow the doctor's instructions.

QUESTION: What if I'm going on vacation where I will be much more active than usual?
Should I eat a lot more to make up for all the exercise? Should I take less insulin?

ANSWER: Adjusting your diet or insulin dosage is hard to do safely. If you know you're
going to be more active than usual, call your doctor and discuss it with him or
her. And be sure you test your blood glucose level regularly to be sure any
adjustments are working.

Writing Handouts for Older Learners

Since many of our patients fall into the older age group, special consideration must be given to making written tools easy to read. Vision deficits and other perceptual problems interfere with understanding, yet these patients have a particular need for written material. Since short-term memory can be a problem for some people in their seventies and eighties, handouts can reinforce material already learned and can minimize confusion over instructions and prescribed treatments.

When preparing education booklets for elderly diabetics, Knight and Kesson found the following guidelines helpful:

- Print should be large.
- Diagrams should be explicit.
- Attempts at activity planning must try to relate to elderly patients' way of life and not leave them struggling to extrapolate from advice to adolescents.
- When describing the signs and symptoms of hypo- and hyperglycemia, it should be made clear that these symptoms may be vague and may coincide with what many people expect of advancing age.
- Advice for dealing with problems should be explicit: more intensive monitoring when ill, instructions for an easily prepared soft diet to maintain carbohydrate intake, exactly when to call the physician.[9]

The use of white space is especially important with older learners; ample spacing separates sections, highlights important points, and provides a rest for the eyes before proceeding to the next set of facts. The length of the material does not seem as important to older learners—they have both more time and patience for reading teaching materials. In Chapter 8 special attention is given to teaching techniques for the elderly, and one of the strategies involves the use of written materials for relearning and reinforcement.

DISPLAYS AND DEMONSTRATION MATERIALS

Displays

Displays include posters, models, mounted illustrations, and other static methods of teaching. These can be permanently displayed in a teaching center, posted on a bulletin board, set up at a health fair, or made portable to be carried to patient rooms. Displays can achieve learning objectives, but they can also be expensive, time-consuming teaching tools. The advantages and disadvantages of a display include:

Advantages
- quick way to promote an idea
- flexible
- portable
- reusable
- stimulates ideas or interest
- attracts people's attention
- can change or influence people's attitudes
- can be made or purchased, depending on your budget

Disadvantages
- time-consuming to prepare
- requires space
- symbolic nature may be misunderstood
- may be cluttered or unclear if it contains too many ideas, words, or pictures
- can be overused
- may be ignored if not carefully displayed or if displayed too long
- can be difficult to transport[10]

The sophistication of your displays depends on the budget available. By using graphic machines such as the Kroy letterer or Merlin in combination with clip art, you can produce professional-looking displays that can be shown with pride anywhere. Exhibit 7-6 is an example of a flier produced in this way to advertise a community class. There are now computer programs available that will produce wonderful lettering and graphic illustrations. Exhibit 7-7 was completely

Exhibit 7-6 Display Produced with a Letterer and Clip Art

Working Parents:
The Search
for Day Care

This class is offered to assist parents of pre-school aged children locate quality child care for working parents.
 • **Types of child care**
 • **Steps for objective selection**
 • **Interviewing skills**
 • **Successful parenting skills for the working family**

Classes to be held: August 15,   2:00-4:00 PM
(choose one date)   October 24, 7:00-9:00 PM
December 3, 2:30-4:30 PM

The class fee is $10.00 per person or $15.00 per couple.

No infants or children will be allowed to ensure Mom and Dad's full concentration on the class content.

Instructor: Darle Moulton, R.N., A.C.C.E.

Pre-registration is necessary.
Childbirth Education Office (818) 397-8478.

Make check payable to: Huntington Memorial Hospital.   **DAY CARE CLASS**
Mail this form with payment to: Huntington Memorial Hospital
                                Childbirth Education Office   CLASS DATE_____
                                P.O. Box 7013
                                Pasadena, CA 91109-7013

Name _____

Address _____

_____ Zip Code _____

Day Phone: (   )_____ Home Phone: (   )_____

Source: Education Department, Huntington Memorial Hospital, Pasadena, California. Reprinted with permission.

Exhibit 7-7 Display Produced by a Computer Package

Community Heartsaver
You May Save Someone You Love

This is a 4 hour class in basic cardiopulmonary resuscitation which will enable you to recognize the signs and symptoms of heart attack, impending cardiac arrest, and when and how to perform lifesaving CPR.

Dates of Class: March 7, 1988   June 6, 1988
April 4, 1988   July 11, 1988
May 2, 1988   August 1, 1988

From 6:00 to 10:00 PM

In the South Room

Fee: $10.00 per person
Coordinator: Louise Drake, RN

For further information, call the Education Department at (818) 397-5041.

computer-generated using a Macintosh computer, a Quark XPress desktop publishing program, and a laser printer.

Expense may stand in the way of using professional-quality displays. The hardware-software package needed to produce Exhibit 7-7 costs about $16,000. A Kroy letterer, tape supply, and clip art subscription total about $4500. If you have a large patient population and an ambitious, professional, patient education program, budgeting for a one-time capital outlay might be well worth the expense.

If such cost is totally beyond your institution's capabilities, consider the purchase of a manual lettering machine such as a Leteron or Letertype. Although the machine is slow and laborious, the lettering produced is excellent. If you have the services of a biomedical artist, all of this will be done for you, but you can produce your own displays with the help of a staff member with artistic talents. One thing to avoid is a hastily scribbled poster or display that you produce with blank posterboard and markers. Patients are part of our sophisticated media-centered culture and expect to see professional-looking materials.

Schroeder lists the following guidelines for designing displays:

- Simplicity and neatness will help get your message across.
- Balance is important. Each side should have the same visual weight.
- Emphasis should be given to your main idea or theme by making it larger, brighter, or bolder.
- Unity emphasizes a single line or direction. Get all parts to relate to each other.
- Shape should relate to your main design.
- Lines attract attention by pulling the eye to a specific focus. Horizontal lines denote solidity, vertical lines suggest strength, curved lines denote movement, and repetition of lines reinforces feeling.
- Texture can be changed by using fabrics, vinyl, burlap, foil, or grass cloth.
- Color attracts attention, but do not overdo it—too many colors clutter and complicate a design.
- Space provides depth and adds excitement and contrast.[11]

The use of these guidelines to create eye-catching displays can pay off with increased patient attention to your message. Keep the displays simple, with the emphasis on important points. And keep your objectives always in the front of your mind—this will help focus the display.

Demonstration Materials

Collecting materials for demonstration ranges from ordering things (such as syringes) to creating mock-ups of equipment. When you teach about actual physical objects, it is often preferable to use the real thing. Models are useful when the real thing is too small, too large, too complicated, too expensive, or unavailable.[12] Models also give patients a chance to practice new skills without running the risk of damaging valuable equipment.

Demonstration as a teaching technique is discussed in Chapter 8. Its value depends on the realism of the simulated activity. The ideal demonstration involves the patient's performing the real procedure with real equipment, but he or she may need to work up to that level. Giving oneself an injection, for instance, is an unpleasant task to many people. Educators often desensitize the patient by beginning with demonstrations on inanimate objects (such as the traditional orange), moving to a model of an arm or leg, and only then going to actual injections of a human being. This method requires more equipment and more syringes, but ultimately it will be more effective.

Realistic models can be ordered from various medical supply companies for many different procedures, from injections to ostomy irrigations to catheterizations. Symbolic models can be made fairly cheaply out of wood, foam rubber, plastic, and other materials stored around the hospital. Enlist the maintenance department to help construct what you need.

AUDIOVISUAL EQUIPMENT AND MATERIALS

What software you purchase depends on what equipment you have to play it on. Each form of audiovisual material has its own strengths and weaknesses.

Sixteen-Millimeter Film Projector

The 16-mm film projector is one of the most common pieces of equipment in hospitals, and many facilities have a large collection of films. Such programs are easily seen, even for vision-impaired people, since the picture size can be adjusted by moving the projector. Picture quality is usually good. The biggest drawback is lack of flexibility. A 16-mm film cannot be altered, so no new information can be added. Periodically review the content of your film collection, and take the hopelessly outdated ones out of service. A film showing incorrect information of course should be pulled, but you also need to consider patient reactions to the film atmosphere. A program filled with fashions of the 1950s or 1960s provokes laughter and detracts from the information.

Another drawback of film is the expense. Most 16-mm films cost about $650—not that costly when you consider that they will be shown hundreds of times, but expensive compared with the $100 to $350 price of most videotapes. It can also be awkward to show films to patients in their rooms. The room must be dark, making note-taking difficult. Complicated setup and operation preclude patients from playing the films independently.

Making 16-mm films yourself is almost impossible, unless your facility has a fully equipped film studio complete with media crew. Send the query cards contained in professional journals to the major film supply companies (such as Roundtable, Pyramid, Oracle, and Churchill) and you will receive catalogs full of their offerings. From those you can then decide to order films for preview or purchase, depending on what is available that meets your needs.

Slide Projector

Slide shows are more flexible than films because changes can be made simply by substituting new slides for old. Although professionally prepared programs can be purchased, one of the advantages of slides is that they can be easily produced by anyone. If you can operate a camera, you can make slides. Close-ups can be used to illustrate key points with slides, and it is simple to back up to review a prior point.

Besides slides that are advanced by hand, slide/sound shows use a synchronized signal to advance the program automatically. The shows require a special tape player, such as a Wollensak, to respond to the taped commands. Slide/sound shows help to avoid the static look of conventional slide programs by employing rapid slide changes to simulate motion.

Although they are cheaper and more flexible than film, slides share some of the same drawbacks. Again the lights must be out for good visibility, and slide projection requires a screen and a good-sized room. One way around both difficulties involves the use of a Caramate projector. This can be used for slides alone or for slide/sound with audiotape. Easy to operate, the Caramate can be set up for individual patient viewing.

When preparing slides, keep your images simple. There is nothing worse than studying an incomprehensible mass of words projected in front of you. Follow these guidelines:

- Illustrate one idea per slide—do not cram several points together and confuse the learner.
- Use pictures, symbols, or diagrams. Long lists or complicated figures should be presented in handout form.

- Keep the proportion of height to width at 2:3. This will keep your slides from looking distorted.
- When lettering for slides, use large, professional-looking letters. Typewriter lettering is hard to read and looks amateurish.
- Photograph with a 35-mm camera for the best-looking slides. If you do not have access to one, you can get fairly good results with even simple cameras (such as the Instamatic) as long as you use slide film.

Overhead Projector

Overhead transparencies resemble slides in their enlargement and isolation of a single fact at a time. The message on clear film is projected onto a screen. Overheads can be seen in lighted rooms, so darkness is not required. Transparencies need the support of verbal explanations, so they generally are used in classroom settings rather than with individual patients. They can be purchased already made or easily created yourself.

Diagrams and figures can be photocopied onto acetate sheets by loading the transparencies into the copying machine paper-feed. Use colored pens (permanent or water-soluble) and different shades of adhesive acetate to create colorful overhead transparencies. Guidelines include:

- Limit each transparency to a single point. If you have heard the rule, "six lines of copy, six words per line," forget it. That is far too many.
- Test readability by having someone hold your originals ten feet away from you. If you can read them, the lettering is large enough. This usually requires letters one-quarter-inch high.

Flipcharts

Flipcharts hold large pads of white paper that can be written on with marking pens. Rarely used for individual patient education, flipcharts are more often helpful in large classes or in meetings during brainstorming sessions to record ideas and input. There are actually such things as prepackaged flipcharts available for purchase, but most people prepare their own, either with large Kroy or Merlin lettering or with markers.

The emphasis in creating flipcharts should be on readability. Lettering must be large, with large amounts of white space. As with any audiovisual tool, use these to emphasize important points and to achieve objectives, not to present large amounts of data that should be in handout form.

Audiotapes

Information recorded on audiotapes has been widely used for teaching purposes. The advantages of audiotapes include ease of preparation, portability, and simple operation. Patients can take tapes home to listen to later. Some hospitals have tape services so that people may call in and choose from a selection of taped topics. These tapes are usually from three to five minutes long and contain information on health topics. The purpose of these services is not primarily educational; most contain a number to call for physician referral and are used as an advertising and public relations tool.

Audiotapes are attractive because of the low cost and extreme ease of production. If you have a tape recorder and a blank cassette and can speak, you can make an audiotape. However, audiotapes tap only one sense—hearing—and can be boring. Anyone who has listened dutifully to the tape of a missed class can testify to how difficult a learning method this is. Keep taped messages short or break them up into individual, short lessons with written assignments or activities to be completed if you want to retain your audience.

Videotapes

More and more health care facilities have videotape players for staff and patient education. Professionally produced videotapes are available from outside companies at reasonable prices. The popularity of television in our culture makes videotape learning generally popular with patients—or at least easier to accept. Videotape is replacing film because of ease of use, portability, lower cost, and high picture quality.

Videotapes can be self-produced if the institution purchases the equipment required. This used to entail a large expense, requiring not only the camera but also a recorder, lights, and a mounting cart. The advent of minicams has made taping not only easier but much cheaper. You can buy an excellent taping package for under $2000.

Of course videotapes have disadvantages, too. Many purchased tapes are too long, exceeding most patients' attention spans and interest levels. If the content is presented in an uninteresting manner—such as the "talking heads" presentation, where a speaker is taped giving a lecture—then it will be uninteresting to the intended audience. Videotape enables you to show demonstrations in close-up, to dramatize possible situations patients may encounter, and to stimulate interest in content by illustrating information rather than simply discussing it. But to succeed it must capitalize on its strengths—motion, color, different shots and angles—all of the things that set this technology apart from more static audiovisuals.

When you tape programs for patients, strive for network-quality production.

You may not achieve it, but such an approach prevents compromises. Never go into a taping project thinking, "Well, it doesn't matter—we're not professionals." It does matter. The first time people laugh at a program you worked hard on, it becomes clear that the time and effort put into such programs pay off.

Use the following guidelines when videotaping:

- Write a script for the program and thoroughly rehearse the actors (even if the only actor is you). This is not the time for *cinéma vérité*.
- If your facility does not have a media expert, hire one on a per diem basis. A video technician will save you time and money in the long run.
- Two cameras and a director unit produce professional videos. The director unit edits the views from both cameras into a seamless whole, enabling you to cut from long shots to close-ups instantly. You can hire someone to edit your tape at an outside facility if your hospital does not have this equipment. If even this is beyond your budget, use a single camera with smooth zoom shots and transitions.
- Keep the objectives of the program always before you. This prevents the production from becoming an end unto itself—you are producing it to teach patients something, not to make a video.
- Keep the program short. The longer the video, the easier it is to lose viewer interest. Most programs should run from five to fifteen minutes—longer than twenty minutes is usually deadly.

Computer-Assisted Instruction

The use of computers for patient education is fairly new and not often seen. Making learning interactive improves retention, and computer-assisted instruction (CAI) simulates the feedback of a live, face-to-face encounter between learner and teacher. In CAI, short bursts of content are presented; then questions are asked about that content, and the learner is guided to the correct answers on any questions missed. At this point there are not many programs available for purchase, but as more hospitals gain access to the technology, more will be produced to meet the demand. CAI programs can be written by patient educators with the help of special software designed to produce learning programs.

There are two main drawbacks to CAI. The hardware and software are expensive; the computer and monitor cost between $1500 and $3000, a printer costs about $500, and software ranges from $40 to $300. A program designed to help you write teaching programs for patients may cost as much as $3000, but of course it can be used over and over to turn out free (after that initial expense) patient education. The second disadvantage is that some adults are not used to computers and may actually fear using them. This "computer phobia" can interfere with learning.

The combination of computers and video is producing some interesting new twists in patient education. A rehabilitation center in Palo Alto, California, has designed a voice-activated video education system for patients with spinal cord injuries. Different programs, on such topics as skin care or bowel training, can be called up by code words alone.[13] This enables paralyzed patients to use the programs without assistance from others.

USING AUDIOVISUAL SOFTWARE

Assessing and Purchasing Outside Materials

Most educators have limited budgets and must select programs for purchase carefully. If you can buy only three software packages a year, you want those films (or videotapes or whatever) to provide the most value for your money. Foster recommends taking the following into consideration when selecting audiovisual materials:

- Who produced the item?
- Was there any input from health professionals?
- Can it be previewed?
- Is the content accurate?
- Does it give a specific group of clients the information they need?
- Are there unintentional hidden messages? Study the images carefully before showing the program.
- Is the price consistent with the educational value? Costly aids may be worth the price if they can be used with large numbers of patients and thus save expensive staff time. Another important cost consideration is how quickly the information will become outdated.[14]

Looking at who produced the item provides insight into its value. If the material is offered by a company that has provided useful, high-quality offerings in the past, ones that have satisfied you and proved helpful to your patients, you have more confidence in it. Materials produced by other hospitals may not be as slick as those done by professional media companies, but they may be written and produced by educators who really know what patients need. The input from health care professionals obviously is important, and in-hospital productions guarantee input from front-line educators directly involved in day-to-day care and patient problems. When you order material from a media company, study the advertisement carefully. Who wrote it? Be wary of programs written by media experts, with health care professionals only "advising." The program may be fine—or it may be a superficial treatment with little practical information.

One way to know for sure, of course, is to preview the material. Alas, the days of the free preview are just about gone, and we have only ourselves to blame. For years companies offered free previews of programs, and health care educators abused them by showing those programs to audiences in direct violation of preview agreements. This was undoubtedly done in a misguided attempt to save the institution some money, but it has resulted in most companies' charging for previews. Some companies have been so badly burned that they no longer even offer the option of previewing. A preview is helpful in judging the quality of the content and its appropriateness for your patients. Often you will find that companies that do not allow previews do have a refund policy stating that if the programs are returned within a certain time period the money will be refunded minus a small preview fee. If you are not sure, call the company and investigate. Try to get some money in your budget for previews. Do not limit yourself only to those few companies still offering free previews—the really elegant materials may be missed. And when receiving programs for preview, abide by the preview agreements. Use the opportunity to judge the material by yourself or with one or two colleagues; do not show it to an audience of patients or staff. Such abuse of previews cheats the company producing the program and is at the very least unethical. It should go without saying that no one *ever* records preview material for later use—that is not only unethical but illegal, and there is simply no excuse for it.

When judging the usefulness of the program, watch not only for accuracy of content but for applicability as well. Will this material meet a need for specific patients? Some programs are too broad, too unfocused, to be really useful for teaching purposes. In trying to meet all needs, they meet none. For example, this book focuses on patient education. If it tried to examine, say, the principles of education, it would lose its focus and possibly be helpful as a text for undergraduate students, but it would be far too general to assist practicing patient educators. On the other hand, programs can be too specific to be cost-effective. Spending $650 for a film on foot care for diabetics would be prohibitive, although one that included foot care as part of the content on diabetic self-care in general might be perfectly practical.

Watching for unintentional hidden messages is both difficult and necessary. These are not obscure cult communications heard when the program is played backwards; the messages are usually well-intentioned pieces of information that can inadvertently mislead patients. In one instance, follow-up calls to new mothers revealed insecurities about giving their babies a bath. Many stated that it seemed "so difficult" and that they were afraid of "making a mistake" or "forgetting something." Upon exploration it was discovered that the film shown to maternity patients about bathing the newborn demonstrated an elaborate procedure involving many steps and numerous changes of towels, blankets, and other linen. Patients received the impression that they had to follow the steps exactly, making the simple and pleasurable act of bathing a baby into an intimidating and stressful chore.

Assessing cost effectiveness in terms of not just initial price but also number of potential viewers is an important part of audiovisual selection. If an aid can cover vital information in a clear, interesting way so that the educator merely needs to review important points rather than teach the entire thing, money is saved. Avoid programs that become outdated quickly. When the autoimmune deficiency syndrome first became a concern, a number of audiovisual offerings came out, only to have the information supplanted by further research. With rapidly changing information, use short-term learning tools such as handouts, slides, and audiotapes rather than film or videotape. Keep your investment small and the material easy to revise.

USING YOUR TOOLS EFFECTIVELY

Choosing the right tools for patient education is a judgment call. Each patient may require a different set of audiovisual aids, a different approach to learning. Using the information garnered from patient assessment, select the tools that will best teach that individual. Pritchett states that the most effective instructional aid is the one that brings the learner closest to experiencing the real thing. Two questions are recommended:

1. What instructional aids do you have that would contribute to this learning situation?
2. Which aids are appropriate for each learning objective?

Be prepared to use several different aids to achieve the same objective, and keep reaching into your "bag of tricks" until you are sure that learning has been achieved.[15]

Research has shown that audiovisual aids can have a positive impact on learning. In one study 210 patients were given a computerized tomographic body scan; 100 received an explanatory leaflet prior to the scan and 110 did not. Patients receiving the leaflet were significantly less worried about the procedure and had fewer misconceptions about what body scanning involved. The leaflet did not reduce their anxieties about the results. The main value of the leaflet was that it told patients exactly what to expect.[16]

Patient package inserts (PPIs) have been studied extensively, and the results reveal that they were widely read, reportedly by 70 percent of all people receiving them. Twenty-two to thirty-two percent kept the PPIs as resources and read them more than once. Although PPIs were effective in increasing people's knowledge about the medicine, they had little or no effect on adherence rates. These findings confirm the results of other studies that more information is appreciated by patients, but that information alone has little effect on behavior.[17]

In another case, a hospital developed a thirteen-minute videotape for preoperative patients covering the evening before surgery, the morning of surgery, and care after surgery. The video is presented in a unit conference room at 7:00 P.M. and again at 7:30 P.M. An outline is distributed to each patient, and a nurse is present to answer questions. At the end of the presentation and discussion, patients sign the outline, attesting that they have viewed and understood the information. The nurse also initials the form, which then becomes a permanent part of the patient's chart.[18]

Ritter reported on a group of ostomy patients receiving self-care education. The program used printed handouts, filmstrips, and demonstrations by nurses. Ninety percent of the patients said the reading material helped with home care, while 95 percent said demonstration of their ostomy care by the nurses was helpful. Only 30 percent of the patients watched the filmstrips; 15 percent said the filmstrips were helpful, 15 percent said not.[19]

No matter what tool you are using, remember the human element. Personal, one-on-one interaction between patient and nurse is probably the most important determinant of success in learning. In one study, three groups of patients were taught with printed material, verbal consultation, or both. Patients receiving the printed leaflet alone scored higher on post-tests than patients receiving the verbal consultation; however, the highest scores were achieved by patients receiving both the printed leaflet and verbal consultations together.[20] Use your audiovisual tools as support and reinforcement for that all-important nurse-patient interaction and ongoing assessment, teaching, and evaluation.

NOTES

1. Edward E. Bartlett, "The New Technology: Boon or Boondoggle?" *Patient Education Newsletter* 6, no. 3 (June 1983): 11.

2. Donna R. Falvo, *Effective Patient Education* (Rockville, Md.: Aspen Publishers, Inc., 1985), pp. 218–19.

3. Marilyn G. Ritter, "Assessing Educational Needs of Ostomy Patients," *Ostomy/Wound Management* 16 (Fall 1987): 15.

4. Barbara Klug Redman, *The Process of Patient Education*, 5th ed. (St. Louis: C.V. Mosby Co., 1984), p. 141.

5. Michael J. Regner, Freya Hermann, and L. Douglas Ried, "Effectiveness of a Printed Leaflet for Enabling Patients To Use Digoxin Side Effect Information," *Drug Intelligence and Clinical Pharmacy* 21 (February 1987): 200–1.

6. Marilyn Boyd, "A Guide to Writing Effective Patient Education Materials," *Nursing Management* 18, no. 7 (July 1987): 56.

7. Falvo, *Effective Patient Education*, pp. 225–6.

8. Redman, *Process of Patient Education*, p. 168.

9. P.V. Knight and C.M. Kesson, "Educating the Elderly Diabetic," *Diabetic Medicine* 3, no. 2 (March 1986): 172.

10. Barbara Schroeder, "Creating an Interesting Display," Resource Sheet Prepared for the AHA/ ASHET Patient Education Liaison Program (Chicago, American Hospital Association, 1987), p. 1.

11. Ibid., pp. 2–4.

12. Redman, *Process of Patient Education*, pp. 165–6.

13. John C. Tang et al., "Interactive Development and Evaluation of an Independently Accessible Video Education System for Rehabilitation," Journal of the American Paraplegia Society 8, no. 2 (April 1985): 39.

14. Susan D. Foster, "Are Commercial Patient Education Materials Right for You?" *The American Journal of Maternal/Child Nursing* 12, no. 4 (July/August 1987): 287.

15. Sue Pritchett, "Effectiveness of Educational Methods," *Patient Education Newsletter* 5, no. 5 (October 1982): 52.

16. C.R. Merrill and A.M. Knox, "Patient Information Leaflets: What Effect?" *Radiography* 52, no. 604 (July/August 1986): 209.

17. "Medication Patient Education," *Patient Education Newsletter* 5, no. 3 (June 1982): 34.

18. Sharon DeWaele et al., "Continuity in Patient Education," *Patient Education Newsletter* 8, no. 4 (August 1985): 8–9.

19. Ritter, "Assessing Educational Needs of Ostomy Patients," p. 15.

20. Regner, Hermann, and Ried, "Effectiveness of a Printed Leaflet," p. 202.

8

Teaching Techniques
For Patient Education

Teaching patients is at once so important and yet so taken for granted that careful examination of different techniques is warranted. Too often educators use only one or two methods that have worked for them in the past. It is human nature to stay with things that are safe and comfortable, but in teaching you need to take a few risks. Trying new teaching techniques expands the educator's repertoire and benefits patients. That unusual approach you have never tried before may be exactly what is needed for a certain individual.

Whatever techniques are used, be sure that your teaching is kept objectives-oriented. Focusing always on objectives keeps you and your patients targeted on results, not on the act of teaching itself. Research indicates that, when learners know what is expected of them, they tend to learn regardless of the teaching methods or media used.[1] However, certain teaching strategies are probably more effective for certain learning tasks than others, although studies on this point are not conclusive.[2]

Patient education involves both one-on-one and group instruction. Techniques for these methods differ. Whether you are teaching a single person or a group, however, certain general principles strengthen learning:

- Organize the material.
- Keep instructions clear and specific.
- Repeat important points.
- Illustrate or demonstrate information.
- Reinforce through written instructions.[3]

ONE-ON-ONE INSTRUCTION

Explanations/Lecture

There really is no such thing as a lecture in one-on-one instruction, since by definition *lecture* implies a group setting. Face to face with a single patient, the educator explains information. This is the most commonly used form of patient education. It is also the most abused. When one thinks of educating patients, the picture that immediately springs to mind is that of patient and nurse sitting together, the patient listening while the nurse talks. But is any learning taking place?

Studies show that patients remember only 7–30 percent of verbally transmitted information.[4] This makes patient education seem pretty hopeless until you consider that a great deal depends on *how* the information is transmitted. As was mentioned in Chapter 7, the proportion of information forgotten increases with the total amount of information given.[5] In many patient contacts the goal seems to be stuffing as much information as possible into the overloaded learner. Some educators boast, "I just spent a solid hour teaching a patient." That is far too long for a single session. Patients need time to process information, to make connections between new facts and things they already know, and to come to terms with the life style changes implicit in the learning. Information should be presented in bite-size bits so that patients can easily digest it. For most patients the ideal length of a single teaching session is about fifteen minutes.

Quality of information is just as important as quantity. Communication is the main determinant of patient satisfaction, and research shows that effective one-to-one counseling significantly increases compliance.[6] The key word is *effective*. In recent studies, physicians reported spending an average of twelve minutes per patient on counseling and discussion, yet taped interviews with the same practitioner showed less than ninety seconds of interactive communication. Researchers also found that, on average, physicians first interrupted patients' statements or questions after only eighteen seconds. When this happened, patients rarely identified other problems.[7]

Educators need to involve learners in one-on-one counseling through questioning and encouragement. Rendon et al. state:

> An environment that affords psychological safety and a sense of security established through respect and acceptance, and that is devoid of impatience and ridicule, is crucial to the learning process. Nursing actions that convey optimistic expectancy, calm certainty, and praise can create an environment in which the client feels capable of success, free to take risks, and motivated to explore new learning tasks.[8]

One of the most important qualities of an effective patient educator is a sense of wonder. Cynicism leads to pessimism, deadly in a teacher. Approach each patient

Table 8-1 Two Different Ways of Reaching the Same Objective

Objective: Perform Blood Glucose Monitoring Using Chemstrips

Approach 1	Approach 2
1. Discuss the relationship between blood glucose levels and symptoms	1. Show patient the equipment to be used and let patient handle it
2. Have patient read booklet on blood glucose monitoring	2. Demonstrate procedure all the way through
3. Discuss content and answer questions	3. Demonstrate procedure again, this time stopping at each step to explain what is happening and why
4. Review steps of Chemstrip procedure, discussing the reasons for each step	4. Answer questions
5. Demonstrate procedure	5. Have patient walk through procedure without actually obtaining blood
6. Answer questions and stress the important points	6. Review importance of accurate results
7. Have patient return demonstration, describing what is being done	7. Have patient perform procedure with coaching from educator
8. Summarize procedure	8. Have patient perform procedure with occasional cues and reminders
9. Have patient test blood glucose again	9. Have staff observe and coach patient through procedure several times
10. Request staff to observe patient's performance each time and give feedback	10. Patient performs procedure without coaching

not as a chore but as a challenge. Every patient you teach can also teach you something about learning, about people. It is all too easy to begin treating patient education almost as an assembly line. Each session becomes more and more like the session before. To combat this sameness, focus on the special qualities and needs of *this* learner. What makes this person unique? How can you vary your approach to mesh with the needs that you have identified?

One-on-one counseling provides opportunities not only to give information but to probe for understanding and for previously unidentified problems. As you tackle each objective, present the information in the way most appropriate for that patient. Table 8-1 shows one objective with two different ways of reaching it. The first patient likes a didactic approach to learning, is very interested in theory, and enjoys studying the information. The second patient has memory problems and is easily confused by a lot of theoretical information. Both need the same basic information, but the methods of reaching the common objective are completely different.

Although there are ten learning steps in each approach, Patient 1 might achieve the objective in one session or at most two sessions. Patient 2 may take four or five sessions to do the same. Both patients need the instructor's full attention, interest, and patience; yet in both cases it might seem tempting to slight the time spent with them. The educator could rationalize that Patient 1 can learn alone simply by reading the material, and so does not need much teaching time. Patient 2, on the other hand, has serious learning problems and could be written off as hopeless. But "why waste my time?" is a poor philosophy for a patient educator.

Use of Reinforcement and Praise

Another thing that every patient needs from educators is positive reinforcement. Even this basic teaching skill can be used effectively or ineffectively. If you nod and say "great" or "good," the patient may sense approval, but you have not succeeded in reinforcing any *specific* behavior. Use reinforcement only when it is justified. Contrived enthusiasm and unfounded praise will be perceived as false.[9]

Link reinforcement directly to the act being reinforced, and make the praise specific to the action. Statements such as, "Good, you remembered to inject air into the vial first this time," and "That's a good question—you have put those pieces of information together," cue the patient to exactly what they did right. Be sure to point out when patients achieve objectives and goals. This highlights progress and gives learners a sense of accomplishment. When there are many skills and a large amount of information to learn, the process can seem never-ending. Progress checkpoints that are recognized and reinforced help to prevent frustration and discouragement.

More tangible rewards can also be used to reinforce learning. Rehabilitation units, chemical dependency programs, and adolescent units have experimented with reward systems using credits toward special privileges, "gold star" charts, even gifts. Acute care settings and outpatient facilities could try variations on a similar reward system. As objectives are achieved, patients could receive small items such as pens, penlights, desk clocks, key chains—the list of small, inexpensive things that could be ordered in bulk is endless. Most items can be ordered with the hospital's name and logo inscribed, thus serving as advertising as well. And almost everyone appreciates a certificate of achievement after completing a course of study, an idea that could be easily adapted to patient education (see Exhibit 8-1).

If the reward approach smacks of behavior modification, it is meant to do just that. The most successful recent studies have employed some behavior modification techniques intended to support compliance in the self-care environment after instruction has ended. It has been demonstrated that behavior-oriented patient education is two to three times more clinically effective than education of a purely didactic nature.[10] Help patients to set goals and rewards for home care as well as formal learning. Outside programs such as weight loss or stop smoking classes are available, many of which employ similar behavior modification theories.

Exhibit 8-1 Certificate of Completion for Patient Education

THIS CERTIFIES THAT

*has satisfactorily completed the course of study
prescribed for graduation from the
childbirth education series of Lamaze classes
in preparation for childbirth.
This certificate is issued by Hometown General Hospital
in recognition of that completion.*

Childbirth Educator   Director of Education

Question-and-Answer Techniques

Of course any educator encourages questions from learners, but questioning can be an active teaching tool over and above the more passive, "Do you have any questions?" Use open-ended questions to stimulate discussion and creative problem solving. This practice encourages independent thought, provides transitions to more complex material, and confirms the learner's ability to contribute to the learning process.[11]

There is really no contest between open-ended and closed-ended questions. A closed-ended question requires a yes or no answer: "Do you understand why you need this medicine?" A negative answer to this requires further probing to discover what specifically is not understood. A positive answer may or may not indicate true understanding. Many learners hesitate to admit that they do not understand something; others may not even be aware that they do not understand. Closed-ended questions are therefore of limited usefulness. Open-ended questions, on the other hand, elicit the patient's own interpretation of the information discussed. "Would you tell me what this medicine will do for you?" brings forth not only the patient's understanding of drug actions, but also his or her personal feelings about benefits and reasons for compliance (or misunderstandings and reasons for potential noncompliance, as the case may be).

Question-and-answer techniques enable you to clear up misunderstanding and get a clearer picture of how patients are processing the information. How do the facts they have just learned fit into their own world view? What linkages are taking place with information previously learned? Careful analysis of questions can identify problem areas and provide clues to what needs to be taught next.

Perhaps you are teaching a patient how to administer insulin. The question, "Tell me your understanding of what insulin does in the body," elicits a correct response followed by: "I saw on the news that they're working on insulin you can swallow. Why can't I have that?" Immediately you see not only an area of misunderstanding triggered by a partially understood mass media story, you also identify an unresolved problem with insulin administration that needs to be addressed. Until the patient's negative feelings are discussed and worked through, little progress will be made in learning about insulin administration.

Discussion of patient questions may be a more powerful tool than we have imagined. Research into education for hypertensive patients raises possibilities that allowing patients to tell their own stories in their own words (as opposed to permitting only "yes" or "no" answers), and giving explanations about illness and treatment, might help to promote blood pressure control.[12] Certainly this technique enables instructors to individualize instruction based on input from each patient.

Demonstration/Return Demonstration

Invaluable for teaching patients how to perform procedures, demonstration requires careful planning. Not only must everything be in working order, the sequence of explanation/demonstration/return demonstration must be individualized for each patient (as illustrated in Table 8-1). Guidelines for effective demonstrations include the following:

1. Lay the groundwork carefully. Patients need to understand the procedure's purpose and sequence as well as the skill steps involved.

2. Prepare equipment in advance. Test everything that will be used, and be sure extra supplies are available in case some become contaminated or broken.
3. Use the real objects if possible. If the actual equipment cannot be used, the models should be as realistic as possible.
4. Use the equipment that the patient will use at home. If the patient has purchased a Glucoscan, it will be confusing and counterproductive to teach blood glucose monitoring using an Accuchek II. This can happen when the hospital uses only one kind of monitor. A patient educator needs at least one of all commonly used machines. If that proves impossible for budgetary reasons, have the family bring in the patient's machine and use it for teaching.
5. Let the patients handle all equipment before requiring them to use it in the procedure. Manipulating syringes, turning machines on and off, closely examining vials or dressings—all these actions help to defuse anxiety and prepare for the actual demonstration.
6. For long procedures, break the demonstration into several sequences, and let the patient master each sequence before moving on to another.
7. Reinforce correct performance in small increments. Success breeds success, so the patient's good performance will build on itself. Do not wait until the whole procedure is finished to praise the patient—praise each step.

Overlearning procedures encourages compliance. Have the patient practice the steps over and over again, not just once or twice. This requires patience on the part of the instructor, especially when learners have trouble mastering a procedure. Remaining encouraging and confident while someone struggles to complete a seemingly simple procedure can be difficult. Holpp has perhaps the best philosophy about it: "The key component of unthreatening practice is that it is not only okay to fail, it is expected."[13] Preceding the demonstrations with a statement about how it takes a while to learn the steps and put it all together may prepare patients for extended practice.

Research on athletes, astronauts, pilots, and other skilled performers has shown that performance improves greatly with mental rehearsal. To facilitate this exercise for patients, encourage them to plan the sequence and timing of the procedure *before* beginning practice. This involves mentally rehearsing the physical movements required for successful performance, visualizing the environment, and feeling the physical sensations associated with the procedure. This mental rehearsal works to implant images of successful performance in the mind.[14]

Self-Studies

Self-studies cover didactic material efficiently and effectively *if* the learners are appropriately chosen. People with good reading skills who enjoy learning from written material will find this method effective and useful. The self-study approach saves teacher time and gives learners a chance to reread and reflect on the information. Learning can be done at a pace comfortable for the patient rather than dependent on the educator's schedule. Perhaps most important, self-studies tap into an adult's sense of responsibility and self-direction, following the principles of adult education.

Writing self-studies takes skill with words as well as with the material. Just as with any handout, the content must be presented clearly and at an appropriate reading level (see the discussion of this in Chapter 7). Use the following guidelines when writing self-studies for patients:

1. Write learner-centered objectives first. This will keep you focused on what is vital to the self-study—information needed to meet the objectives. Eliminate everything else.
2. Break the information into small blocks, with frequent checkpoints and pauses where the learner can check for understanding and review as needed. A programmed learning method can be used to achieve this purpose (see Exhibit 8-2 for an example of a self-study using the programmed format).
3. Keep it short. A huge, book-length manuscript is intimidating and demotivating. The longer the self-study, the less likely it is to be read. Limit the infor-

Exhibit 8-2 Excerpt from a Patient Self-Study

A "heart attack" is actually caused by loss of blood supply to a part of the heart muscle. When the arteries supplying oxygen and nutrition to the heart become narrowed, as was discussed earlier, a small clot or bit of plaque can get in the bloodstream and block an artery. This stops part of the heart muscle's air and nutrients and the heart muscle becomes damaged.	
	CHECKPOINT Part of the heart muscle can be hurt when something blocks the _____ supplying oxygen and food.
When this damage happens, the muscle sends pain messages to the brain, and the heart has to work harder because part of it is hurt. This causes the symptoms (things the person feels) of a heart attack: 1. Crushing pain in the chest, shoulder, arm, or jaw 2. Shortness of breath 3. Feeling of indigestion or nausea 4. Sweatiness, anxiety, or fear	ANSWER: Artery

Exhibit 8-3 Self-Study Post-Test

QUIZ

1. List the top three risk factors contributing to heart disease:
   a. _____
   b. _____
   c. _____
2. What can you do to make your life style healthier and lower your risk for heart disease? Name three things:

   _____
   _____
   _____
   _____
   _____

3. Explain in your own words what happens to the heart when a person has a "heart attack":

   _____
   _____
   _____
   _____
   _____
   _____
   _____
   _____

4. List at least three symptoms of a heart attack:

   _____
   _____
   _____

---

mation to "need to know" items, while ruthlessly pruning the "nice to know" from your material. A self-study for diabetics that contains "the history of insulin" is inefficiently prepared—however interesting the story, diabetics do not need to know it to care for themselves.

4. Use a post-test to encourage learning. Just being asked to read something does not always motivate people to do so. Knowing that a test must be completed lends more urgency to the material. Exhibit 8-3 shows some questions from a post-test for the self-study in Exhibit 8-2. An open-book approach to testing is usually effective and much less threatening to most people.

Of course all information covered in a self-study should be verbally reviewed by the educator. This gives the educator a chance not only to check that the patient read the material but also to probe for misunderstandings and elicit patient questions. Again, there is no substitute for person-to-person contact in patient education. Whether the self-study is provided on paper, on video, or through a computer (and computer-assisted instruction is simply high-technology self-study), educator and patient must interact to ensure high-quality instruction and enhanced compliance.

Journal Writing and Review

This little-used technique provides a chance for patients to write their own thoughts about their illness and what it means to them. Especially helpful for people with long-term illnesses, journal writing and review use a diary format to elicit patient feelings. Not everyone is comfortable with such an approach, nor is it appropriate for every learner, but for selected patients it can be both educational and enlightening.

Patients having trouble adjusting to a long-term or debilitating illness are the chief candidates for journals. For those who already keep a diary, this approach is ready-made, but such people are in the minority. Journal writing involves recording daily happenings and how one feels about these happenings. A record of emotions is the valuable and educational part—without the feelings, the journal becomes merely a dry list of events (which can itself indicate the strength of the feelings involved).

Educators must prepare patients carefully for journal keeping. The purpose should be made clear: it is a way to explore what is happening to you and how it is affecting your life. Adding that many people have found it beneficial helps the patient to understand that this technique is accepted and used with others. Other helpful guidelines include the following:

- Set a time limit of a few days. If the patient agrees to write down what is happening and the feelings involved with those happenings for two or three days, you have accomplished a great deal.

- Provide a framework for the journal. Rather than ask the patient to jot down thoughts on a tablet or spare notebook, provide a booklet guiding the journal keeper through the process (see Exhibit 8-4 for an example of a journal format).

- Suggest that the patient select a certain time of day to do the writing. Some people like to write at night before dinner or before bedtime. Others do their best writing first thing in the morning, after sleeping on what happened the day before. Each person needs to find the time that works best and then do all journal writing at that time to establish the habit and prevent writer's block.

- Review the journal entries. This is the most important part of journal keeping, and it should be done jointly by patient and educator. As both read over the entries, the meanings of recorded events should be explored. Questions such as "How did you feel when that happened?" or "That would have made me feel awfully frustrated," should elicit patient reactions. Another useful question is "How do you feel now as you read this?"

Exhibit 8-4 Excerpt from a Journal Format

Remember to take a little time each day to write in your journal. When we go over it later we'll talk about how this information can be helpful to you.

DAY 1
How did your day start? What has changed since you became ill? How do you feel about these changes?

Do people treat you differently now? If so, how? Why do you think this is? How does it make you feel?

Resist the temptation to psychoanalyze the patient or the journal. You are exploring the impact that the illness is having on the patient and how he or she is adjusting. That is a task difficult enough to accomplish without attempting complex analyses which few people are equipped to do.

GROUP INSTRUCTION

Teaching patients in a group is done more frequently in outpatient settings than in acute care facilities. Many patient educators believe that individual instruction is much more effective and so are reluctant to group patients together. Little research has been done to discover whether this belief is true. In one study, middle-aged men needing to lose weight were seen ten times over an eighteen-week period. They were given weight-reduction materials covering such educational strategies as stimulus control, social support, keeping food diaries, and making gradual changes in eating habits. Half of the men were selected randomly to learn about the materials in individualized teaching sessions lasting ten to twenty minutes. The other half attended group classes/discussions that were one to one and a half hours long. Both approaches were effective in significantly influencing behavioral and physiological measures.[15]

Group instruction enables patients to interact with others in the same situation, expanding viewpoints and perhaps making them feel not quite so alone and vulnerable. Discovering that others are encountering and coping with the same problems you have can be a liberating experience. As we discuss the various group-teaching strategies, keep in mind that patient interaction is the key to their effectiveness.

Lecture

Lecture is merely an expanded version of the one-on-one explanations given to individual patients. However, lecturing to groups sometimes brings out the worst in educators. Analyses of courses for patients given by physicians have shown that physicians often disconcert patients by starting their lectures with abstract, theoretical explanations and not tackling the more concrete aspect of the problem until the session is almost over, when attention is already wavering.[16] Throw out all of the old role models from college days, when professors droned on about abstract theories and regurgitated information from a textbook. Patient education requires a fresh approach.

Studies have shown that the lecture can be used effectively to help learners develop the ability to apply concepts and to generalize, so use lecturing as a way of relating information to the overall picture and for clarifying difficult relationships.[17] Use your expertise to explain things that patients find puzzling or obscure. In order to accomplish this, follow these guidelines:

- Learn as much about the topic as you can. Do not rely on your current knowledge—research new information constantly to stay abreast of new findings and to keep your presentation fresh.

- Notes in outline form can help to keep your lecture on track, but do not write the lecture out word for word. That leads to reading the content rather than interpreting it. Nothing is more boring than sitting and listening to someone read a speech. Exhibit 8-5 shows helpful lecture notes.

- Bring *yourself* to the lecture. As you research the information, filter it through your own knowledge and experience. Interpret the material in light of how you have seen it apply to patients.

- Anticipate the questions and problems patients might have. Again, your own experience will cue you to these. Provide explanations and extra attention to content areas that cause confusion.

- Use audiovisual tools to highlight important points and to illustrate information that does not lend itself to easy verbal explanations, but do not overuse these tools. A lecture that leans too heavily on audiovisual fireworks often proves distracting rather than enlightening.

Exhibit 8-5 Lecture Notes in Outline Form

BREAST-FEEDING TIPS

I. INTRODUCTION
   A. Welcome and introduction of participants
   B. Review instructor background and qualifications

II. BENEFITS OF BREAST-FEEDING
   A. For mother
   B. For baby

III. CARE OF THE BREASTS DURING PREGNANCY
   A. Support
   B. Hygiene measures
   C. Nipple care
   D. Preventing problems

IV. STARTING BREAST-FEEDING
   A. "Latching on"
   B. Timing of feedings
   C. Supplemental feedings—yes or no?
   D. Care of the breasts

V. CONTINUING BREAST-FEEDING
   A. Observing baby
   B. Resources if problems develop
   C. Breast-feeding and day care
   D. Weaning

As you put together the lecture, keep the objectives always in mind. Just as with written materials, you need to prune everything that does not contribute directly to what patients need to know. Once you have the content together and your notes made, rehearsal ensures perfection. One expert on presentation skills has stated that "Thinking is the first principle of good rehearsal."[18] Run through your lecture mentally before you do it physically. Picture yourself giving the lecture, reacting to questions, making your points. Now rehearse physically. Deliver the lecture, using the audiovisual aids that you will actually use when learners are present. This enables you to manipulate the overhead transparencies or the slide control and adjust your timing. Keep in mind, however, that the actual class will take much longer; the presence of learners adds time through questions and discussion.

The day of class, arrive at the classroom at least thirty minutes before starting time. This gives you a chance to set the seating and equipment the way you want it. Test all audiovisuals, getting videotapes fast-forwarded past leaders to the starting point of the actual content and slides and overhead transparencies focused.

Greet participants as they arrive and help them through any sign-in procedures. Think of yourself as the host, and go out of your way to make them feel welcome. An atmosphere is being established that will carry through the entire course.

Discussion

Once class is under way, discussion becomes your greatest ally. Discussion can be effective for

- developing appropriate patient self-management techniques for increased adherence to prescribed regimens
- assisting patients to use appropriate resources
- reducing the risks leading to health problems
- minimizing the effects of an illness and avoiding its recurrence
- orienting people to seek early screening and treatment
- sharing peer support, guidance, and reinforcement[19]

These purposes are achieved as learners exchange feelings and opinions about content areas. Both formal and informal discussion takes place in the classroom, and both kinds stimulate learners to think for themselves and to bring their own experiences into the exchange. The more you can draw participants into a discussion, the more active their learning will be. Limiting learning to passive listening, whether one-on-one or in a group, will literally limit learning. After two days, most people forget at least 75 percent of what they have heard.[20] When they internalize the topic by reflecting on its personal meaning for them through discussion, retention is bound to be greater.

The success or failure of discussion rests mainly on the instructor. Establish the purpose of a particular discussion at once, usually by defining the topic clearly. Effective discussion guidelines include the following:

- Encourage full participation by asking the quiet ones nonthreatening questions such as "How have you seen that work?" or "What does that make you think of?"
- Keep the discussion on target. If the group wanders into irrelevancies or disagreement, pull them back with a nonpunitive remark such as "Let's get back to our topic," or "How does that relate to _____?"
- Do not let one or two people dominate the discussion. Thank them for their input, but direct attention to others by asking them to comment on points just made. You may need to say, "Let's hear what someone else thinks about that," or some similar remark.

- Reinforce contributions by making positive remarks about the comments. Even if the remark seems redundant or obvious, you are rewarding effort, not quality. Provide reinforcement by saying such things as "That's interesting," "Good," "Good point," or even "Thank you."
- As the discussion draws to a close, summarize the points made by the group. This provides closure and gives worth to the group's efforts.

Small Group Work

Small groups can be used to discuss issues brought up in class, to share experiences, and to work on joint projects related to self-care or class content. They should be used only if small group work is the most effective way to achieve an objective. Groups provide peer support and reinforcement and are useful for changing attitudes and exploring new patterns of behavior.

For small groups to work effectively, the instructor must provide clear guidelines. What exactly is to be accomplished? What is the time frame? How will the group know it has been successful? Follow these suggestions:

- Have group activities thought out ahead of time and thoroughly planned. Springing things on the spur of the moment (or worse, just to fill time) usually results in an unsatisfying experience.
- Keep the groups small. Six members is an ideal group size. More than ten in a group causes lack of participation by shy participants.
- Instruct groups to choose someone who will report results back to the class as a whole. This recognizes group efforts and provides everyone with new insights into the topic or problem.
- Record group results on flipchart pages that can then be posted around the room for the rest of the session. A written record may stimulate new ideas as people read over it later.
- In a series of classes, consider using small groups as a way of tracking progress. In each session, participants report to their group what happened since the last class, what successes or problems they have had, and what they did about them. Group members can then offer peer reinforcement, support, and suggestions for future action.

Role Playing

In role playing a simulated situation is set up, with class participants then pretending to be characters within that situation. The roles are acted out until some sort of resolution is reached or until the instructor calls a halt. Usually used to gather insights on interpersonal problems, role plays can be difficult to run effectively and must be very carefully planned and executed.

Many people feel self-conscious during role playing, and some even feel threatened by the potential for embarrassment or self-exposure. For these reasons, the decision to use role play is one not lightly made. What will role play accomplish? What objectives will it achieve *more effectively* than other learning methods? Some examples of role playing in a patient education setting include participants playing the roles of physician and patient to learn how to talk with and ask questions of the doctor; patients acting as family members to learn how to handle pressures and temptations concerning diet or life style; or participants practicing assertive statements in various simulated situations.

To ensure a positive outcome, instructors must structure the experience carefully.

- Provide enough information for the participants. Descriptions of the situation and the characters should be fairly detailed if you want participants to react productively. Exhibit 8-6 is an example of role play instructions for a group of adolescent patients with diabetes.
- Never start a session with a role play. The group needs time to "warm up" and get used to each other and the instructor.

Exhibit 8-6 Instructions for Role Play

Each participant in the role play receives one of the following instruction sheets:

You are a high school senior. Recently you became ill and had to be hospitalized, and the doctor told you that you have diabetes. You have learned about diet and exercise, and you give your own insulin. You also check your blood glucose level twice a day and are doing well at keeping the diabetes under control. You haven't told any of your friends about the diabetes yet.

You are a high school senior. Your best friend was quite ill recently and had to be hospitalized. You visited the hospital. Since he/she came home you've wondered what was wrong. Your friend hasn't said anything about the illness. You know a little bit about diabetes— insulin injections and special diets are required, and some sports figures and celebrities have it.

You are a high school senior. One of the people in your section of the band is also in several classes with you. You know him/her pretty well, although you don't hang around together. You know nothing about diabetes, but it sounds frightening to you.

SITUATION: The three of you were talking together when suddenly the first character became very dizzy and ill. The school nurse came and said, "Oh, yes, you're the one with diabetes." Afterward you meet again. What happens?

- Spend a few minutes with each role player to be sure each understands the part.
- Assign a role to everyone in the class. Those who are not actually participating should act as observers. Observers need specific instructions: "List the assertive and nonassertive statements made by the people in the role play," or "Notice how each person contributes to the conversation and be prepared to give each feedback on the positive and negative aspect of his or her behavior."
- The most important part of any role play is the debriefing that takes place after it. Conducted by the instructor, this activity enables participants to discuss the meaning the role play had for them; for the observers, to share their perceptions about what happened. End the debriefing with a summary of what was discussed and the objectives accomplished by the role play.

Games

Games enable participants to review material and work through simulated situations in a format that many people find interesting and exciting. Few commercial games for patients are available, but you can create your own with just a little effort. As with any teaching strategy, games should accomplish objectives. They can range from very simple crossword puzzles to elaborate games that incorporate competition and active learning (see Exhibit 8-7 for the rules of such a game).

To compose games, follow these guidelines:

- Write the objectives first, to stay on target.
- Model your game on a commercial one, such as Bingo or Monopoly. This not only makes it easier to create, but patients will recognize the source and find it easier to play.
- Make the rules clear and explicit. Write them out in enough detail that someone could play the game even if you were not there.
- Try to make the game flexible enough to handle different-size groups. If you can fashion the game to enable small groups to play as if they were single participants, the game will be even more useful.
- When the game is over, discuss what was learned from the experience and what it meant to the participants. This is the most important part of any game playing.
- When you compose a game, test it with a group before using it in class. These "pilot" participants will have valuable insights on how well the game works and how it should be changed to make it work better.

Exhibit 8-7 Rules for Patient Education Game

LIFETIME

INSTRUCTIONS: Each player selects a colored token and rolls the dice for the first turn. The highest number goes first, and turns proceed clockwise from the first player. A turn starts by rolling the dice and making that many moves on the board.

RULES: Follow the instructions given on the square landed on. If you land on a CHANCE square, take a CHANCE card from the stack and follow its directions.

1. Each time you "visit a doctor" you must give up an INSURANCE card and write the date of the visit on your personal record list.
2. From time to time you must make decisions based on instructions from the board or CHANCE cards. Remember to take what has happened to you before into consideration. For instance, if vision problems develop but you have visited the eye doctor in the past six months (be sure this is recorded on your personal record list), you may choose a PREVENTION card and serious damage will be prevented.
3. When asked to make a diet selection, use the DIET BOARD. The instructor will give you a point total for your selection. Add these points to the others you win in the game.
4. Keep track of insulin points and exercise points as you play. Remember these must not outweigh each other and should remain within the limits set at the beginning of the game.
5. If you become "ill," a decision must be made about what action you will take. Inaction is also a choice here.
6. If you are "hospitalized," you may get out by using a PREVENTION card, giving up 10 points, or choosing to remain in the hospital for the next three turns, after which you will be automatically discharged.
7. The first player to accumulate 100 points wins.

Demonstrations/Return Demonstrations

All of the principles of demonstration discussed earlier in this chapter under "One-on-One Instruction" apply to group learning. Demonstrations in the classroom are more difficult because not everyone in the group may be able to see clearly. For instance, demonstrating blood glucose testing to a group of twelve people would be ineffective because probably half of the group would not be able to see the buttons and readouts. However, a video or film demonstrating the procedure could show extreme close-ups of the equipment and the steps. The group then could be separated into pairs to practice the procedure under instructor supervision.

Everyone in the group must not only be able to see the procedure but also be able to practice it and receive feedback about performance. If this cannot be done, demonstration is probably not a good choice of strategy. No matter how careful the explanation, someone in the group will misunderstand. This can be caught and corrected in return demonstration, but without that follow-up people will leave the class still unsure about the procedure (or worse, will believe that they know how to do it and habitually will perform the procedure incorrectly). The need to manipulate the equipment and walk through the actual procedure cannot be overemphasized. If this is impractical, the content should be taught individually rather than in a group.

Support Groups

These groups provide opportunities for participants to share experiences, feelings, resources, and support with each other. They can be offered for patients with similar diagnoses (such as diabetics, cancer patients, and patients with chronic obstructive pulmonary disease), for family members (AlAnon for family members of alcoholics, for instance), or for home caregivers (parents of child diabetics or patients with cystic fibrosis, or caregivers of patients with Alzheimer's disease). Although participant interactions are the most important part of meetings, the leader plays a vital role.

A support group leader states the purposes of the group, gets participants to introduce themselves, and keeps the conversation moving in productive directions. This includes redirecting topics, tactfully ending monologues or hostile exchanges, and ensuring that everyone gets a chance to share. It is an extremely difficult and taxing role. Some people believe that only psychologists should serve as group leaders, but many successful groups have been run by registered nurses or social workers.

Before initiating a support group, assess the need for such a group through questionnaires, interviews, or marketing surveys. Decisions must be made on length of sessions, group composition, time periods (during the workday, in the evening, on weekends?), location, and enrollment procedures. If you will be acting as group leader, plan the first session in detail. How will you begin the session? What "ice-breaking" activities will be used? How can you encourage discussion? Have a number of questions/projects/activities to use if the group is very quiet. There is nothing worse than running out of things to do halfway through a program, so do not let it happen to you. As with any learning activity, debriefing is an important component, so allow time at the end for summary, questions, and final comments.

DEALING WITH SPECIAL SITUATIONS

Teaching Older Patients

It has been estimated that 80 percent of the elderly do not comply with their drug regimens, and that only 30 percent of older patients adhere to their prescribed diets. Approximately one-third of people over 65 suffer from significant hearing loss. Besides correctable visual acuity problems, there is an increased incidence of color blindness in the elderly, who have difficulty distinguishing blue/yellow shades.[21] Consider the problems these factors create in, say, teaching an older patient home blood glucose monitoring with Chemstrips. Even people with no visual problems sometimes have difficulty in deciding which shade on the bottle is nearest to that on the strip. But if you had had trouble hearing the instructions in the first place, could not read the directions well because the print was so small, and *then* tried to distinguish one shade of blue-green (a mixture of blue and yellow) from another, imagine the frustration and potential for error.

When teaching older patients, adjust teaching strategies to compensate for sensory deficits. This does not mean yelling. Often people with hearing problems have one side that is more impaired than the other. Find out which ear hears better and direct your voice to that side. Experiment with vocal pitch. Can the patient hear better if your voice is pitched lower than normal? Higher? Visual acuity problems require simple size adjustments. Examine large-print books from the public library to see how big handout copy should be. A special typewriter element can be purchased to redo reading material. In extreme cases, magnifying glasses can be used to assist vision-impaired patients.

As people grow older they become more resistant to change and increasingly more cautious. The elderly are less likely to attempt a response to a new learning stimulus unless they are relatively sure that it will be correct. Older patients are also at a disadvantage when pressed with complex tasks under time constraints. Performance becomes more congruent with that of younger people when time limits are removed.[22]

The implications for education are clear. Older patients need more time for learning—not longer teaching sessions, but more short sessions, with time for reflection and rest between sessions. Logical organization of material, with each piece of information linked to the other, will help older patients retrieve the data from their memories. Positive reinforcement creates a climate of success and helps to overcome the tendency toward caution.

Perhaps the most important impact on education for any patient, but particularly for the elderly, is the interaction between educator and patient. Video and film presentations are not as popular with the elderly as they are with younger patients.[23] The warmth of human contact can be as much a reward as any praise or certificate you give. Discuss the patients' feelings about what they are learning and what problems they foresee. Incorporate their past experiences into present teaching, to help them link the new information to knowledge and skills they already possess and to tap into the wealth of information they carry within them. This can only be done one-on-one, educator to patient.

Teaching Illiterate Patients

It is estimated that there are twenty-five million American adults who cannot read. A recent study in a public hospital found that only 40 percent of the patient sample could read at the sixth grade level.[24] When dealing with illiterate patients, all of your carefully prepared reading materials are useless. The sheer volume of information that must be learned without reliance on reinforcement from written instructions seems daunting, but even more daunting is the fact that you may have difficulty identifying these patients. Adult illiterates generally try to hide the fact that they cannot read, and they may deny illiteracy if you ask them about it.

What are some signs that illiteracy exists? Do not use socioeconomic measures to determine it—illiteracy is found in all levels of society. One of the coping methods is to agree with everything; if you ask whether the patient understands, the answer will always be yes. Because illiterates lack the data base usually obtained from reading, their comprehension is slower and less complete. They tend to have a narrow perspective related only to personal experience. Another sign of illiteracy is extreme restlessness—a sign of stress when the patient is threatened with the possibility of having to admit to illiteracy.[25] When you do suspect a literacy problem, use extreme tact and avoid any hint of disapproval or impatience. You want to be perceived as a helping person, not a judge.

Teaching strategies for illiterate patients include the following:

- Teach the smallest amount possible to achieve the objectives.
- Make your points as vivid and explicit as possible.
- Teach one step at a time.
- Have the patient restate and demonstrate the procedure.
- Repeatedly review information and procedures.[26]

Limiting your content can be frustrating—the patient is not receiving everything needed. But with limited reading ability only the basics will be retained, so it makes sense to stress the most vital information. Make explanations memorable through the use of simile and story telling. The basic principles of demonstration, of course, hold true for these patients as well; but the steps will need to be stated and restated, and shown and reshown, since written reinforcement will not be available. Realistic drawings or photographs can illustrate the steps of a procedure or outline information about a condition. One inexpensive yet effective method of instruction and reinforcement that patients can take home with them is an audiotape. Record procedures and instructions on audiotape, along with a phone number they can call for answers to questions. Use any strategy you can think of to assist these patients to learn the information needed for effective self-care.

A CHALLENGE FOR CHANGE

Many different teaching techniques have been discussed in this chapter. Some may be old friends—strategies you have used often and feel comfortable implementing. Now, a challenge: choose at least one technique you have never used and try it in your teaching. Change and learning lead to growth, for educators as well as patients.

NOTES

1. J. Segall Ascher et al. *Systematic Course Design for the Health Care Fields* (New York: John Wiley and Sons, Inc., 1975), p. B-130.

2. Mary Louis Donaldson, "Instructional Media As a Teaching Strategy," *Nurse Educator* 4, no. 4 (July–August 1976): 18.

3. Donna R. Falvo, *Effective Patient Education* (Rockville, Md.: Aspen Publishers, Inc., 1985), pp. 153–4.

4. Debra L. Phairas and Judith N. Peeples, "Advice on Informed Consent," *Patientvision Update* 3, no. 2 (Winter 1988): 8.

5. Barbara Klug Redman, *The Process of Patient Education*, 5th ed. (St. Louis: C.V. Mosby Co., 1984), p. 132.

6. "Communicating with Patients about Medicine," *Patientvision Update* 3, no. 2 (Winter 1988): 5.

7. Ibid.

8. Diane C. Rendon et al., "The Right To Know, the Right To Be Taught," *Journal of Gerontological Nursing* 12, no. 12 (December 1986): 37.

9. Matthew Cahill, ed., *Patient Teaching* (Springhouse, Pa.: Nursing87 Books, 1987), p. 67.

10. Steve A. Mazzuca, "Diabetes Care and Education: A Creative Approach," *Patient Education Newsletter* 6, no. 6 (December 1983): 1.

11. Lawrence Holpp, "Technical Training for Nontechnical Learners," *Training and Development Journal* 41, no. 11 (October 1987): 56.

12. James E. Orth et al., "Patient Exposition and Provider Explanation in Routine Interviews and Hypertensive Patients' Blood Pressure Control," *Health Psychology* 6, no. 1 (1987): 40.

13. Holpp, "Technical Training for Nontechnical Learners," p. 56.

14. Kathleen A. Curtis, "Imagery for Skill Improvement," *Clinical Education Outlook* 1, no. 3 (Spring 1988): 2.

15. R.W. Jeffrey et al., "Weight and Sodium Reduction for the Prevention of Hypertension: A Comparison of Group Treatment and Individual Counseling," *American Journal of Public Health* 73 (1983): 691–3.

16. J.P. Assal, "Self-Management of Diabetes: A Therapeutic Success But a Teaching Failure?," *Diabetic Medicine* 2, no. 5 (September 1985): 421.

17. Jean Hayter, "How Good Is Lecture As a Teaching Method?," *Nursing Outlook* 27, no. 4 (April 1979): 274.

18. W.A. Mambert, *Effective Presentations* (New York: John Wiley and Sons, Inc., 1976), p. 250.

19. Helen S. Ross, "Group Discussion Methods," *Patient Education Newsletter* 5, no. 1 (February 1982): 7.

20. Martin M. Broadwell, *The Supervisor As an Instructor: A Guide for Classroom Teaching*, 2nd ed. (Reading, Mass.:Addison-Wesley Publishing Co., 1970), p. 47.

21. P.V. Knight and C.M. Kesson, "Educating the Elderly Diabetic," *Diabetic Medicine* 3, no. 2 (March 1986):170.

22. Rendon et al., "The Right To Know," p. 35.

23. Knight and Kesson, "Educating the Elderly Diabetic," p. 171.

24. Annette Walker, "Teaching the Illiterate Patient," *Journal Of Enterostomal Therapy 14*, no. 2 (March–April 1987): 83.

25. Ibid., pp. 84–85.

26. Ibid., p. 85.

9

Outpatient Instruction

The tools and techniques for outpatient instruction are the same as those for inpatient instruction, and both have been covered in preceding chapters. This chapter discusses the special circumstances that arise because of the nature of outpatient settings.

REIMBURSEMENT FOR OUTPATIENT EDUCATION

Patient education done on an inpatient basis is considered part of required services (along with food and nursing care) by most third-party payers. For a long time outpatient education was not directly reimbursable, but that is changing. On September 1, 1983, Michigan Blue Cross/Blue Shield approved Medicare reimbursement of outpatient diabetes education programs sponsored by hospitals. Under the Michigan Diabetes Control Project run by the state department of public health, a diabetes policy advisory council was established. This came about through a task force put together by hospitals working with Blue Cross/Blue Shield in 1979. The task force established standards to assure quality and continuity of services. The circumstances under which Medicare could legally reimburse were that the services

- be integral to care
- be furnished by a physician or by personnel under medical supervision and under a physician's order
- meet reasonable and medically necessary criteria
- provide essential knowledge to the patient that aids in treatment[1]

131

Perhaps the most important lesson to come out of this effort was the necessity of following a course acceptable to the third-party payer when establishing standards and protocols. The initial rationale of the hospitals seeking reimbursement had emphasized the preventive and cost-effective benefits of diabetes education. It was only when the task force acknowledged Medicare's legal constraints and began emphasizing education as integral to care that the state intermediary and Medicare officials could address education as a potentially reimbursable service.[2]

Patients are often willing to pay for outpatient education themselves if the cost is within their means. At one hospital, for instance, diabetes education is prescribed by physicians on prescription blanks, which patients then bring to outpatient registration. Just as if they were receiving radiology or laboratory services, they are registered and sent to the diabetes educator's office for instruction. At the end of the session the educator reports the length of teaching, and billing is handled in the same way any other outpatient service would be. The rate charged is $30.00 per hour, and patients have been willing to pay for several half-hour sessions. In this instance, patients evidently see a direct link between the services offered and results at home, which is perhaps the single most important determinant of willingness to pay. If a definite link can be established between teaching efforts and results, all payers, whether direct or third-party, will find reimbursement easier to approve (see Chapter 11 for evaluation methods to establish this link).

SURGICENTERS/DAY SURGERY SETTINGS

Developed to eliminate costly presurgery admissions to acute care hospitals, outpatient surgery centers are rapidly expanding. These units, once used for minor procedures such as gastrointestinal studies and minor cyst removals, now handle plastic surgery, gynecological procedures, cardiac catheterizations, hernia repairs, and neurological procedures—including percutaneous discectomies. The list can only expand as surgeons develop safer ways of performing procedures and the pressure for fewer hospitalizations continues.

One of the results of this increased use of outpatient surgery is, of course, decreased professional observation and care. Patients and families must know what to watch for, when to call the physician, how to care for wound sites, and what medicines are required when. This increased need for instruction is coupled with decreased time for teaching. Nurses in outpatient surgery settings need an organized system for delivering patient education, so that no patient can "fall through the cracks" and fail to learn safe home care.

A head nurse in one day surgery unit set up an effective and efficient teaching procedure for her staff without requiring a huge time commitment. She began by meeting with high-use physicians. Their input totally changed the printed instructions she had drawn up in rough draft form. The teaching system began with a preoperative telephone call to each patient. Made the day before surgery, this call enabled nurses to confirm arrival time, ans˟₁er questions, and review important preoperative instructions. After the surgical procedure, nurses reviewed postoperative instruction sheets with each patient, tailoring them to the individual. One or two days after surgery, phone calls were made to the patients to ask them how they were feeling and whether they had any questions or problems. The head nurse states, "If the patient had a specific problem on the day of surgery, I ask about this. This has been a popular part of the program with patients."[3]

It is important not just to develop such a program but to institutionalize it. Write a procedure and policy for the teaching program; build it into your orientation classes, into the quality assurance system, into staff performance appraisals. Make it an expected—even demanded—part of patient care. The following questions need to be answered:

- What instruction should our patients receive?
- What tools will we use?
- What objectives will be set for each patient?
- Who will be responsible for
  1. setting objectives,
  2. coordinating instruction,
  3. giving instruction,
  4. conducting follow-up?
- How will teaching/learning be documented?
- How will it be evaluated?

These questions must be answered in any teaching situation, but they are especially critical in outpatient settings where time is so limited.

OUTPATIENT CLINICS

Outpatient treatment centers traditionally have been viewed as places dedicated to patient education as well as to treatment. Besides learning about self-care, patients can receive education about such preventive topics as nutrition, birth control, and child care. Some clinics charge for this, others offer it as a community service. Kulik and Mahler believe that patients should be screened carefully before such preventive information is offered. Because acutely ill people do not have the energy to focus on prevention of future illnesses, clinics dealing with acute illnesses rather than with routine physical examinations may not be the best choice psychologically for dissemination of material. When suffering from an acute illness, people generally feel more vulnerable to other diseases and less interested in acquiring prevention material.[4]

Since most clinics deal with illnesses, most education focuses on the patient's adjustment to treatment and self-care. The same principles of patient education used in any other setting are applicable to outpatient clinics. Problems arise because of the episodic nature of clinic visits. During one appointment a patient will be seen by one person; the next time, someone different. To maintain continuity of teaching as well as care, documentation becomes vital. Exhibit 9-1 is an example of an educational checklist that could be used in a clinic setting. Exhibit 9-2 is a goal-oriented teaching plan that serves a similar purpose.

Exhibit 9-1 Education Checklist for a Clinic Setting

PATIENT EDUCATION CHECKLIST

As the patient receives instruction, please check off the appropriate items and record the date and your initials.

CHECK	TEACHING/LEARNING ACTIVITY	DATE	INITIALS
_____	Explanation of diagnosis/condition	_____	_____
_____	Explanation of prognosis	_____	_____
_____	Explanation of treatment plan	_____	_____
_____	Medication instructions	_____	_____
	Demonstration of procedures (list procedures):		
_____	_____	_____	_____
_____	_____	_____	_____
_____	_____	_____	_____
_____	_____	_____	_____
_____	_____	_____	_____
_____	_____	_____	_____
_____	Other (Specific problems or learning needs):		
_____	_____	_____	_____
_____	_____	_____	_____
_____	_____	_____	_____
_____	_____	_____	_____

Exhibit 9-2 Education Documentation Form for Clinics

PATIENT TEACHING PLAN

Name: _____ Age: _____

Physician: _____

Diagnosis: _____

Teaching Goals: _____

_____

_____

_____

List teaching actions and patient reactions at each visit:

_____

_____

_____

_____

_____

_____

_____

_____

_____

_____

_____

_____

_____

_____

_____

Helping Children to Cope with Procedures

Clinics dealing with children face trickier educational activities. Estimates of behavioral disturbances resulting from health care-related experiences range from 10 to 92 percent, with as many as 32 percent needing treatment for long-term disturbances such as regressive behavior, increased dependency, excessive fear, sleep or eating disturbances, anger, enuresis, or social withdrawal.[5] Anyone who has worked in a pediatric clinic has encountered such behaviors in the patients. How can children be better prepared for treatments and procedures?

Studies have demonstrated that, for children who had not previously experienced hospital or dental procedures, simply having the child review a videotape of a peer undergoing a shortened version of the impending events reduced anxiety and improved cooperation. However, the timing of the preparation was critical. Children below the age of seven became more emotionally aroused if they were prepared one week in advance, but the more immediate the preparation, the better the benefits for the child. Researchers also found that children under the age of three actually became more anxious and anticipated more fear and pain when they were shown a slide/tape program about their procedure. Since instruction can increase anxiety inadvertently, great care must be taken to individualize education to the child. Other strategies that have been found to help children include enlisting the help of parents. When parents assist the child to learn, there is greater parent satisfaction and improved child cooperation. Younger children also need to have concrete experience with the instruments to be used.[6]

PHYSICIANS' OFFICES

Much depends on the physician's philosophy about patient education in an office setting. Many physicians are committed to instructing patients about their condition and care. Others see education as a low priority. Scheduling appointments so that patients are seen too close together is an expression of the latter philosophy. With just a few minutes per patient, little instruction can be given. Other factors influencing office instruction include:

- physician's level of knowledge about educational activities
- staff knowledge and expertise
- resources available
- system for follow-up and reinforcement

Physician's Level of Knowledge

Is the doctor aware of the principles of effective teaching? That people have different learning styles? That "talking at" people may not be the best teaching strategy? There are physicians who are very much aware of how people learn best and who are very well attuned to the individual. If your physician(s) is not knowledgeable about patient education methods (which are not covered in most medical schools), you may have a teaching job to do on your employer before you can teach patients. Try things on your own initiative—put together a teaching plan, get some handouts—and keep track of the results. Since most physicians are results-oriented, a positive outcome to your interventions should make an impression.

Staff Knowledge and Expertise

Staff knowledge and expertise vary, along with the motivation to perform educational activities. Why not take advantage of this variance, allowing the people who enjoy patient teaching to take over that aspect of care while others take more of the technical/procedural tasks. Subscribing to journals, making books available on patient education, and conducting inservice meetings on the topic are other ways to encourage more staff participation. Of course, the most effective way of getting staff action is for patient education to be an expected part of the job, tied into salary adjustments and performance appraisals.

Resources Available

If your office carries a few diet sheets mimeographed in small print as your entire stock of patient education materials, it is time to reassess things. Diet instructions are fine, but they need to be readable and supplemented by human directions. Some offices are now stocking videotapes and/or slide/sound programs for instruction, as well as pamphlets, books, and instruction sheets. Just remember, if audiovisual programs are used they should be an adjunct, not the be-all and end-all. Sticking a patient in a room with a videotape is not patient education. Explain the purpose of the program, including what patients should watch for and what they will do with the information later. Then meet with them after the program to review the content and answer questions.

System for Follow-up and Reinforcement

Just as in any outpatient setting, offices need a method of keeping track of what has been taught and how the patient is doing. The more physicians and office staff see the patient, the more crucial this becomes. Setting goals and recording achievements in the patient record should be done by physician and/or patient educator, and a checklist similar to that in Exhibit 9-1 can be used as well. Methods of evaluation are covered in Chapter 11.

EMERGENCY DEPARTMENTS/URGENT CARE CENTERS

Emergency departments and urgent care centers suffer problems somewhat different from those of other outpatient units because of extreme time pressures. Patients admitted to emergency units are not only traumatized by injury or illness but also frightened about even *being* in that setting. The urgency of the physical problems can drive all other priorities away, and yet patients who are sent home unable to care for themselves properly can undo all of the high-technology, highly professional emergency care they received.

Since the setting hardly allows extended teaching time, printed instructions are a must. Exhibits 9-3 and 9-4 show samples of emergency department instruction sheets. These sheets reinforce verbal instructions once the patient is home. Teaching can be done while dressing wounds, applying casts, or helping the patient to dress, thus using time efficiently and effectively. Record whatever teaching was done on the patient's chart. If standardized instruction sheets are used, a form such as shown in Exhibit 9-5 can be used to simplify documentation.

Some emergency units have teaching rooms stocked with information sheets, pamphlets, and videos covering topics such as wound care. Others have rooms especially designed for children, for teaching about such procedures as suturing and casting. Melamed found that children who were to have same-day surgery directly from the emergency department were better prepared when they viewed a distracting film that explained nothing about the surgery.[7] Including inexpensive videotapes of Disney cartoons or other child-oriented entertainment can help as both a distractor and an anxiety reducer.

HOME CARE TEACHING

In home care nursing, patient education must be viewed as one of the top responsibilities, if not *the* chief goal of the home care nurse. The differences between priorities of hospital nurses and those of home care nurses (whether working for a visiting nurse association or a private agency) were detailed in recent research. A

Exhibit 9-3 Emergency Unit Instruction Sheet

CARE OF YOUR SUTURES

There are a few simple things you need to do to care for yourself and prevent problems. Be sure to follow these directions exactly to help your wound heal quickly.

1. Keep the dressing dry. Do not let any water get on it—protect it during washing. Don't take a shower until the dressing has been removed by the doctor. If the dressing does get wet, replace it with a piece of dry sterile gauze.

2. If there is no dressing, keep the wound clean. Do not touch or pull on the stitches.

3. You may have some clear or reddish-brown draining—this is normal. If thick green or yellow fluid comes from the wound, call _____

4. Some pain and stiffness is normal. If the area becomes very swollen or extremely painful, call the above number.

INSTRUCTIONS ON YOUR MEDICINE: _____
_____
_____
_____
_____
_____

ADDITIONAL INSTRUCTIONS: _____
_____
_____
_____

Come back on _____ at _____ to see the doctor.

number of hospital discharge planners and an equal number of home health nurses were studied. Discharge planners see their primary responsibility as assisting patients toward a plan of care, which includes very specific means and techniques necessary to support care. Home health nurses holistically focus on primary care in the home, including patients' physical care, health teaching, and promotion of patients' independence.[8]

Fifty percent of the home health nurses believe that at least half of the patients discharged from hospitals (whether or not they are referred to a home health nurse) are not able to manage their care adequately in the home. According to discharge planners, lack of resources (people, money, or equipment) was the primary barrier to self-care or family care, while a knowledge deficit about care is viewed as the primary barrier by home health nurses. When asked about the quality of communication between the two groups, 55 percent of the discharge planners described quality as very good or excellent, while only 35 percent of the home health nurses answered in this way.[9] One might speculate that the differing priorities of the two

Exhibit 9-4 Emergency Unit Instruction Sheet

CARE OF YOUR CAST

There are a few simple things you need to do to care for yourself and prevent problems. Be sure to follow these directions exactly.

1. Some pain and swelling is normal. If the areas around the cast swell so much that the skin becomes numb or discolored, or if the pain becomes very severe, call _____

2. Keep the cast elevated as much as you can. You should be able to move your fingers/toes at all times—if they become numb or won't move, call the above number.

3. Keep the cast dry. This means no showers while you have the cast. You may take baths as long as the casted area remains out of the water at all times.

4. If the cast becomes wet and gummy, or begins to crumble or crack, call the above number.

INSTRUCTIONS ON YOUR MEDICINE: _____

_____

_____

_____

_____

ADDITIONAL INSTRUCTIONS: _____

_____

_____

Come back on _____ at _____ to see the doctor.

---

groups (specific versus holistic) predisposes to communication problems.

Teaching in the home needs to be planned and documented. It is probably the most underdocumented skilled service because most nurses in home care do not recognize the scope and depth of the teaching they do. Nurses tend to view much of their teaching as common-sense suggestions.[10] Developing an education plan similar to those developed in acute care settings will highlight teaching actions. After visiting the patient's home, the following steps should be taken:

1. Assess the needs of patient and family.
2. Set goals for patient education, discuss them with the clients, and win agreement.
3. Document the goals, teaching/learning actions, and time lines for completion.
4. Implement the plan.

Exhibit 9-5 Teaching Documentation Form

```
┌─────────────────────────────────────────────────────────────────────┐
│                       PATIENT EDUCATION NOTES                         │
│  Name: _____    │
│  Number: _____ Date of Service: _____    │
│  Diagnosis: _____    │
│  Seen by: _____    │
│  Treatment: _____    │
│  _____    │
│  _____    │
│                                                                       │
│  Instruction Sheets Given: _____    │
│  _____    │
│  _____    │
│                                                                       │
│  Verbal Instructions Given: _____    │
│  _____    │
│  _____    │
│  _____    │
│  _____    │
│  _____    │
│  _____    │
│                                                                       │
│  Patient Reactions: _____    │
│  _____    │
│  _____    │
│  _____    │
│  _____    │
│                                                                       │
│  Follow-up Scheduled:   NO_____   YES_____   WHEN_____    │
└─────────────────────────────────────────────────────────────────────┘
```

5. Evaluate the patient's/family's ability to carry out self-care.
6. Document the results.

Teaching is built into home care. As dressings are being changed, baths given, or medications injected, home health nurses give instruction along with nursing care. Actually seeing the home environment gives you a tremendous advantage in assessing potential problems and creating solutions. Evaluation also becomes easier, because you can follow the results of your teaching on future visits. Perhaps the single most significant advantage that home care nurses have is the close relationship that develops between them and their patients and the patients' families. The trust and friendship not only makes what the nurses teach have more impact, but also makes clients more motivated to comply, since someone significant to them will be following up on their results.

NOTES

1. Richard H. Danielson, John K. Beasley, and Randall S. Pope, "Diabetes Education Payment: The Michigan Experience," *Patient Education Newsletter* 7, no. 3 (June 1984): 7.

2. Ibid., p. 8.

3. Pam Borich, "A New Outpatient Surgery Patient Teaching Program," *Patient Education Newsletter* 8, no. 4 (August 1985): 5.

4. James A. Kulik and Heike I.M. Mahler, "Health Status, Perceptions of Risk, and Prevention Interest for Health and Nonhealth Problems," *Health Psychology* 6, no. 1 (1987): 26.

5. Barbara J. Melamed, "Individualizing Preparation for Medical Procedures," *Patient Education Newsletter* 7, no. 3 (April 1984): 5.

6. Ibid., pp. 5–6.

7. Ibid., p. 6.

8. Leslie A. Drew, Diane Biordi, and Dee Ann Gillies, "How Discharge Planners and Home Health Nurses View Their Patients," *Nursing Management* 19, no. 4 (April 1988): 68.

9. Ibid., p. 70.

10. Diane J. Omdahl, "Preventing Home Care Denials," *American Journal of Nursing* 87, no. 8 (August 1987):1032–3.

10

Documenting Patient Education

LEGAL RISKS OF INADEQUATE DOCUMENTATION

Everyone involved in health care knows that documentation is important—but why? Time spent in charting could be better spent at the bedside—at least, that is what many caregivers believe. But documentation not only provides other team members with the information they need to care for patients, it also protects you from lawsuits.

The key rule for documenting educational activities is the same as that for any other nursing activity: if it is not written down, it did not happen. If legal action is brought against you or the hospital, the way in which you documented your actions may be your only protection. In one case, a child was burned by a heating pad after his mother incorrectly carried out the nurse's instructions for applying it. The nurse was charged with malpractice. But the nurse had both provided and documented patient teaching; she had even documented the mother's response to her teaching. The court found no grounds for malpractice because the nurse had maintained reasonable standards of care by providing instruction.[1] If evidence had not been found in the chart supporting the nurse's testimony, the outcome of the case could have been quite different.

Throughout this chapter on documentation, remember that your teaching actions do not exist unless they appear in the written record. Whether you work in an acute care hospital, outpatient setting, extended care facility, or patient homes, lack of instruction (or lack of documentation of instruction) can lead you to the losing end of a lawsuit.

143

REIMBURSEMENT AND DOCUMENTATION: A VITAL RELATIONSHIP

In any situation where third-party payers provide reimbursement of services, documentation plays a vital role in obtaining payments. Whether Medicare, Medicaid, or private insurance is involved, the claims examiner will peruse the records and base the payment decision on what is documented there. The most common reason for denial is documentation that does not give all of the facts. The record must show that the patient and the services met the requirements of Medicare, for example. Information must be complete and accurate and must reflect the care actually given on every visit.[2]

Omdahl believes that teaching is probably the most underdocumented skilled service because most nurses do not recognize the scope and depth of the teaching they do.[3] Think about all of the teaching activities you perform with your patients—not just the formal sessions with audiovisual tools and objectives, but the informal explanations of care that are made during a bath, the answers provided while administering a medication. Are *all* of those teaching actions documented? Most of us would have to answer no.

Throughout the rest of this chapter, examples are shown of different charting systems and how they can be adapted to record patient education activities. Whatever system is in use in your setting, remember that a few minutes spent in documenting your teaching actions and the patient's responses can make a tremendous difference both legally and financially.

CHARTING SYSTEMS AND PATIENT EDUCATION

Standard Charting Systems

Still the most widely used, standard charting systems incorporate a graphics sheet for recording vital signs, elimination, and hygiene activities; a fluid balance sheet for intake and output; a medication administration record; and nursing notes on which narrative statements about patient activities and observations are recorded. In this system there is no overall coordination. To see links between a medication that was given because an observation was made, causing a change in intake and output and/or vital signs, you would have to trace laboriously the sequence of events through many different forms—a paper chase that few take the time and trouble to do.

Patient education activities usually are recorded in the nursing notes in this system. Exhibit 10-1 shows some examples of charting teaching/learning actions. The difficulty with this system, of course, is trying to follow the teaching plan and its results from start to finish. With so many other notes and observations intermixed, tracing patient education activities is difficult.

Exhibit 10-1 Patient Education Charting in Nurses' Notes

Time	V.S., Treatments	Narrative Notes
0715	Pt. Educ.	Drew up + injected insulin mixed dose. Still needs to be reminded about injecting air into vial before withdrawing dose. Stated, "I don't think I'll ever get used to this. I just hate needles." Will speak to Dr. Smith about getting air injector. Left vials of water + syringes c̄ pt. Instructed to practice drawing up doses. Reviewed foot care. Allow pt. to wash his own feet tomorrow — watch for complete drying of feet + toes.
		A. Nurse, RN

One way around this problem is to separate patient education notes from nursing notes. Some hospitals have a form for "treatment activities" such as respiratory services, physical therapy, social workers' visits, and other allied professional activities. If the patient educator is required to chart on these "allied progress notes," the sequence of activities and results is easier to follow. But this method carries a tremendous disadvantage—few nurses read this part of the chart. One patient educator working with this system expressed frustration: "I'll visit the patient, do a complete assessment, talk to the doctor and the patient's nurse, document very completely—and then the next day be asked by another nurse why I haven't seen the patient yet."

Another strategy that has been tried involves a special form used just for patient

Exhibit 10-2 Documentation Page of a Teaching Plan

OBSERVATIONS: _____

_____

_____

_____

PROBLEMS ENCOUNTERED: _____

_____

_____

_____

PATIENT REACTIONS: _____

_____

_____

_____

_____

FAMILY REACTIONS: _____

_____

_____

_____

FINAL SUMMARY: _____

_____

_____

_____

_____

education. In Chapter 5 a patient education form was shown in Exhibit 5-4. The documentation of such a plan would be done on a second page (see Exhibit 10-2). This system has the advantage of isolating patient education activities from the rest of the observations and treatments, so that implementation of the plan can be followed clearly. That very advantage is also its disadvantage: the documentation is separate from the nursing notes and may or may not be read by all of the staff. It also adds yet another form to an already-crowded chart. These disadvantages can be overcome if reading (and adding to) patient education documentation becomes an expected part of nursing practice at institutions where these kinds of charting systems are practiced, but this must be instituted by nursing administration and enforced by nursing managers.

NURSING CARE PLANS AND PATIENT EDUCATION

Should patient education be included on the nursing care plan (NCP)? The answer would seem to be an automatic and resounding yes, but in actual practice that is not always the case. Too many NCP systems consist of card stock Kardexes, where the patient's diagnosis, age, sex, physician, medications, treatments, and diagnostic tests are written in pencil. These are used for giving reports to other shifts (usually a dry recitation of what tests the patient is to have, when the last pain medication was given, and how much is left in the intravenous bottle.) When the patient is discharged, the NCP is thrown away. Most systems call for problem identification and implementation of a plan to meet those problems (including patient teaching). But with too little time and too much to do, these sections are often left blank or have a perfunctory "Relieve post-op pain" or "Help with adjustment to illness" scribbled on them.

A workable care planning system must start with the following premises:

- It will contain useful information.
- It will be part of the permanent record.
- It will serve as a communication tool for all health care workers.
- It will be available when needed.

Useful information implies something that will improve patient care. It also should be something that is found nowhere else. Incorporating the plan for patient education into the NCP is practical *if* it becomes a permanent part of the record. If the NCP is destined to end up in the trash, why should anyone invest time and effort into developing a plan of care? To have the care plan serve as a communication tool, all disciplines should be able both to read it and to add to it. Sometimes the care plans are guarded as jealously as the nursing notes, with the similar result that no one reads them except the nurses. Social workers, physical therapists, and other health care professionals may have valuable insights about patient care that belong on the care plan.

The point about accessibility brings up the whole issue of what form a care plan should take and where it should be kept. The flip-open Kardex is probably the most widely used form, although separate notebooks seem to be gaining in popularity. Regardless of form, the practice has always been to keep all NCPs together in a central location, with one Kardex or notebook per team or per wing. This facilitated giving reports in some little room off the nurses' station while patients wondered where all the nurses had gotten to. It also ensured that anyone wanting to consult or add to the care plan had to go running around looking for it somewhere in the station.

The trend is now toward a more patient-centered system of documentation. More and more you will find NCPs kept in each patient's room, in a charting cabinet or drawer. Some hospitals also keep the graphics sheet, fluid balance sheet, medication administration record, and nurses' notes in the same area. Anyone caring for the patient can consult the clipboard or other holder for whatever information they need, and charting can be done without leaving the room. Reports are given during walking rounds as the nurses move from room to room, seeing the patients as well as hearing about them. The advantages for documenting your patient education activities are obvious: teaching/learning activities can be written down right after they happen, minimizing the risk that they will be forgotten or charted incompletely. The education section of the care plan can be consulted to see what action comes next, what reaction the patient had to the last session, or what follow-up and reinforcement are needed. Changes to the plan can be made immediately.

Exhibit 10-3 shows one way in which the education section of the care plan can be designed. The teaching plan concept shown in Exhibits 5-4 and 10-2 can also be adapted to NCP form. If the care plan is kept as a permanent part of the patient record, charting can be done directly onto it, thus saving nursing time and encouraging more complete documentation.

PROBLEM-ORIENTED SYSTEMS

The problem-oriented system of documenting patient care was developed in 1968 by Dr. Lawrence L. Weed of Cleveland Metropolitan Hospital in an effort to better coordinate the health team's approach to each patient. One nursing leader advocates it because, if properly used, it facilitates patient care; publicly documents evidence of nursing contributions; and leaves sufficient permanence for accountability, peer review, and clinical nursing research. The nurses' records show evidence of the entire nursing process: assessment, formulation of problems, for-

Exhibit 10-3 Education Section of NCP

Expected Outcomes for This Patient: _____
_____
_____
_____
_____

Teaching Needed before Discharge: _____
_____
_____
_____
_____
_____
_____
_____
_____

Referral (Social Worker, Dietitian, Home Health, Etc.): _____
_____
_____

Other Information: _____
_____
_____
_____

mulation of solutions, intervention, and evaluation.[4]

After the patient is assessed, a problem list is developed from the data collected. Each problem is assigned a number, which is referred to in all documentation. Exhibit 10-4 shows a typical problem list. Interventions are then planned to solve the problems. Sana and Judge delineate priorities as follows: "The plan for each problem states specifically how the care planner is going to approach the problem in regard to (1) diagnostic plan, (2) therapeutic measures, and (3) patient education."[5] All observations, actions, new interventions, and evaluations are made in the progress notes using the number and title of the pertinent problem(s). All disciplines chart on the progress notes using the same format.

The acronym for this charting format is SOAP:

S— Subjective observations (patient's viewpoint)
O—Objective observations (caregiver's viewpoint)
A—Analysis of observations (what do they mean in relation to this problem?)
P—Plan (what are the next steps needed?)

Exhibit 10-4 Problem List in Problem-Oriented System

Name: _Jane Doe_   Age: _35_

Diagnosis: _Diabetes Mellitus_

Physician: _Faber_

PROBLEMS LIST

No.	Problems	Identified	Resolved
1.	Elevated blood glucose levels.	6-15-88	
2.	Impaired vision due to retinal damage	6-15-88	
3.	Weakness in Ⓡ arm	6-15-88	
4.	No visitors; Husband has not called since admission.	6-18-88	

At first glance this may seem rather cumbersome, but after working with the system for a while, most nurses evaluate it positively. Repetitive observations such as vital signs, neurological checks, and cast care are put on flow sheets rather than made part of the narrative SOAP notes.

Exhibit 10-5 SOAP Notes for a Patient with Diabetes

No.	Notes and Observations
1.	S: Expresses doubts about being able to give herself insulin.
	O: Hands shake when she handles equip. Averts eyes when receiving injections
	A: Very apprehensive about injections. Does not seem to have adjusted to Dx; has learned about diabetes but seems resistant.
	P: Pt. to practice injecting water into silicone model. Will speak to Dr. Faber about this problem. Do not have pt. give own injection yet.
4.	S: Spoke wistfully about roomate's visitors.
	O: Has received no visitors since admission + no phone calls. Appears depressed.
	A: Needs family contact. Husband is not visiting or calling.
	P: Talk to pt. about family for clues on situation. Speak to Dr. Faber. Spend extra time c̄ pt. Encourage socialization.

Exhibit 10-5 shows sample SOAP notes related to the problem list in Exhibit 10-4. Linking all charting to a problem (or problems) makes a coherent whole out of the chart rather than a series of random observations and activities. Patient education will still be used as an intervention for several—perhaps all—of the problems. This weaves patient education documentation throughout the entire chart and involves the entire care team in teaching the patient.

NURSING DIAGNOSIS SYSTEMS

Nursing diagnosis is a development of the nursing process and professional nursing practice. In an effort to define independent nursing practice, the North American Nursing Diagnosis Association (NANDA) developed a list of nursing diagnoses, as well as a system for implementing them in practice. The list of approved diagnoses is updated every two years; the next NANDA meeting will be in 1990.

Alfaro defines nursing diagnosis as "an actual or potential health problem (of an individual, family, or group) that nurses can legally treat independently, initiating the nursing interventions necessary to prevent, resolve, or reduce the problem."[6] Medical diagnoses focus on identifying diseases, while nursing diagnoses focus on iden'ifying human responses and alterations in the patient's ability to function as an independent person.[7] To use a patient education example:

Medical Diagnosis	Nursing Diagnosis
Diabetes	Knowledge deficit: Insulin therapy

Nursing diagnoses are worded as two-part statements: (1) The label is the diagnostic category or nursing diagnosis term that describes the health problem, and (2) the etiology describes the possible cause(s). This statement must be supported by clinical information obtained during assessment.[8] For example, the label "Airway clearance, ineffective" might be accompanied by the etiology "related to decreased energy or fatigue" or "related to presence of tracheobronchial obstruction or secretions." Working with the NANDA list, almost all patient problems can be classified by using their terminology.

At first glance this system seems complicated. But the list of diagnoses quickly becomes familiar, and a little practice enables you to identify patient problems that can be handled independently versus ones that require collaboration with the physician or other health care professionals. Use of the nursing diagnosis promotes professional nursing practice by standardizing terminology nationwide and defining just what constitutes nursing care as opposed to medical care or the care provided by dietitians, physical therapists, or any other group of practitioners.

As an example of how this system might work in a patient education context, if a patient demonstrates lack of knowledge about some aspect of care, the nursing diagnosis category would be *knowledge deficit*. This is defined as "the state in which the individual experiences a deficiency in cognitive knowledge or psychomotor skills that alters or may alter health maintenance."[9] One etiology that might accompany the nursing diagnosis would be "knowledge deficit: related to lack of exposure," which further defines it as "inadequate understanding of information or inability to perform skills needed by an individual to practice health-related behaviors."[10]

The nursing actions required by this nursing diagnosis would involve assessment of needs, planning, implementation of teaching/learning activities, and evaluation of results, as described elsewhere in this book. Notice how this follows the nursing process. Such nursing action takes no more time than other methods of providing care while clearly defining professional nursing practice.

Suggested documentation for the nursing diagnosis of "knowledge deficit: related to lack of exposure" include:

- client's verbalization of what he/she knows/does not know
- expressions of need to know, motivation to learn
- learning objectives
- methods used to teach client
- information imparted
- skills demonstrated
- client's response to teaching
- documentation including evaluation of each expected outcome[11]

Many books and articles are available on nursing diagnosis and how to implement such a system of care. With its emphasis on independent nursing practice, nursing diagnosis seems an ideal partner for professional patient education efforts.

DOCUMENTATION OF DISCHARGE PLANNING

Discharge planning continues to grow in importance as more third-party payers move to contract payments. Modeled on the diagnosis-related groups (DRGs) used by Medicare, contracts use a prospective payment system—hospitals receive a flat rate for services, regardless of what the actual charges might be. Prospective payment systems put tremendous pressure on the hospital to discharge patients as quickly as possible.

Drew, Biordi, and Gillies state that discharge planning should be expanded to ensure that unnecessary readmissions do not occur and to meet the demands for continuity of care at lower costs. Hospitals need to develop treatment protocols for their most costly DRGs. If discharge planning is included in protocols, the true costs of DRGs are likely to be better understood.[12] As part of this development process, forms should be thought out that will document the teaching and preparation of home care.

Exhibit 10-6 shows a form that might be used to record discharge planning. This form can be filled out by the discharge planning coordinator, but it probably will be more effective if it is completed by the people actually caring for the patient. Time will be saved by putting parts of the form in a checklist format. Remember that whatever form you design serves as legal protection as well as simple documentation (see Chapter 1 for another example of a discharge planning documentation form).

Exhibit 10-6 Discharge Planning Form

Name: _____ Age: _____

Diagnosis: _____

Physician: _____   Pred. date of discharge: _____

Instruction materials given: _____

_____

_____

_____ Medications explained   _____ Treatments demonstrated

_____ Diet instructions given   _____ Equipment ordered

_____ Follow-up appointment scheduled   Date: _____

                                        Time: _____

_____ Community resources contacted   Which: _____

_____

Patient problems: _____

_____

_____

_____

Interventions: _____

_____

_____

_____

_____

_____

_____

_____

INFORMED CONSENT AND PATIENT EDUCATION

Although informed consent is really a medical responsibility, so many health care systems involve nurses and patient educators that a brief discussion of the issue seems in order. Physicians have a legal directive to inform patients of the benefits and risks involved in the plan of treatment before beginning that treatment. Although this has been required for quite some time, there is still considerable misunderstanding about informed consent.

A recent study found that only 2.5 percent of all malpractice claims submitted during a five-year period involved informed consent. Treatment without consent (except in some special cases) constitutes a civil battery. Even if there is no harm to the patient, a physician who violates the rule of consent would still be liable for battery, since the essence of battery is touching without consent.[13] Nurses can be liable for battery as well—for example, when a nurse gives an injection that the patient has refused to accept.

Before patients can give a reasonable informed consent, they must understand not only the procedure to which they are consenting but also any risks involved, as well as alternatives that might be available. In one study it was found that most physicians and patients thought of informed consent as meaning that patients were "informed" about their conditions and treatments. Only eleven percent of the public and few physicians mentioned treatment alternatives, risks, or patient choice or treatment preference.[14]

Many physicians assume that detailed disclosure of risks may increase patient anxiety, treatment refusal, and incidence of side effects. But studies show that limited disclosures and one-sided exchanges between physicians and patients are correlated with noncompliance and poorer medical outcomes.[15] Rimer decided that informed consent studies prove that:

- Patients want detailed information about their conditions.
- So far, no negative consequences have been found with disclosure.
- Physicians generally disclose less information than patients want to know.[16]

Patient educators can improve the process of informed consent by helping the institution to develop a standardized approach. If you read samples of consent forms from different organizations, you will find that many of them use pedantic language with many difficult medical terms. Forms should be simplified and should include risks and treatment alternatives. Frequently performed procedures can have standardized forms with information preprinted on them. A form with blank spaces where physicians may write in appropriate information can be used for other procedures (see Exhibit 10-7 for an example).

Besides developing consent forms, patient educators can also develop teaching materials about groups of procedures. Patients receiving handouts or booklets about their conditions and the treatment modalities available will be better able to discuss issues with the physician. In preparing these materials, remember the legal requirements of informed consent:

- the diagnosis
- the kind, purpose, and expected outcomes of the proposed treatment
- the risks and consequences of the proposed treatment
- any alternative treatments and their attendant risks and benefits
- the prognosis if no treatment is given (in some jurisdictions)[17]

Brenner and Gerken believe that standardizing the information provided to patients accomplishes two goals: a uniform consent process, and good will between

Exhibit 10-7 Sample Informed Consent Form

CONSENT FORM

I, _____ , consent to the
treatment/procedure _____ .

to treat my condition of _____ .
_____

I understand that _____ ,
the physician performing the treatment/procedure, his/her assistants, and all people working
under his/her direction will perform the above-named treatment/procedure and any emergency
treatment that might be required. I also consent to any anesthesia required for this procedure
(Insert type of anesthesia here: _____).

The expected outcome(s) of this treatment/procedure is/are

_____
_____
_____ .

The following risks and consequences may occur: _____
_____
_____

The following alternative treatments are available: _____
_____
_____

If this treatment/procedure is not done, the following consequences will result: _____
_____
_____

_____   _____
Patient Signature   Physician Signature

(If a parent or guardian signs, relationship: _____

---

the professional staff and hospital administration as concern for the informed consent process is demonstrated by providing means for its improvement.[18]

The majority of informed consent studies have examined what patients recall following the informed consent interview. The results show consistently low levels of patient understanding immediately after they sign the consent form.[19] Of course, improving educational materials and making consent forms clearer and more complete will help to improve patient understanding, but it is a nursing responsibility to assess the effectiveness of the informed consent process.

Ask patients to explain, in their own words, what the physician told them. If they are unclear about small details (such as the exact definition of a term, or what exactly will occur in the preoperative or postoperative period), clarify these for them. But if your evaluation reveals basic misunderstandings about diagnosis, treatment, or prognosis, the physician must be asked to return and rediscuss the entire process with the patient. Information about patients' understanding (or lack of understanding) should be documented in the patient record, as should any actions taken (such as notification of the physician).

Problems with the informed consent process must be addressed and corrected—the legal risks are too great for physicians and hospitals alike. As patients and families grow more sophisticated and knowledgeable about health care, patient education and informed consent will be not only more necessary but more in demand from consumers.

NOTES

1. Carol E. Smith, "Patient Teaching: It's the Law," *Nursing87* 17, no. 7 (July 1987): 67.

2. Diane J. Omdahl, "Preventing Home Care Denials," *American Journal Of Nursing* 87, no. 8 (August 1987): 1032.

3. Ibid., p. 1033.

4. Josephine M. Sana and Richard D. Judge, eds., *Physical Appraisal Methods for Nursing Practice* (Boston: Little, Brown Co., 1975), p. 25.

5. Ibid., p. 26.

6. Rosalinda Alfaro, *Application of the Nursing Process: A Step by Step Guide* (Philadelphia: J.B. Lippincott Co., 1986), p. 59.

7. Ibid., p. 66.

8. Cynthia M. Taylor and Sheila S. Cress, *Nursing Diagnosis Cards* (Springhouse, Pa.: *Nursing87*, Springhouse Corporation, 1987), p. v.

9. Lynda Juall Carpenito, *Handbook Of Nursing Diagnosis* (Philadelphia: J.B. Lippincott Co., 1985), p. 42.

10. Taylor and Cress, *Nursing Diagnosis Cards*, p. 61a.

11. Ibid., p. 61b.

12. Leslie A. Drew, Diane Biordi, and Dee Ann Gillies, "How Discharge Planners and Home Health Nurses View Their Patients," *Nursing Management* 19, no. 4 (April 1988): 67.

13. Carolyn E. Cotsonas, "Informed Consent in Perspective," *Patient Education Newsletter* 5, no. 2 (April 1982): 13.

14. Donna R. Falvo, *Effective Patient Education* (Rockville, Md.: Aspen Publishers, Inc., 1985), pp. 195–6.

15. R.R. Faden, et al., "Disclosure of Information to Patients in Medical Care," *Medical Care* 19 (1981): 732.

16. Barbara Rimer, "Informed Consent Education: The Role for Patient Education," *Patient Education Newsletter* 8, no. 3 (June 1985): 2.

17. Cotsonas, "Informed Consent in Perspective," p. 13.

18. Lawrence Brenner and Elizabeth Gerken, "Informed Consent: Myths and Risk Management Alternatives," *Quality Review Bulletin* 12, no. 12 (December 1986): 425.

19. Rimer, "Informed Consent Education," p. 2.

11

Evaluating Patient Education

Evaluating the results of an education program is neither easy nor always comfortable. It is tempting to let evaluation slide, particularly in patient education, where people can say with some justification that any efforts will have benefit. But developing a systematic evaluation plan not only enables you to prove that your efforts have worth, it also provides information about any changes needed to make the program more effective. As we look at evaluation methods, we need to focus on two aspects of evaluating patient education: (1) evaluating effectiveness for the patient and (2) evaluating program effectiveness.

EVALUATING EFFECTIVENESS FOR THE PATIENT

The Three Dimensions of Evaluation

People performing evaluations tend to focus on easily measured things such as written tests. While written tests certainly serve a valuable purpose, evaluation needs to be approached from a standpoint both broader and, at the same time, more practical. Douglass and Bevis state that "the ultimate purpose of individual evaluation is to provide the learner with a guide for accomplishing a stated goal."[1] When we perform learner evaluations, we are trying to discover whether learners have achieved the objectives—have they learned what they need to know to perform self-care? Taking it one step further, can they (and will they) perform effective self-care at home?

Looking at it from that point of view, you can see that we should evaluate learners to:

159

1. determine whether they are assimilating information as it is being taught
2. determine whether they remember information after it has been taught
3. determine whether they can use the information in day-to-day life

Each of these is a separate function, requiring a different approach. While learners are being taught there should be a planned review of progress built into each session. Another review of objective achievement should be made at the end of the teaching process, when the patient is ready for discharge. Yet another evaluation should be made to check actual patient progress. Keep these three phases in mind as we discuss different evaluation methods and approaches.

Analysis of Evaluation

Evaluation can be analyzed in one of four ways:

Reaction—measuring the responses of learners to the content and to the
        instructor
Learning—measuring the acquisition of knowledge
Behavior—measuring the change in skills occurring as a result of learning
        activities
Results— measuring the life style changes resulting from learning activities[2]

Each of these analyses requires different methods of evaluation.

Reaction

In classroom settings, reaction is measured by "evaluations" that are passed out to the group at the beginning of class and collected at the end. These forms ask for participants' reactions to such things as organization of content, behavior of the instructor, and helpfulness of handouts. Reaction sheets are rarely used for individual patients, yet the information they provide might prove helpful. Exhibit 11-1 is an example of a reaction form that could be distributed to patient learners.

The value of this information must be decided by the people involved. Sometimes reaction forms provide few concrete data about changes needed to make learning more effective. Watch for patterns. If a number of patients list the same negative reaction to something, a change is probably indicated. For instance, if one patient finds a certain procedure confusing, it probably means that the patient had a problem with this area of learning. If several patients state that they found the same procedure confusing, the problem probably lies with the way in which the procedure is taught.

Another point involving patient reactions to learning is the impact of patient edu-

Exhibit 11-1 Reaction Form for Patient Learners

REACTION FORM

Please fill out this form and return it to your nurse. The information will help us find better ways of helping people. Thanks for your help!

1. Were you given the information you need to care for yourself at home?
   YES _____ NO _____

2. Were your questions answered promptly?
   YES _____ NO _____

3. Do you know how to do all the procedures you need to do at home?
   YES _____ NO _____

4. Was the patient educator courteous and helpful to you?
   YES _____ NO _____

5. Did your nurses give you information and answer your questions?
   YES _____ NO _____

COMMENTS: _____
_____
_____
_____
_____

DO YOU HAVE ANY QUESTIONS OR CONCERNS ABOUT YOUR CARE?
IF SO, PLEASE LIST: _____
_____
_____
_____

---

cation on patient satisfaction. It has long been assumed that patient education activities increase satisfaction, but one study found a moderately high inverse relationship between teaching patients self-care measures and the patients' satisfaction with nursing care. Learning self-care measures, while providing patients with independence and control over their situation, may induce feelings of dissatisfaction because of needed modifications of life style, alterations in self-image, or patient expectations of nursing care and sick role behavior.[3] This may be simply a case of "truth hurts," but a negative reaction to teaching efforts can be devastating to the educator.

If reaction forms are used, the information provided must not be taken personally. Use them to analyze reactions to presentations, audiovisual materials, and nurse-patient interactions. Use them to collect data on which to make changes in the program if needed. But do not use them as a basis for judging self-worth or teaching ability. If a problem exists with your teaching strategies, it will show up on other evaluation measures.

Learning

Assessing learning enables you to check retention and understanding of content presented to the learner. This is accomplished through testing. A test is defined as "any systematic procedure that provides descriptive data on one or more people."[4] Well-constructed tests help to

- assess participant progress
- diagnose difficulties
- measure the effects of the content
- determine the effectiveness of the methods and materials used in teaching.[5]

Written Tests. Base your tests on the objectives. Written tests are classified as multiple-choice, true-false, matching, fill-in-the-blank, and essay. Follow a few simple rules to write test items in the different categories.

Multiple-Choice Items. In a multiple-choice test, only one answer is correct. The other choices are called "distractors," and their purpose is exactly that—to distract test takers from the right answer if they do not know the content being tested. Writing multiple-choice questions requires careful phrasing to prevent two common problems: (1) making the question confusing or obscure or (2) making the question a dead giveaway. An example of the first would be:
The pancreas produces:
    a. Trypsin
    b. Insulin
    c. Enterokinase
    d. a, b, d
    e. a, c, d
    f. All of the above
This is a poor test item for two reasons. First, it is confusing to the reader, requiring several readings and backtrackings to distinguish the correct answer. Second, from a patient education standpoint it is asking a useless question. Who cares if the patient can tell the difference between different enzymes and hormones? This item is not written from an objective (unless the objectives are obscure and poorly written). It sounds more like a question from a freshman anatomy and physiology examination—and not a very good one at that.

An example of a "giveaway" test item would be:
When testing your blood glucose level, you find it is 625. You would:

a. Eat a small amount of protein
b. Repeat your morning dose of insulin
c. Call your physician
d. Do nothing

This question borders on the absurd. Three of the choices are so blatantly wrong that the correct answer leaps out at the test taker, but worse than that, the question is not realistic. It implies that someone with a blood glucose reading of 625 would still be reasoning without impairment by not providing a choice of "carefully rerun the blood glucose test," since an incorrectly performed test would be the most likely cause of such asymptomatic extreme hyperglycemia. If a lower value had been used, the question might be usable as written.

Write multiple-choice items so that all of the choices seem reasonable and possible, so that only knowledge of the content can guide the test taker to the correct answer. This is not easy. In fact, good multiple-choice questions are among the most difficult to write, simply because there are so many ways to go wrong.

Pitfalls to avoid include:

1. The grammatical giveaway. Here the phrasing of the question clues the person to the right answer.

    The most serious foot problem for a diabetic is:
    a. Bunions
    b. Calluses
    c. An ulcer
    d. Corns

    Simply reading "is bunions," "is calluses," "is corns" tells the test taker that he or she must be incorrect. "An ulcer" is the only choice that is grammatically correct. This one can sneak up on you, so read all questions aloud to prevent its slipping by.

2. The "all of the above" trap. This one needs no example, since we have all run into it innumerable times. Any canny test taker knows that if one of the choices is "all of the above," that choice is nearly always the correct answer. For this reason, and because such questions can be confusing as well, avoid the use of "all of the above," and "none of the above." They are usually the sign of a lazy test writer.

3. The "alphabet soup" attack. An example of this was shown earlier. Here the question becomes a confusing morass of "a, d, and e" or "b, c, and f," etcetera. Simplify these questions by pulling choices into another question or changing to a non-multiple-choice format.

4. The "apples and oranges" gambit. The correct answer is given away because it blatantly does not match the other choices.

    A good exercise program for a diabetic might include:
    a. Hurdling

    b. Marathon running
    c. Ski jumping
    d. Brisk walking
5. The double negative. These questions are stated in the opposite way of most
    items, leading to learner confusion and error.

    Name the food not recommended on a diabetic diet:
    a. Nonfat milk
    b. Bananas
    c. Chicken
    d. Milk chocolate candy

    Not only does the desired answer usually leap out at the learner, but even
    well-written questions of this sort require a double-think that test takers may
    find difficult. Try another type of question if possible. If you have decided
    that only multiple-choice will do (perhaps because you are using a standard-
    ized grading format of some kind), emphasize the elimination nature of the
    question through boldface or underlining: "All of these are correct
    EXCEPT" or "From the choices below, pick the one that is <u>not</u> _____."
6. The "statistics game." An easy pitfall to slip into, this one involves choosing
    correct numbers.

    The number of diabetics in the United States is now more than:
    a. 1,000,000
    b. 5,000,000
    c. 10,000,000
    d. 25,000,000

    A very little thought lets the test taker safely choose *a*. There *must* be "more
    than" 1,000,000 diabetics in the United States, so that answer has to be
    counted as correct. Again, this is an example of lazy test writing.

There are other problems that can develop with multiple-choice questions, but
these are the most common. Multiple-choice tests are difficult to write and require
time and effort to do so correctly. Think through the purpose of each question carefully; choose intelligent, reasonable-sounding distractors; and phrase the question
so that it will not give away the answer. Exhibit 3-4 in Chapter 3 contains examples
of some multiple-choice questions that require knowledge of content to answer.
With any test, administer it first to several colleagues—they may catch problems
that you were too close to see. If any question is missed consistently by patients,
either the question is poorly written or that area of content is not being covered
adequately.

True-False Items. True-false questions require that a simple judgment be made
by the test taker—is this statement correct or incorrect? Examples of such questions include:

Diabetes is considered a disease of the endocrine system.
        TRUE   FALSE
The beta cells of the islets of Langerhans produce insulin.
        TRUE   FALSE

There are three main problems with true-false questions. First, requiring a yes or no answer tends to lead to simplistic statements. Second, it is much easier to write true statements than false ones, which leads to a preponderance of true answers and often makes the false ones sound absurd ("The back of the neck is a good site for insulin injections"—this is an actual question from a test for patients!). Third, it is easy to fall into negative statements ("Do not stop taking your insulin dosage if you become ill") that mislead the test taker. Ask yourself why you are choosing a true-false format. Is it just to make grading easier? What will these questions accomplish that another form would not accomplish better? If true-false is still your choice, think through the statements carefully and read them aloud to yourself and others before using them.

Matching Items. Matching requires straight recognition of parallel facts or related items. Two lists are given in no particular order, and the learner is asked to match items in the list that relate to each other. Exhibit 11-2 is an example of a matching test question. Most test takers enjoy matching items and find them less confusing than other forms of questions. Still, care must be taken to make the choices clear and unambiguous. The two lists should relate directly to one another, and items that might be answered more than one way should be dropped.

Fill-in-the-Blank Items. These questions differ from the preceding types because fill-in-the-blank questions require recall rather than recognition. The learner receives cues from the words surrounding the blank space and is asked to place the appropriate word in that space. For example, "Insulin acts to carry _____ through cell membranes." These are not always easy to grade if the instructor delegates the task to a secretary or clerk. The instructor may have put the word *glucose* down on the test key as the desired response. But what if the patient writes *sugar* as the answer? Is that acceptable? Will the secretary be able to make such judgments?

Learners find fill-in-the-blank questions stressful. Being put on the spot to come up with just the right word can be anxiety-producing. Still, these items can determine whether the test taker really knows the information or is just taking cues from the accompanying material (which is one reason that multiple-choice is jokingly called "multiple-guess" by college students). Bluffing does not work with fill-in-the-blank—you either know the correct answer or you do not. For this reason these questions must be carefully worded to make the desired answer the only one that really fits. Add enough clues in the statement to point to the answer if the learner knows the content. If more than one answer fits, then allow both as correct on the grading key.

Exhibit 11-2 Matching Test Question

Match the following foods with the correct nutritional classification:

1. Ground beef _____

   a. Protein
2. Bread _____

   b. Carbohydrate
3. Salad dressing _____

   c. Fat
4. Apples _____

5. Cauliflower _____

6. Pork chops _____

7. Butter _____

8. Eggs _____

9. Pineapple chunks _____

10. Cottage cheese _____

11. Sour cream _____

12. Bacon _____

Essay Items. These questions require learners to state an answer in their own words. Most people shudder when encountering essay questions; visions of blue books and overzealous college professors rise in the memory. Yet these items can help to detect a true understanding of complex issues. Patients are forced to apply their own interpretation to things rather than just parroting memorized data. You can minimize negative reactions to these questions by focusing on one issue per item and by stressing that you want *short*, pertinent answers.

Exhibit 11-3 is an example of several essay questions. Note the short space provided for the answers—another cue that long, rambling responses are not desired. Some people still will try to "cover ignorance with words," using run-on answers to try to bluff their way through a question. You should be able to spot these as you correct them, so that you can get back to the learner and clear up the misconceptions.

One big disadvantage to essay questions (besides the added time learners take to answer them) is that they must be graded by the instructor. Each answer must be read, assessed, and corrected by hand by the person who wrote the items. Another disadvantage lies in the skills required by the learner. Essay questions are totally inappropriate for illiterate or semiliterate patients, and even people who can read

Exhibit 11-3 Sample Essay Questions

1. Describe the symptoms of a low blood sugar level, and explain what you would do if these symptoms occurred.

2. List the areas of the body where you can safely inject insulin.

3. Explain the effects of exercise on insulin needs in a diabetic.

and write may have difficulty with them. Essay items require the ability to write down thoughts in an organized way and to think in an abstract fashion. They are not for everyone.

Pretests and Post-tests. Pretests attempt to discover what knowledge learners bring with them into the learning situation. By using similar tests before and after teaching has taken place, knowledge acquisition as a result of the teaching can be demonstrated. Segall et al. have developed a system for analyzing the results of pretest and post-test scores using the same instrument:

High errors on pretest, low on post-test = probably good questions, shows change after instruction.
Low errors on pretest, high on post-test = either the item is ambiguous or instruction was misleading.
High errors on pretest, high on post-test = poor item or unsuccessful teaching.
Low errors on pretest, low on post-test = probably too easy—should not have been included.[6]

Judicious use of pretests can save instructor time and effort by indicating what areas need not be covered (or covered only minimally) because the patient already knows that information. Discovering this also makes learners feel successful; it is ego-boosting to have your knowledge of something recognized. You will retain patients' attention longer if you are not repeating information they already know.

Oral Tests. In some situations oral testing may be the strategy of choice. Oral testing obviously is necessary for patients with reading problems, and it is also helpful in reviewing material during teaching sessions and in testing people with "test anxiety"—those who become immobilized when faced with a written test.

Tips for oral tests include:

- Make your questions specific to the patients' particular life style.
- Pose your questions tactfully, so that patients will not feel they are being grilled.
- Phrase the questions objectively to avoid giving away certain answers.
- Try to ask hypothetical questions about how the patient will respond to situations after discharge.[7]

Simulations. Simulation tests may be written or oral; they ask the patient to review a simulated situation and (given the constraints posed by the situation) react to it in a real-life manner. Simulations not only test learners' recall of information, they also review and reinforce the learned material. By allowing patients to confront realistic situations, simulations preview problem-solving skills and enable educators to assist in developing alternatives and new approaches.

To write a simulation, choose a situation that requires critical thinking and demonstrates behaviors based on objectives. For instance:

> You are invited to a big holiday party. There will be a magnificent catered buffet, open bar, and baked Alaska and champagne for dessert. You want to go, but are afraid you'll get carried away and blow your diet, sending your blood sugar sky-high. What will you do?

Keep the simulation short, to avoid confusion and allow more time for discussion of alternatives. But provide details (such as the baked Alaska and champagne) to make it more real and more interesting.

Zufall found that since simulation tests are purposely designed to represent reality, learners find them more relevant than conventional tests and tend to become more involved.[8] They are certainly less threatening than most written tests. Simulation tests can be presented as simple discussions of learned material, yet they can highlight problems for further review and clarification. If patients have to make judgments and apply new information at home, trying these skills out in a safe setting with the educator present only makes sense.

Value of Testing for Knowledge Changes. Testing can certainly help educators measure gains in knowledge levels, but unfortunately they prove nothing about whether patients will apply their knowledge to self-care. Zufall suggests increasing test relevance by asking the following questions:

1. Did the test represent a problem that the learner may encounter, and did the material presented help the learner to deal with it?
2. Were the questions in proportion to the importance of the behavior that the program attempted to develop?[9]

With those questions as guidelines, simulation testing of realistic self-care di-
lemmas seems to be the method of choice. Other types of tests, particularly when
used in a pretest/post-test format, may be beneficial for justifying the teaching program and supporting patients' self-esteem, but the more real-life-oriented the test
the more valuable it will be. Such testing of learning should be interlaced with
evaluations of behavior and results.

Behavior

When you measure behavior, you are looking for a change in actual abilities, not
just in knowledge. The most commonly used evaluation of behavior is the return
demonstration. Observing patients demonstrate blood glucose testing, insulin injection, or other skills proves conclusively that they either can or cannot perform
these skills correctly. This observation of behavior change is a vital part of patient
education.

Bailey and Claus describe the three major limitations of observation as

1. subjectivity of the observer
2. the presence of an observer (a variable that may alter the situation)
3. fragmentary reporting resulting from the problem of observing and recording
   information at the same time [10]

Subjectivity of the Observer. Observer subjectivity affects not only evaluation
but patient performance and morale   as well. For instance, perhaps the patient
educator has worked long and hard teaching a patient how to draw up and inject a
mixed dose of insulin. The patient has had a great deal of difficulty learning this,
but by dint of incredible effort and concentration manages to achieve it successfully. The return demonstration is slow and shaky, but all of the steps are there and
no serious breaks in technique occur. The educator praises the patient, and both
feel a sense of achievement, of finally getting somewhere. The next day someone
else observes the patient perform the procedure. Rushed and impatient, this observer criticizes the slowness, tells the patient the syringe should be handled *this*
way, and snaps "Don't push it through the skin like that—do it fast, with a flick of
your wrist!" (The patient's wrist has not been able to flick for twenty years.) The
result: a devastated, demoralized patient and an educator back at square one.

One way to prevent these things from happening is through thorough communi-
cation, both verbally and in writing, with everyone involved in the patient's care.
Inform everyone of the patient's progress and need for support and encouragement.
If everyone is on the same wavelength, subjectivity will be minimized.

Presence of an Observer. The presence of an observer may do one of two
things: either throw the patient completely off stride by creating a "test anxiety," or
put the patient on his or her best behavior, creating an unrealistic situation. A ner-
vous, trembling patient throwing over-the-shoulder glances to see if you approve

will be unable to concentrate on the procedure. This can usually be relieved by repetition of the procedure along with gentle reinforcement and support, gradually desensitizing the learner to the anxiety-creating event.

Much worse, because the demonstration is misleading and at the same time soothing to the educator, is the patient who performs perfectly while being watched but who lets things slide once he or she is home. Unfortunately, these patients are almost impossible to identify. About all you can do to minimize this ever-present concern is to reinforce the importance of correct technique and to instruct at least one family member about the procedure. This person can then act as a "quality control" monitor, if willing to do so.

Fragmentary Reporting. This is not such a problem in patient education as in working with the staff, because the procedures become second nature to the educator and the reporting is usually limited to simple "can do it/cannot do it" charting. Yet observation can be made more effective by using such things as checklists and rating scales to direct both observations and evaluations of performance. Exhibit 11-4 shows an example of a performance checklist for use with patients; Exhibit 11-5 is an example of a rating-scale performance sheet. Both help to standardize the observations to be made, as well as either implicitly (in Exhibit 11-4) or explicitly (in Exhibit 11-5) stating the standards of performance.

Exhibit 11-4 Performance Checklist

PERFORMANCE CHECKLIST

PERFORMANCE	IF DONE
Washes hands	
Reads label of vial	
Rotates vial to mix insulin	
Draws up and injects air into vial	
Draws up correct dosage	
Checks for air in syringe	
Rotates sites appropriately	
Chooses usable site	
Cleanses skin	
Allows skin to dry	
Inserts needle at correct angle	
Injects entire dose	
Handles site care appropriately	
Disposes of syringe	
Enters dosage into personal record	

Exhibit 11-5 Rating-Scale Patient Performance Sheet

PERFORMANCE RATING SHEET		
1 = Has to read procedure; leaves out steps or gets steps in the wrong order. Contaminates equipment or stick sites.		
2 = Has to occasionally refer to written procedure. Performs procedure slowly but gets steps in order. Contaminates equipment or stick sites only occasionally.		
3 = Performs procedure correctly without referring to written materials, with all steps in order. Rarely contaminates equipment or stick sites.		
SKILL	RATING	COMMENTS
Calibrates machine		
Runs high/low QC* tests		
Prepares machine		
Washes hands		
Prepares site		
Performs finger/ear stick		
Covers pads with blood		
Wipes strips correctly at proper time		
Inserts strip into machine		
Double-checks reading with color comparison		
Records results on own personal record		
*QC, Quality control.		

Results

Measuring results—the permanent changes in life style resulting from patient education—is the most valuable and the most difficult phase of evaluation. This is a longer-term evaluation than measuring reaction, learning, or even the behavior change seen immediately after teaching. Results involve long-term behavior change, change that sustains itself without educator reinforcement.

Redman found there are a number of units by which behavior can be measured. The most common are speed, accuracy, probability of occurrence, originality, persistence, amount, and correctness. Of these, the measurement of persistence is often neglected, leaving us with little knowledge about retention of health teaching.[11] Because measuring results requires follow-up in the home setting, educators often rationalize that they have neither the time nor the ability to conduct such appraisals. Actually, the most vital requirement is the will to evaluate for results; if that is present, time can be found and methods created.

Techniques for Results Evaluation. Techniques for results evaluation are discussed starting at the simplest and moving to the more difficult. Remember, none of these techniques is impossibly hard to do. It may take a little rearranging of your schedule, but mostly it takes rearranging priorities and beliefs about evaluation.

Phone Interviews. One of the simplest and least time-consuming methods involves follow-up phone calls to discharged patients. While teaching them in the acute care setting, ask them to participate in the follow-up program and obtain their phone numbers; then call periodically to see how they are doing. Calls can be made at set intervals, such as two days after discharge, a week after discharge, two weeks from then, and so on.

This method of follow-up not only enables you to check on compliance, it also allows you to review and reinforce learning and to answer questions. Patients usually appreciate the calls. Just giving your phone number to patients and telling them to call if problems arise does not work as well. Many patients feel awkward about calling, rationalizing that the educator is too busy to be bothered.

The disadvantages to this method of evaluation are twofold: (1) you are relying on patients' self-reports, which may or may not be accurate; and (2) verbal follow-up tends to be disorganized and haphazard. Both disadvantages can be minimized with the use of a form for documenting telephone follow-up. Exhibit 11-6 is an example o such a form. Using such an evaluation makes follow-up consistent and enables you to compare data collected each time and to assess the accuracy of self-reporting. These forms can also be used as evidence that patient education efforts are successful.

McCormick and Gilson-Parkevich recommend three other methods for results evaluation:

Self-Report Diary. The self-report diary could include a symptoms checklist, prescribed medications records, a list of activities, health services utilization, problems, and experiences related to health management; it is similar to but more comprehensive than the journal mentioned in Chapter 8.

Patient and Family Self-Appraisal. Through personal interviews or written instruments, patient and family are asked questions on the actual use of behaviors learned. Patients rate their behaviors in terms of successful applications, deficiencies in behavior, and further education needed to maintain health.

Inspection of Medical Records. If patients return for follow-up visits at outpatient facilities or physicians' offices—or if they are visited by home care nurses—ask to examine the documentation for evidence of successful implementation of instruction.[12]

Exhibit 11-6 Form for Documenting Telephone Follow-up

TELEPHONE FOLLOW-UP

Name: _____

Phone: _____   Discharge Date: _____

Physicians: _____

Diagnosis: _____

1. List medicines and frequency; ask patient for pill count on at least two prescriptions:

   Pill count correct?   Yes _____   No _____

2. Ask patient: When did you last perform _____

   _____?

   Compliant _____   Noncompliant _____

3. Ask patient what problems have been encountered since discharge:

   What has been done to cope with these problems?

4. Ask patient what additional information would have been helpful to receive while in the hospital:

5. Ask patient for any other questions or suggestions:

Physical Evidence. Yet another way of evaluating results is looking for physical evidence. All of the preceding methods involve subjective reporting on the part of patients, family members, and health care providers. Physical evidence, on the other hand, involves actual measurement of objective results. For instance, Bradshaw recommends instructing home care personnel (or the patient and family) to do periodic pill counts. Compliance with medication regimens is said to have occurred if the pill count is correct, if the medication appears to be working both objectively in controlling symptoms and subjectively to the satisfaction of the patient, and if the prescription is successfully refilled.[13]

Other physical evidence that could be measured includes: blood levels of drugs, blood pressure measurements, blood glucose levels, and changes in physical abilities (such as those shown by treadmill tests or strength measurements). It might be argued that there is no way to prove a direct link between these changes and patient education. But if you teach a patient the importance of, for instance, regular exercise and diet to control blood pressure, and that patient (1) recalls the information on a written test; (2) reports taking a brisk twenty-minute walk four times a week and sticking to a low-sodium, controlled calorie diet; and (3) subsequent blood pressure readings are significantly lower, then cause and effect can be pretty clearly linked. This example illustrates the importance of using different types of evaluation with the same patient and of leaving a "paper trail" of consistent documentation when you evaluate.

EVALUATING PROGRAM EFFECTIVENESS

When program effectiveness is evaluated, more issues are examined than just patient outcomes. Program evaluation investigates the results of patient education efforts, leading to change and revision as necessary. This process of investigation can help you answer these questions:

1. Did my actions make a difference?
2. Was it worth the effort?
3. What should be changed to reach the objectives?[14]

These questions give us three elements of program evaluation:

1. evaluation of instructor effectiveness
2. evaluation of cost/benefit ratios
3. changes needed to make the program more effective

The third element is especially important to keep in mind. Unless revisions take place based on the outcomes of evaluation, you might as well save your efforts. Evaluation for its own sake is meaningless.

Dunn believes that evaluation should not mean heavy-handed judgment of whether one is doing a good or bad job; he states:

> Evaluation tells us which parts of the program are working and which are not; it helps us to decide how to capitalize on strengths and to minimize weaknesses. And ultimately, in a field demanding unusual enthusiasm and commitment for a frequently repetitive and frustrating service role, evaluation can provide the necessary stimulus for new energy and new directions.[15]

Measuring Instructor Effectiveness

Some patient educators believe that instructor effectiveness is implied by successful patient results. Certainly a case can be made for that belief, but unless specific assessments are made of instructor performance, how can there be any improvement? Surely there is no educator alive who is perfect, with no need for any change. Evaluations of instructor effectiveness should be designed to identify areas for improvement and to reinforce positive activities.

Who Should Evaluate?

In reality, everyone involved evaluates instructor performance: patients, family members, staff members, physicians, the instructor, and the instructor's supervisor. Patients and family members evaluate through reaction forms, patient questionnaires, letters to the hospital, and comments made to the staff and to their physician. The staff and physicians usually evaluate through comments and suggestions; it is rare for written input to be volunteered. Yet valuable insights may be lost without some method of periodically soliciting staff and physician reactions to patient instruction. Exhibit 11-7 is an example of a questionnaire that could be used to get staff and physician views of the patient educator's efforts. Notice that the questionnaire is phrased to minimize the discomfort that anyone might feel about assessing another professional's performance. An open-ended format stimulates more feedback than a checklist or rating form. Rating forms make the process more uncomfortable for everyone with their "excellent," "good," "fair," "poor" arbitrary judgments. You want information on which you can base change, not a report card.

Exhibit 11-7 Staff/Physician Questionnaire

PATIENT EDUCATION FEEDBACK FORM

Please share your ideas and suggestions to help improve our patient education program. Your input is very much appreciated.

1. How has the patient education program helped patients?

2. What problems have occurred in connection with patient education?

3. Are there any changes in policies or procedures that you think would be helpful?

4. Is there any way the patient education section could help you with the patient teaching activities you perform in the course of your work?

Further comments and suggestions:

Instructor self-evaluation goes on continuously. After each session with a patient, educators analyze (consciously or unconsciously) how it went. What seemed to work with this patient? What did not work? What modifications to the usual content were required? Most instructors have an internal script that they follow, based on what has worked in the past. Changes are made spontaneously, according to individual patient needs. Any change that proves extremely successful may eventually be incorporated into this standard internal script. Bringing this continuous process onto the conscious level and making it a formal part of post-teaching analysis aids positive change.

Evaluation by the supervisor is more difficult. How can you make what is essentially a subjective process more objective? How can evaluation of another professional be a learning experience rather than an ordeal? Perhaps neither of these aims can be achieved entirely, but a procedure can be developed that will help. First, base evaluations on job standards, not on some arbitrary measure of performance. Since the data collected will be used as a performance appraisal, the utilization of previously established and communicated standards is not only more fair, but more helpful. Second, use the same form to guide each evaluation, to encourage consistency by raters and ratees. Exhibit 11-8 is an example of such a form.

With this form the observer checks off the appropriate column regarding each standard. If the instructor being observed meets the standard, no further comment is necessary. However, if the standard is not met, or if performance exceeds the standard, the observer comments on what exactly was done. Using the standards minimizes an observer's tendency to operate off what he or she normally does in class, forcing a focus on the instructor's style and activities, not on the observer's preferences.

The form is reviewed with the instructor after the teaching session. The form's structure enables this discussion to pinpoint exactly what was done right as well as any areas needing improvement, thus reinforcing good performance as well as providing guidance if a problem exists.

Cost/Benefit Evaluation

Program analysis that focuses on measures of productivity and the benefits derived is more difficult to perform than instructor evaluation. McCormick and Gilson-Parkevich identify two different dimensions:

1. Level of activity may be expressed in terms of numbers of patients and families participating, hours of instruction provided, and number of teaching aids used. This information is strictly descriptive; it does not comment on the effectiveness of efforts to bring about learning objectives or patient compliance. Activity levels may show that we

have been working hard, but do not reveal whether the efforts have made a difference in the lives of patients.
2. Results of patient education programs begin to demonstrate the *value* of patient education. Results may be reported in terms of reduced length of stay, compliance with instructions, increase in knowledge and skills, and reduction in repeated hospitalizations.[16]

Activity Levels

Too many patient educators fail to keep track of how they spend their time. Not only is this unwise from the standpoint of justifying your existence to the administration, it also handicaps you in analyzing what should be changed. Rykwalder believes that recording your activities and the time devoted to each can be an effective means of evaluating how you manage your time. This record can suggest the need to reallocate time to priority areas and to delegate tasks to staff members. It can also comprise part of the documentation substantiating your need for support staff.[17]

Exhibit 11-9 is an example of such a record. By using this record you not only can keep track of your activities and the time spent on each, but ultimately you can calculate productivity. Record statistics for six months. From those statistics, calculate the average time needed to teach one patient. That will give you a standard by which to measure productivity. For instance, perhaps you find that it takes an average of four hours to teach a new diabetic patient, two hours for a repeat patient, and one hour for follow-up (these numbers are purely for the purpose of example—your findings may be entirely different). The more patients you see, the higher your productivity. If you start to take longer and longer to accomplish teaching, productivity drops. If you start spending more time in meetings or other activities not directly related to patients, productivity drops. This helps to keep you focused on your prime directive: patient teaching.

Results Of Patient Education

In assessing the results of patient education, Rykwalder suggests that you answer the following questions:

1. What is it I'm doing?
2. What outcomes are being achieved?
3. What resources are being expended?[18]

The first two questions have already been answered—your instructor log shows what you are doing, and your patient evaluations demonstrate the outcomes being achieved. Keeping track of resources being expended involves recording all expenses: equipment, handouts, audiovisual materials (initial cost divided by

Exhibit 11-8 Instructor Evaluation Form

PATIENT/FAMILY TEACHING SKILLS AUDIT STANDARDS

EDUCATION OBSERVER: _____   JOB TITLE: _____

PATIENT EDUCATION INSTRUCTOR: _____   DATE: _____

ITEM AND STANDARD	EXCEEDS STANDARD	MEETS STANDARD	DOES NOT MEET STANDARD	COMMENTS/ CORRECTIVE ACTION
1.0 RAPPORT 1.1 Introduces self to patient. 1.2 Uses "small talk" to open conversation and establish initial rapport. 1.3 Queries patient to discover feelings about illness, hospitalization, and health care beliefs.				
2.0 NEEDS ASSESSMENT 2.1 Uses open-ended questions to elicit patient's existent knowledge of his/her condition. 2.2 Notes misconceptions for correction (presently or in the future). 2.3 Identifies learning needs.				
3.0 GOAL SETTING 3.1 Establishes need to know and attempts to elicit patient/family agreement.				

3.2 Sets realistic long- and short-term goals with patient/family.

3.3 Working from the goals, develops behavioral objectives for the patient and sets time line for accomplishment.

3.4 Communicates goals and objectives in writing to rest of health care team.

4.0 TEACHING

4.1 Dressed appropriately: clean, neat, and appropriate for activity.

4.2 Introduces subject with reaffirmation of importance of topic to patient.

4.3 States performance objectives to be accomplished.

4.4 Uses a variety of teaching techniques (lecture, discussion, demonstration, question-and-answer, diagrams, etc.).

4.5 Displays concerned, interested, encouraging attitude.

4.6 Uses appropriate language/vocabulary.

4.7 Encourages questions and answers them clearly and simply.

4.8 Seeks reasons for inaccurate learner comments and explores issues.

4.9 Allows for periods of physical activity.

4.10 Uses adult learning principles.

4.11 Allows learner to pursue special interests when possible.

4.12 Gives appropriate feedback.

4.13 Provides checkpoints and summary.

4.14 Keeps material pertinent and individualized to patient.

5.0 *DOCUMENTATION*

5.1 Documents each patient interaction in patient record.

5.2 Communicates with health care team verbally and in writing on patient's progress in achieving objectives.

5.3 Follows up on other team members' actions and reinforcement of learning.

5.4 Makes appropriate entries on Patient Care Plan to keep learning plan updated.

6.0 *EVALUATION*

6.1 Conducts frequent assessments of patient's learning through questioning, written quizzes, etc.

6.2 Uses return demonstrations by the patient for evaluation of learning and as an opportunity for reteaching important points.

6.3 Arranges for follow-up and evaluation of learning with other health team members.

6.4 Arranges for at least one method of long-term follow-up (post-discharge) with the patient, physi-

PATIENT INSTRUCTOR LOG								
NAME: _____ WEEK OF _____								
(Figures to the nearest 0.25 hour)								
Number of Patients Seen: _____								Total
ACTIVITY	MON	TUE	WED	THU	FRI	SAT	SUN	TOTAL
CONSULTATION WITH PHYSICIANS/STAFF								
ASSESSMENT OF NEW PATIENTS								
INSTRUCTION/REVIEW								
DOCUMENTATION OF PATIENT TEACHING								
CLASSROOM TEACHING								
OTHER: (Research, meetings, etc.)								
NONPRODUCTIVE HOURS (Vacation, holiday, ill, LOA, workshops)								
TOTAL HOURS								
TOTAL HOURS WORKED (Total hours − nonproductive hours)								
EDUCATION UNITS								GOAL

To determine productivity, divide hours worked by education units, then divide that number into the productivity standard or goal.

number of uses), and—most important—labor. Instructor time is the most costly part of patient education. That is why using it wisely is so important.

Another part of results calculations involve measurements of factors such as length of stay, repeat hospitalizations, and cost of hospitalizations. You can discover data like these not only from your own hospital but also from organizations such as the American Diabetes Association, American Heart Association, and American Lung Association. The federal government also keeps statistics on Medicare and Medicaid patients. Comparing average length of stay for patients with and without education could document concrete financial benefits from the use of your program.

In a review of length of stay and cost data for a twelve-month period in 1983 through 1984, Walton came up with these figures for diagnosis-related group (DRG) 294, diabetes mellitus, age 36 or older:

> Reduction in length of stay: 1.7 days
> Per diem cost: $283.00
> Benefits from reduced length of stay: $481.10/patient

In reporting this benefit from the patient education program, Walton clarified that the benefit was not really *cost savings* (money that could be put in the bank and saved), but rather *cost avoidance* (money not spent).[19] This is an important distinction to make, especially if you are dealing with financial people.

Another benefit that is difficult to ascertain but certainly valuable is the increased health and prolonged life brought about by patient education. One longterm study was carried out in a large hospital in Copenhagen: it tried to ascertain the cost/benefit ratio for outpatient supervision for 20 years after diagnosis on survival rates of people with juvenile diabetes mellitus. With an average of 4.4 annual outpatient follow-up visits, which included instruction, the duration of diabetes survival was prolonged by nearly twelve years compared with a control group. The benefit of this prolongation was ten times the cost of the follow-up.[20]

Quality Assurance/Risk Management Issues

The increased emphasis on quality assurance by the Joint Commission on Accreditation of Healthcare Organizations and other regulatory bodies almost forces educators to develop standards and measurements for implementing a quality assurance program. Not only will such a program stand you in good stead with regulatory agencies, it can also be used as a risk management tool to minimize legal risks and ensure quality patient care.

Brown and Villalaz-Dickson recommend the following steps in setting up a quality assurance program for patient education:

1. Design the study in terms of scope and focus.
2. Establish criteria to measure quality and appropriateness of patient education. Use statements that reflect structure, process, or outcomes.
3. Gather the data identifying
   a. methods for each criterion
   b. frequency of data collection
   c. who will collect the data
   d. sources of the data (patient interview, chart review, or direct observation)
4. Summarize and interpret the data. Compare the level of performance with the level of acceptability.
5. Take definitive action and follow-up. Analysis of findings should lead to recommendations for improvement such as
   a. revision of procedures or program methods
   b. inservice education
   c. management reinforcement
   d. new resources or teaching tools [21]

Table 11-1 is an example of a quality assurance plan for patient education. Notice all of the required elements: criteria, methods, frequency of data collection, sources of data, and who will collect the data. With a plan like this, there is no guesswork about what will be done when. Results are reported to the department quality assurance committee and are summarized for the hospital-wide quality assurance committee. This ongoing feedback is accomplished in an organized, simple manner when a well-thought-out plan is in place.

PLANNING PROGRAM CHANGES BASED ON EVALUATION RESULTS

The many evaluation methods discussed in this chapter can provide you with a wealth of data about your patients and the overall patient education program. Making changes based on those data is the whole purpose of evaluation. If no changes are made, if nothing constructive is done with the information, then the evaluations might just as well not have been done.

Content changes should be made cautiously. Watch for definite patterns from a number of patients before making any sweeping changes. Variations in teaching strategies can be made much more easily—you can judge from patient reactions and retention of material whether or not the changes are working. Remember with teaching activities, however, that the individual patient must be considered. What works well with one person may fail with another. Learning can be influenced by so many factors—learning style preference, motivation, intelligence, age, disabilities, and state of health, for example—that flexibility on the teacher's part is

Table 11-1 Quality Assurance Plan for Patient Education

Criterion	Method	When	Source of Data	By Whom
Patient Satisfaction	Questionnaire	Every other mo.	Patient	Patient educator
	Interviews	Every 6 mo.	Patient	Coordinator
Instructor performance	Audits	Every 6 mo.	Observation of teaching	Coordinator
Learning	Written tests	Test every patient for 1 mo./yr.	Patients' test scores	Patient educator
Physician/staff satisfaction	Survey	Every 6 mo.	Medical staff Nursing staff Allied health professionals	Patient educator

the only constant requirement of teaching.

Program changes generally involve others. Instructors can change content or approaches, but adding major activities (such as a new teaching program for patients with amyotrophic lateral sclerosis) requires approval from an advisory committee, physicians, the administration, or sometimes all of them. A typical procedure for adding to, deleting from, or making a major change in a patient education program might include the following steps:

1. Survey physicians, staff, and possibly patients for input on the proposed change(s).
2. Collate results to determine patterns and identify consensuses.
3. Prepare a proposal and present it to the appropriate people, such as
   a. patient education advisory committee
   b. other committees, such as nurse practice committee or policy and procedures
   c. administrators
   d. medical Executive Committee
4. If approved, develop policies and procedures for the program.
5. Repeat the approval process.
6. Conduct an information blitz to publicize the newly available program to physicians and staff.
7. Implement the program.

This process is time-consuming and often frustrating. Circumventing it almost ensures program failure. One group of patient educators had trouble getting together with their physician advisory group, so they gradually developed the habit of making changes on their own. Unfortunately, when the physicians inevitably discovered what had happened, the resultant flap almost destroyed the program. It survived, but it was cut drastically. The educators now must have every handout, every slide, every detail of the program scrutinized and approved in advance.

As was stressed in Chapter 1, you can avoid this fate by involving significant and powerful people from the beginning. Do not waste your carefully planned and carried out evaluations—use the information obtained to make your program stronger, more effective, and famous throughout your institution.

NOTES

1. Laura Mae Douglass and Em Olivia Bevis, *Nursing Leadership In Action* (St. Louis: C.V. Mosby Co., 1974), p. 55.

2. John W. Newstrom, "Employee Training and Development," in *Encyclopedia of Professional Management* (New York: McGraw-Hill Book Co., 1978), p. 291.

186   HANDBOOK OF PATIENT EDUCATION

3. Lillian R. Erickson, "Patient Satisfaction: An Indicator of Nursing Care Quality?" *Nursing Management* 18, no. 7 (July 1987): 33.

4. Stuart M. Shaffer, Karen L. Indorato, and Janet A. Deneselya, *Teaching in Schools Of Nursing* (St. Louis: C.V. Mosby Co., 1972), p. 44.

5. Dorothy L. Zufall, "Testing: A Creative Experience for Learners and Educators," *Cross-Reference* 7, no. 2 (March–April 1977): 8. 6

6. Ascher J. Segall et al., *Systematic Course Design for the Health Care Fields* (New York: John Wiley & Sons, Inc., 1975), p. B-97.

7. Matthew Cahill, ed., *Patient Teaching* (Springhouse, Pa.: Nursing87 Books, 1987), p. 77.

8. Zufall, "Testing: A Creative Experience," p. 9.

9. Ibid.

10. June T. Bailey and Karen E. Claus, *Decision-Making in Nursing: Tools for Change* (St. Louis: C.V. Mosby Co., 1975), p. 106.

11. Barbara Klug Redman, *The Process of Patient Education*, 5th ed. (St. Louis: C.V. Mosby Co., 1984), p. 205.

12. Rose-Marie Duda McCormick and Tamar Gilson-Parkevich, *Patient and Family Education* (New York: John Wiley & Sons, Inc., 1979), pp. 172–3.

13. Susan Bradshaw, "Treating Yourself," *Nursing Times* 83, no. 3 (February 11, 1987): 40.

14. Roger Kaufman and Susan Thomas, *Evaluation without Fear* (New York: New Viewpoints, A Division of Franklin Watts, 1980), p. 29.

15. Stewart M. Dunn, "Reactions to Educational Techniques: Coping Strategies for Diabetes and Learning," *Diabetic Medicine* 3 (1986): 427–8.

16. McCormick and Gilson-Parkevich, *Patient and Family Education*, p. 154.

17. Annette Rykwalder, "Productivity Management: An Essential Tool," *Patient Education Newsletter* 8, no. 4 (August 1985): 2.

18. Ibid.

19. Barbara G. Walton, "Assessing the Benefits of Patient Education," *Patient Education Newsletter* 8, no. 4 (August 1985): 7–8.

20. T. Deckert et al., "Importance of Outpatient Supervision in the Prognosis of Juvenile Diabetes Mellitus: A Cost/Benefit Analysis," *Diabetes Care* 1 (1978): 281–4.

21. Linda Brown and Sandra Villalaz-Dickson, "How Does Patient Education Interface with Quality Assurance?," *Patient Education Newsletter* 8, no. 6 (December 1985): 3–4.

12

Patient Education: Nursing's Future?

GROWING IMPORTANCE OF PATIENT EDUCATION

In the past ten years patient education has burgeoned from something performed "when there was time" to a major enterprise in health care. A 1981 survey showed that 60 percent of all hospitals have a person specifically designated with responsibility for coordinating hospital patient education functions.[1] The percentage now is probably much higher. A full-time patient educator is coming to be seen as a necessity by more and more hospitals. Large institutions may have a whole staff of full-time instructors supervised by a patient education coordinator.

Whether you are that coordinator or whether you are trying to get a program started in your institution, it is vital to focus attention on patient education and its benefits. By using needs assessment strategies, you can prove that the patients need your skills. But an important part of building and sustaining a program involves selling it to the "power people" in your organization.

Creating Visibility for Patient Education

Gilroth recommends that the patient education coordinator participate on hospital committees such as quality assurance, medical education, and discharge planning. These committees give you information on what is going on in the organization and let you interact with department heads and important staff members. Another recommended strategy is to communicate with hospital decision makers on a regular basis. Provide briefings to top administrators, explaining the department's accomplishments, problems, and needs. Part of this communication involves developing personal relationships with managers and medical staff. One coordinator "works the halls"—on her way to meetings she takes advantage of informal encounters with physicians to update them on the progress of their patients, subtly reminding them of how patient education contributes to patients' recoveries and rehabilitation. Developing strong interpersonal networks gains support from the informal power structure that exists in every organization.[2]

It is all too easy for patient education to fade into the background. Some coordinators and instructors even prefer it that way. Their philosophy is, "if they do not know we are here, we cannot get into trouble." Unfortunately, the reality is "out of sight, out of mind"—and out of the budget. When money gets tight, the first thing to go is often education. This is shortsighted, to be sure, but it is a hospital reality. If patient education is not kept visible with administration and the medical staff, it will be perceived as an expensive luxury rather than a patient necessity. Keep this from happening by publishing your successes. Letters from satisfied patients are especially useful in your efforts to portray the value of the program. New approaches, new handouts, a different way of doing things—let people know about the changes in the program via newsletters, inservice classes, presentations to management groups, and staff meetings—even coverage in the local news media, if you can manage it. Newspapers often seek local stories, and human interest articles about successful patient education efforts might interest an editor. You will never know unless you contact one. Even local television stations often have health reporters who might like to come out to interview you.

National Patient Education Week is a good hook to use. In 1988 it was held November 6–12. The American Society for Healthcare Education and Training (ASHET) suggests working with a metropolitan hospital council to sponsor a citywide proclamation, possibly even a citywide patient education fair for consumers. Even in your own hospital, you could feature different types of free screening programs for patients and staff in outpatient areas, waiting areas, or the cafeteria. Free blood glucose testing and blood pressure measurement are always popular. Use tent cards on tables and trays to announce the week. Other ideas include organizing a "patient education tour" for the board of trustees, auxiliary, and administrators to update them on the extent of patient education programming; developing special displays in patient waiting rooms and putting together special information displays in cooperation with the public library; and offering nutrition quizzes and other information to patients and staff.

Defining Nursing's Role in Patient Education

Another facet of patient education in the hospital setting involves defining where it fits into nursing practice. Do nurses perceive patient education as valuable and as something they are supposed to do, or do they tend to believe that "the patient educator should do that." In one instance a staff nurse called to order the patient educator to teach blood glucose monitoring to a patient. Upon being told that the educator was on vacation she asked plaintively, "Then what can we do? How will the patient learn?" Something has gone wrong when this happens—in communicating expectations, in defining nursing practice, and in providing patient care.

In one survey nurses expressed satisfaction in performing patient education, but experienced frustration that so much was informal and lacking in efficiency, effectiveness, and quality control. They also reported experiencing difficulty in locating and gaining approval for courseware and tools to educate patients.[3] Obviously, the more organized your program and the more accessible the resources, the more staff participation is likely to result.

Besides developing standards for patient education and building these into standards of care and job standards/performance appraisal forms, provide plenty of help and training for the nursing staff. This can take the form of periodic seminars on teaching techniques and disease entities from a patient education viewpoint, short-unit inservices, or conferences on specific patients. One of the most popular offerings is nursing grand rounds. At Huntington Memorial Hospital in Pasadena, California, nursing units take turns putting on monthly grand rounds. These revolve around one patient, with different staff nurses presenting the problems, planning, and interventions used with the patient. The education needed by patient and family is always an important part of the presentation. Because nursing grand rounds are completely staff-presented, each session focuses on the issues and concerns important to nurses. So far each meeting has been attended by anywhere from 90 to 150 nurses. These sessions are an hour long, from noon to 1:00 P.M., and sandwiches, beverages, and cookies are provided for the audience. If you have not yet tried nursing grand rounds, seriously consider doing so.

Other ways to increase staff involvement include creating task forces to tackle problems in patient education; using staff members as authors or advisors for patient education materials and as actors in audiovisual productions; writing letters of appreciation to the supervisors of staff members participating in patient education activities; providing certificates, small awards, or other forms of recognition for excellence in patient education; providing a format for sharing new ideas and effective teaching strategies (newsletter or memos).[4] Provide key units with teaching carts containing patient education materials, to make it easier for staff members to have access to the resources they need for effective patient education. If you have the budget for it, you could provide a cart for every unit, but few hospitals can do that. More often seen is a cart for each broad topic of patient education: for example, the diabetes education cart, the maternity teaching cart, and the chemotherapy teaching cart. If you use the teaching cart concept, be sure to publicize to all staff, not just the ones on the home units, just where these are kept, what they contain, and how they can be used. The carts can then be borrowed by other units if a patient who needs teaching on that particular subject comes in.

CAREER LADDER CONCEPTS AND PATIENT EDUCATION

Many hospitals are bringing career ladder programs into their nursing departments. With a career ladder program, the usual methods of determining raises and promotions are discarded. Instead, nurses wishing to progress up the career ladder must take responsibility for their own practice by documenting their achievements and convincing a committee of peers that they have met the critieria for the next step. Typically, a career ladder program would have titles for the steps, such as clinical nurse I, clinical nurse II, clinical nurse III, and clinical nurse IV. This provides a way to be promoted and yet stay at the bedside, rather than having to move into management in order to progress.

A nurse wishing to move from one step to another must meet stated critieria covering such areas as education, clinical experience, hospital involvement, and special projects. Each nursing department must develop its own criteria for the different levels, but each step up the ladder obviously should require more effort and more responsibility on the part of the nurse. Patient education can play an important part in the areas of hospital involvement and special projects. Participating on committees and task forces could be part of the requirements for hospital involvement. Developing a special project on patient education (such as that shown in Exhibit 12-1) would carry special weight because benefits to patients can be so clearly identified and documented. Act as a resource for nurses planning these projects, and both patients and staff will reap the rewards.

PATIENT EDUCATION AS A PROFESSIONAL PRACTICE ISSUE

Bioethical Considerations

As nursing becomes involved in issues such as the right to die, maintaining anencephalic fetuses for use as donors for infants requiring organ transplants, religious controversy about treatment, and other bioethical considerations, professional practice becomes more difficult. Right and wrong are not necessarily clearcut in these instances, and feelings often run high on both sides of the issues.

Most hospitals now have (or are developing) bioethical committees to review such issues and to set policies and procedures to guide staff actions. If you have not already done so, become a member of this group. Patient education could play a vital part in developing factual, nonpartisan presentations of the options available to patients and families faced with life or death decisions. Patient educators can also work with staff educators to keep employees informed of the current status of such issues in the institution and what their roles may be.

Exhibit 12-1 Special Project for Career Ladder Promotion

CAREER LADDER PROJECT

PURPOSE: Develop a preoperative teaching class to be given to all patients having inpatient surgery.

ACTIONS:

1. Meet with nurse clinician group to brainstorm possible content areas.
2. Analyze results and outline tentative behavioral objectives.
3. Feed objectives back to group for approval.
4. Write tentative class outline based on objectives.
5. Take objectives and outline to Patient Education Committee for physician input.
6. Revise objectives and outline.
7. Write class, choosing teaching strategies and composing handouts.
8. Take class content and handouts to Patient Education Committee for approval.
9. Make any necessary revisions.
10. Set up system for tracking patients and getting classes scheduled on a regular basis for all surgical units.
11. Present two-hour seminar to nurse clinicians about program; clinicians will tell staff about program and how to make it accessible to patients.
12. Implement program.
13. Evaluate results of program.
14. Present results to Patient Education Committee and clinician group.
15. Make necessary revisions to program.

METHODS OF EVALUATION:

1. Pretests and post-tests will be used for all patients to test knowledge gain and retention.
2. A randomly selected 20 percent of all patients in the program will be interviewed to get feedback on the preoperative teaching program.
3. Reaction sheets will be collected from all people participating.
4. Staff will be surveyed after three months to obtain their assessment of patient knowledge of surgery and postoperative care and of patient reaction to the class.

Role of the Nurse in Patient Education

Since patient education is viewed as an independent nursing function, expanding this area of practice makes good sense for the profession. Indeed, educating patients could be argued as the true future of nursing. With increasing consumer sophistication, concern for health issues, and demand for information, patient education bids are soon to move out of hospitals and into independent practice. A number of nurses run their own businesses, offering seminars and private teaching sessions to consumers.

One such nurse, a breast-feeding consultant, not only teaches classes on breast-feeding, but also conducts sessions where the client brings her baby and the consultant guides both through the process of breast-feeding. It may take one session or several, but her clients are 100 percent successful at breast-feeding. This nurse grosses more than $60,000 per year.

As another example, Donna Hill-Howes, R.N., M.S., discovered that people like to learn about health issues through the media, a less-threatening, more convenient, and comfortable environment for learning. She now hosts a San Francisco Bay area health talk show called "Your Vital Signs." Ratings and reviews have been extremely favorable, and the show is currently negotiating for syndication in many parts of the country. Ms. Hill-Howes says,

> Interestingly, my research revealed that many diabetics first learned that their disease can cause blindness from programs they saw on television. Today the question is: Why not television—and why not a nurse?[5]

Other independent practitioners offer childbirth classes, diabetes education, general health training in health club settings, or specific teaching topics for several groups of physicians, who contract for their services in teaching patients and families. The possibilities can only expand.

Building Support for Patient Education

Nursing Education Programs. Patient education needs to receive more emphasis in basic nursing programs. In too many instances, lip service is paid to it in class, but precious little patient education actually occurs when the students are in the clinical area. Instructors must set realistic learning objectives for patients and conduct teaching sessions to create role models for the students. Then, as the students develop their own teaching plans, instructors can offer advice and critique the teaching that takes place. Without a conscious effort to stress the importance of patient education to student nurses, nothing effective is likely to happen.

As an example of ineffective student intervention, one nursing student on a bachelor of science program had written a care plan for a patient who was terminally ill. It contained entries taken right out of a textbook: "Assist patient with dying process," "Maintain dignity," "Use comfort measures." For a teaching plan, she wrote, "Assist daughter with anticipatory grieving." The only problem was that no one had told the daughter that her mother was dying, and when the student left the teaching plan in the room and the daughter read it—well, upset is a mild word for what occurred. How could such a thing happen? Very easily, if students are taught to parrot theory rather than shown how to apply theory to real-life situations. This student needed someone to show her how to assess a situation, how to set behavior-specific objectives, and how to approach an unpredictable learning situation with sensitivity and flexibility. Unless instructors in basic preparatory programs emphasize the importance of patient education in professional nursing practice and *show* students how to implement education plans with real patients, our new graduates will suffer under a tremendous handicap—and so, of course, will their patients.

Continuing Support for Patient Educators. Professional patient educators often feel isolated, since many work alone (as far as the job description goes). Maintain interest and enthusiasm for the job through networking with other patient educators. Join some professional organizations such as the American Society for Healthcare Education and Training (ASHET); the Diabetes Teaching Nurses (DTN); the American Association of Diabetic Educators (AADE); or the American Association for Continuity of Care (AACC), a discharge planning group. As you go to meetings and listen to presentations about new methods of patient education, interest in the job rekindles. The most valuable benefit of these meetings, however, comes from interaction with other educators. Exchanging ideas and anecdotes sparks new creativity toward problems that previously seemed hopeless.

Another way to support yourself is through attending continuing education workshops on the subject of patient education. Unfortunately, these can be hard to find. Not many seminars on this topic are currently available. One way around this is to coordinate your own workshop. Put together some interesting speakers on current patient education topics, inviting people from outside your institution as well as your own staff. Charging an attendance fee will help you to recoup your costs.

The final strategy is one that at first glance may seem frightening—writing for publication. Nurses constantly seek new ways of educating patients. Why not share methods that have worked for you through the medium of professional journals? Choose a topic that you have not read about lately; query the editor of a journal that seems most appropriate, and, if you receive a positive answer, write the manuscript and submit it. Not only will you benefit the profession, publishing your ideas will also help you to grow as an educator and as a nursing professional.

FUTURE TRENDS IN PATIENT EDUCATION

Trends in Reimbursement

As has been mentioned before, inpatient education is not separately reimbursable by most third-party payers, being lumped in as part of the general diagnosis-related group (DRG) rate. In one survey of hospitals, costs spent on patient education ranged from 20 to 56 percent of total hospital education costs, averaging 29 percent. Almost all of the costs were for time spent in teaching patients rather than for materials.[6] What can you do to increase cost recovery for your hospital?

Johnson and Grubb recommend developing a plan that identifies and analyzes the DRGs most commonly seen in your hospital that can benefit from patient education programs. The top twenty diagnostic categories probably include over two-thirds of the patients on Medicare DRGs. Patient education for these categories should be explored first. Differentiate among patient education, family education, and community health education so that you can be sure that only the patient education component is included as part of the cost system. Patient education elements that can be proved to improve the speed of recovery of patients or to reduce the cost of care will be more likely to be approved for reimbursement.[7] Diabetic inpatient programs meeting the standards set up in November 1983 by the National Diabetes Advisory Board have been reimbursed by Blue Cross/Blue Shield and Medicare in several states.[8]

A survey indicated that 96 percent of the Blue Cross plans and 90 percent of the Blue Shield plans cover patient education when it is provided as part of treatment. Preventive health education services are covered by 73 percent of the Blue Cross plans and 65 percent of the Blue Shield plans.[9] Gaining reimbursement is not easy, however. Enlist the aid of community hospital associations to make it community practice, and apply as a group.

Develop standardized patient education protocols to make documentation easier. Since outpatient education *is* reimbursable, Breckon recommends careful attention to appropriate billing. For example, if the outpatient visit were for "diabetic follow-up to evaluate injection technique and adherence to diet," it would be more likely to be reimbursed than if it were for "diabetic education."[10]

There are other ways to reduce the costs of patient education and to enable the hospital to increase volume and develop new sources of revenue. Market patient education materials to other institutions. Offer fee-for-service outpatient classes and private sessions. Some patient educators have packaged patient education materials with necessary equipment that is charged separately to the patient (self-care kits such as Hickman catheter kits and ostomy kits).[11]

New Opportunities

New trends in health care demand new approaches to patient education. Mathews identified the significant future opportunities in patient education as:

- Aging consumers and longer life spans will require more chronic illness programs and services for older adults.
- Increased needs for women's services suggest new areas for education, such as coping with menopause, parenting classes, etc.

- Wellness programs will continue to grow in demand—and education is a major component.
- More home care and expansion of educational services will be offered to physicians' offices.[12]

Your own area and institution's specialties can provide more ideas for new programs and services. Keep abreast of the trends in health care through reading and seminars, and be especially aware of what is coming in your own hospital. For example, if an in vitro fertilization program is being developed, talk to the people planning it to explore possible patient education needs. Stay proactive, not reactive. The field of patient education is limited only by your own imagination and energy. In other words, the field that you have chosen is almost unlimited. Enjoy yourself, and bring innovation and creativity to the people who need it most—your patients.

NOTES

1. Patricia Mathews, "Patient and Community Health Education," *Journal Of Healthcare Education And Training* 2, no. 2 (Special Issue 1987): 30.

2. Barbara Gilroth, "Creating Greater Visibility To Strengthen the Hospital's Patient Education Program," *Promoting Health* 8, no. 1 (January–February 1987): 6–7.

3. Alice P. Farmer, "Costs and Benefits of Hospital Education Programs, Part 2," *Journal of Healthcare Education And Training* 3, no. 1 (1988): 18.

4. Gilroth, "Creating Greater Visibility," pp. 7–9.

5. "R.N. Hosts Television Talk Show," *Southern California Nursing News* 1, no. 3 (June 1988): 1.

6. Farmer, "Costs and Benefits of Hospital Education Programs," p. 17.

7. David A. Johnson and Allen Grubb, "Patient Education and DRGs: An Administrative Perspective," *Patient Education Newsletter* 7, no. 3 (June 1984): 6.

8. Mathews, "Patient and Community Health Education," p. 31.

9. Survey Report, *Blue Cross and Blue Shield Plan Support for Health Education* (Chicago: Blue Cross/Blue Shield, 1979), p. 11.

10. Donald J. Breckon, *Hospital Health Education* (Rockville, Md.: Aspen Publishers, Inc., 1982), p. 151.

11. Mathews, "Patient and Community Health Education," p. 31.

12. Ibid., p. 30.

Bibliography

"Communicating with Patients About Medicine." *Patientvision Update* 3, no. 2 (Winter 1988): 5.

"How To Shorten Your Patient's Hospital Stay Safely." *NursingLife* (July–August 1986): 49–52.

"Medicare Study Finds Health Education Benefits." *Patient Education Newsletter* 6, no. 5 (October 1983): 7.

"Medication Patient Education." *Patient Education Newsletter* 5, no. 3 (June 1982): 34.

Policy and Statement: The Hospital's Responsibility for Patient Education Services. Chicago: American Hospital Association, 1982.

"R.N. Hosts Television Talk Show." *Southern California Nursing News* 1, no. 3 (June 1988): 1–3.

Akhtar, Tasleem. "Patient Compliance and the Need To Improve It." *Journal of the Pakistan Medical Association* 36, no. 11 (November 1986): 276–7.

Alfaro, Rosalinda. *Application of the Nursing Process: A Step by Step Guide.* Philadelphia: J.B. Lippincott Co., 1986.

Anderson, Robert M. "The Personal Meaning of Having Diabetes: Implications for Patient Behavior and Education." *Diabetic Medicine* 3 (1986): 85–89.

Ascher, J. Segall, et al. *Systematic Course Design for the Health Care Fields.* New York: John Wiley & Sons, Inc., 1975.

Assal, J. P. "Self-Management of Diabetes: A Therapeutic Success But a Teaching Failure?" *Diabetic Medicine* 2, no. 5 (September 1985): 420–2.

Bailey, June T., and Karen E. Claus. *Decision-Making in Nursing: Tools for Change.* St. Louis: C.V. Mosby Co., 1975.

Bartlett, Edward E. "Consultation Corner." *Patient Education Newsletter* 5, no. 1 (February 1982): 5.

————. "The New Technology: Boon or Boondoggle?" *Patient Education Newsletter* 6, no. 3 (June 1983): 11.

Berg, Melvin. "Patient Education and the Physician-Patient Relationship." *Journal of Family Practice* 24, no. 2 (February 1987): 169–72.

Bergman, A. B., and R. J. Werner. "Failure of Children To Receive Penicillin by Mouth." *New England Journal of Medicine* 268 (1963): 1334–8.

Bertakis, Klea D. "An Application of the Health Belief Model To Patient Education and Compliance: Acute Otitis Media." *Family Medicine* 18, no. 6 (November/December 1986): 347–50.

————. "Educational Impact of a Family Practice Clinic Patient Medical Advisor Booklet." *Family Medicine* 18, no. 4 (July/August 1986): 210–12.

Blaes, Stephen. "Patient Education Protects from Malpractice Claims." *Patient Education Newsletter* 7, no. 6 (December 1984): 8–9.

Blalock, Susan J., Brenda M. DeVellis, and Charlotte Friedberg. "Helping Patients Cope with Arthritis." *Patient Education Newsletter* 7, no. 6 (December 1984): 7–8.

Bluhm, Judy. "Helping Families in Crisis Hold On." *Nursing87* 17, no. 10 (October 1987): 44–46.

Borich, Pam. "A New Outpatient Surgery Patient Teaching Program." *Patient Education Newsletter* 8, no. 4 (August 1985): 4–6.

Boyd, Marilyn. "Patient Education: Whose Territory Is It?" *Patient Education Newsletter* 7, no. 6 (December 1984): 1–2.

————. "A Guide to Writing Effective Patient Education Materials." *Nursing Management* 18, no. 7 (July 1987): 56–57.

Bradshaw, Susan. "Treating Yourself." *Nursing Times* 83, no. 3 (February 11, 1987): 40–41.

Breckon, Donald J. *Hospital Health Education*. Rockville, Md.: Aspen Publishers, Inc., 1982.

Brenner, Lawrence, and Elizabeth Gerken. "Informed Consent: Myths and Risk Management Alternatives." *QRB* 12, no. 12 (December 1986): 420–5.

Broadwell, Martin M. *The Supervisor As Instructor: A Guide for Classroom Training*, 2nd ed. Reading, Mass.: Addison-Wesley Publishing Co., 1970.

Brown, Candace S., Robert G. Wright, and Dale B. Christenson. "Association between Type of Medication Instruction and Patients' Knowledge, Side Effects, and Compliance." *Hospital and Community Psychiatry* 38, no. 1 (January 1987): 55–60.

Brown, Linda, and Sandra Villalaz-Dickson. "How Does Patient Education Interface with Quality Assurance?" *Patient Education Newsletter* 8, no. 6 (December 1985): 3–4.

Brown, Sharon A. "An Assessment of the Knowledge Base of the Insulin-Dependent Diabetic Adult." *Journal of Community Health Nursing* 4, no. 1 (January 1987): 9–19.

Budlong-Springer, Alexis S. "Enhancing Patients' Social Support Systems." *Patient Education Newsletter* 6, no. 6 (December 1983): 5–7.

Bullough, B. "Nurses As Teachers and Support Persons for Breast Cancer Patients." *Cancer Nursing* 4 (1981): 221–5.

Butterfield, Patricia. "Nursing Interventions Aid Patient Transition from Hospital to Home." *Idaho R.N.* 10, no. 2 (March–April 1987): 12–13.

Cahill, Matthew, ed. *Patient Teaching*. Springhouse, Pa.: Nursing87 Books, 1987.

Carpenito, Lynda Juall. *Handbook of Nursing Diagnosis*. Philadelphia: J.B. Lippincott Co., 1985.

Carpenito, Lynda Juall, and T. Audean Duespohl. *A Guide for Effective Clinical Instruction*. Wakefield, Mass.: Nursing Resources, 1981.

Centers for Disease Control. "Impact of Diabetes Outpatient Education Program—Maine." *Morbidity and Mortality Weekly Report* 31 (1982).

Cirincione, Sandra. "Dealing with Diabetes: A Family Affair." *Countdown IX*, no. 2 (Spring 1988): 10–13.

Conway-Rutkowski, Barbara. "The Nurse: Also an Educator, Patient Advocate, and Counselor." *Nursing Clinics of North America* 17, no. 3 (September 1982): 455–66.

Corkadel, Linda, and ReNel McGlashan. "A Practical Approach to Patient Teaching." *Journal of Continuing Education in Nursing* 14, no. 1 (January 1983): 9–15.

Cotsonas, Carolyn E. "Informed Consent in Perspective." *Patient Education Newsletter* 5, no. 2 (April 1982): 13–15.

Curtis, Kathleen A. "Imagery for Skill Improvement." *Clinical Education Outlook* 1, no. 3 (Spring 1988): 2.

Dai, Yu-Tzu, and Marci Catanzaro. "Health Beliefs and Compliance with a Skin Care Regimen." *Rehabilitation Nursing* 12, no. 1 (January–February 1987): 13–16.

Danielson, Richard H., John K. Beasley, and Randall S. Pope. "Diabetes Education Payment: The Michigan Experience." *Patient Education Newsletter* 7, no. 3 (June 1984): 7–8.

Davis, M. S. "Physiologic, Psychological, and Demographic Factors in Patient Compliance with Doctor's Orders." *Medical Care* 6, no. 2 (1968): 115–22.

Day, J. L., et al. "Diabetes Patient Education Workshops." *Diabetic Medicine* 2 (1985): 479–83.

DeBaca, Vicki. "So Many Patients, So Little Time." *R.N.* 50, no. 4 (April 1987): 32–33.

Deckert, T., et al. "Importance of Outpatient Supervision in the Prognosis of Juvenile Diabetes Mellitus: A Cost/Benefit Analysis." *Diabetes Care* 1 (1978): 281–84.

DeHaes, W. F. M. "Patient Education: A Component of Health Education." *Patient Counseling and Health Education* 4, no. 2 (1987): 95–102.

DeWaele, Sharon, Lois Hortsman, Vicki Ligney, and Jan Tardiff. "Continuity in Patient Education." *Patient Education Newsletter* 8, no. 4 (August 1985): 8–9.

DiMatteo, M. Robin, Ron D. Hays, and Louis M. Prince. "Relationship of Physicians' Nonverbal Communication Skill to Patient Satisfaction, Appointment Noncompliance, and Physician Workload." *Health Psychology* 5, no. 6 (1986): 581–94.

Donaldson, Mary Louis. "Instructional Media As a Teaching Strategy." *Nurse Educator* 4, no. 4 (July–August): 18.

Dorsky, Lori Toranto. "Using Dolls To Prepare Children for Surgery." *Patient Education Newsletter* 7, no. 2 (April 1984): 4–5.

Douglass, Laura Mae, and Em Olivia Bevis. *Nursing Leadership in Action.* St. Louis: C.V. Mosby Co., 1974.

Drew, Leslie A., Diane Biordi, and Dee Ann Gillies. "How Discharge Planner and Home Health Nurses View Their Patients." *Nursing Management* 19, no. 4 (April 1988): 66–70.

Dunn, Stewart M. "Reactions to Educational Techniques: Coping Strategies for Diabetes and Learning." *Diabetic Medicine* 3 (1986): 419–29.

Engelhardt, Barbara. "Problem Solving (and Teaching) toward Objectives." *AD Nurse* 2, no. 2 (March/April 1987): 18–19.

Eriksen, Lillian R. "Patient Satisfaction: An Indicator of Nursing Care Quality?" *Nursing Management* 18, no. 7 (July 1987): 31–35.

Faden, R. R., et al. "Disclosure of Information to Patients in Medical Care." *Medical Care* 19, (1981): 718–33.

Falvo, Donna R. *Effective Patient Education.* Rockville, Md.: Aspen Publishers, Inc., 1985.

Farmer, Alice P. "Costs and Benefits of Hospital Education Programs, Part 2." *Journal of Healthcare Education and Training* 3, no. 1 (1988): 17–19.

Feuer, Louis C. "Discharge Planning: *Home* Caregivers Need Your Support, Too." *Nursing Management* 18, no. 4 (April 1987): 58–59.

Fink, D., et al. "The Management Specialist in Effective Pediatric Ambulatory Care." *American Journal of Public Health* 59, no. 3 (1969): 527–33.

Foster, Susan D. "Teaching Patients To Manage Complex, Long-Term Care." *The American Journal of Maternal/Child Nursing* 12, no. 1 (January/February 1987): 57.

————. "Evaluating Patient Learning." *The American Journal of Maternal/Child Nursing* 12, no. 2 (March/April 1987): 131.

————. "Are Commercial Patient Education Materials Right for You?" *The American Journal of Maternal/Child Nursing* 12, no. 4 (July/August 1987): 287.

Freudenberg, Nicholas. "Addressing the Environmental Barriers of Patient Adherence." *Patient Education Newsletter* 7, no. 3 (June 1984): 9–10.

Garity, J. "Learning Styles Basis for Creative Teaching and Learning." *Nurse Educator* 10 (1985): 12–15.

Gentile, M. G. "Dietetic Education and Assessment of Compliance in Patients with Chronic Renal Insufficiency." *Contributions to Nephrology* 55 (1987): 36–45.

Germer, S., et al. "Do Diabetics Remember All They Have Been Taught? A Survey of Knowledge of Insulin-Dependent Diabetics." *Diabetic Medicine* 3 (1986): 343–5.

Gilroth, Barbara. "Creating Greater Visibility To Strengthen the Hospital's Patient Education Program." *Promoting Health* 8, no. 1 (January–February 1987): 6–9.

Glanz, Karen. "Nutrition Education for Risk Factor Reduction." *Patient Education Newsletter* 7, no. 6 (December 1984): 3–5.

Green, L. W., D. M. Levine, and S. Deeds. "Clinical Trials of Health Education for Hypertensive Outpatients: Design and Baseline Data." *Preventive Medicine* 4 (1975): 417.

Greene, Sylvia M. "Removing Health Service Ritual and Increasing Patient Satisfaction." *Perioperative Nursing Quarterly* 3, no. 1 (1987): 17–22.

Harwood, A., ed. *Ethnicity and Medical Care.* Cambridge, Mass.: Harvard University Press, 1981.

Hayter, Jean. "How Good Is the Lecture As a Teaching Method?" *Nursing Outlook* 27, no. 4 (April 1979): 274.

Heins, Joan M., Judith Wylie-Rosett, and Susan Green Davis. "The New Look in Diabetic Diets." *American Journal of Nursing* 87, no. 2 (February 1987): 196–8.

Higgins, Millicent. "Learning Style Assessment: A New Patient Teaching Tool?" *Journal of Nursing Staff Development* 4, no. 1 (Winter 1988): 14–18.

Hinthome, Rita. "Teaching Nurses How To Teach Patients." *Nursing Management* 14, no. 9 (September 1983): 30–33.

Holland, Stevie. "Teaching Patients and Clients." *Nursing Times* 83, no. 3 (January 23, 1987): 59–62.

Holpp, Lawrence. "Technical Training for Nontechnical Learners." *Training and Development Journal* 41, no. 10 (October 1987): 54–57.

Holvey, Sherman M. "The Diabetes Education Team in the Management of Non-Insulin-Dependent Diabetes Mellitus." *Metabolism* 36, no. 2, suppl. 1 (February 1987): 9–11.

Hughes, Barbara. "Diabetes Management: The Time Is Right for Tight Glucose Control." *Nursing87* 17, no. 5 (May 1987): 63–64.

Jeffrey, R. W., et al. "Weight and Sodium Reduction for the Prevention of Hypertension: A Comparison of Group Treatment and Individual Counseling." *American Journal of Public Health* 73 (1983): 691–93.

Johnson, David A., and Allen Grubb. "Patient Education and DRGs: An Administrative Perspective." *Patient Education Newsletter* 7, no. 3 (June 1984): 5–6.

Johnson, Larry, and Mark A. Hahn. "Patient Education Programming for Psychiatric Patients." *Patient Education Newsletter* 7, no. 4 (August 1984): 8–9.

Karam, Sister Judith Ann, Steven M. Sundre, and George L. Smith. "A Cost/Benefit Analysis of Patient Education." *Hospital & Health Services Administration* 31, no. 4 (July/August 1986): 82–90.

Kaufman, Roger, and Susan Thomas. *Evaluation without Fear.* New York: New Viewpoints, A Division of Franklin Watts, 1980.

Kemp, Jerrold E. *Instructional Design.* Belmont, Calif.: Lear Siegler/Fearon Publishers, 1971.

Kempe, Alice R. "Patient Education for the Ambulatory Surgery Patient." *Association of Operating Room Nurses Journal* 45, no. 2 (February 1987): 500–507.

Kendall, Sally. "Helping People To Stop Smoking." *Professional Nurse* 1, no. 5 (February 1986): 120–23.

Kennett, Alison. "Informed Consent: A Patient's Right?" *Professional Nurse* 2, no. 3 (December 1986): 75–77.

Kilo, Charles. *Educating the Diabetic Patient*. New York: Science & Medicine Publishing, 1982.

Kirscht, J. P., and I. M. Rosenstock. "Patient Adherence to Antihypertensive Medical Regimens." *Journal of Community Health* 3 (1973): 115–24.

Knight, P. V., and C. M. Kesson. "Educating the Elderly Diabetic." *Diabetic Medicine* 3, no. 2 (March 1986): 170–73.

Kolb, David A. *Learning Style Inventory*. Boston: McBer and Co., 1976.

Kramer, Marlene, and Claudia Schmalenberg. "The First Job . . . A Proving Ground." *Journal of Nursing Administration* 7, no. 1 (January 1977): 12–17.

Kriewall, Beth, and Kathryn Trier. "Consultation Corner." *Patient Education Newsletter* 7, no. 1 (February 1984): 8.

Kulik, James A., and Heike I. M. Mahler. "Health Status, Perceptions of Risk, and Prevention Interest for Health and Nonhealth Problems." *Health Psychology* 6, no. 1 (1987): 15–27.

Logue, Jacquelyne H. "Patient Education Challenges in Home Care." *Patient Education Newsletter* 7, no. 5 (October 1984): 3–4.

Lucey, David, and Elspeth Wing. "A Clinic Based Educational Programme for Children with Diabetes." *Diabetic Medicine* 2, no. 4 (July 1985): 292–5.

Mager, Robert F. *Preparing Instructional Objectives*, 2nd ed. Belmont, Calif.: Fearon Publishers, 1975.

Mambert, W. A. *Effective Presentations*. New York: John Wiley & Sons, Inc., 1976.

Mathews, Patricia. "Patient and Community Health Education." *Journal of Healthcare Education and Training* 2, no. 2, special issue 1987: 30–33.

Mazzuca, Steven A. "Diabetes Care and Education: A Creative Approach." *Patient Education Newsletter* 6, no. 6 (December 1983): 1–3.

McCormick, Rose-Marie Duda, and Tamar Gilson-Parkevich. *Patient and Family Education*. New York: John Wiley & Sons, Inc., 1979.

McKenzie, Leon. "The Supervisor As Learner: The Study Process." *Health Care Supervisor* 5, no. 4 (July 1987): 43–53.

Melamed, Barbara G. "Individualizing Preparation for Medical Procedures." *Patient Education Newsletter* 7, no. 3 (April 1984): 5–6.

Merrill, C. R., and A. M. Knox. "Patient Information Leaflets: What Effect?" *Radiography* 52, no. 604 (July/August 1986): 209.

Mezzanotte, E. Jane. "A Checklist for Better Discharge Planning." *Nursing87* 17, no. 10 (October 1987): 55.

Minkler, Meredith. "Social Support and Health: Programmatic Implications." *Patient Education Newsletter* 5, no. 3 (June 1982): 32–33.

Moughton, Mona. "The Patient: A Partner in the Health Care Process." *Nursing Clinics of North America* 17, no. 3 (September 1982): 467–79.

Narrow, Barbara W. *Patient Teaching in Nursing Practice*. New York: John Wiley & Sons, Inc., 1979.

Newstrom, John W. "Employee Training and Development." *Encyclopedia of Professional Manage-*

ment. New York: McGraw-Hill Book Co., 1978.

Nihil, Joy. "Community Education Program Helps Clients Help Themselves." *Nursing and Health Care* 8, no. 2 (February 1987): 113–15.

O'Connor, Andrea B. *Nursing: Patient Education*. New York: American Journal of Nursing Co., 1979.

Omdahl, Diane J. "Preventing Home Care Denials." *American Journal of Nursing* 87, no. 8 (August 1987): 1031–3.

Orth, James E., et al. "Patient Exposition and Provider Explanation in Routine Interviews and Hypertensive Patients' Blood Pressure Control." *Health Psychology* 6, no. 1 (1987): 29–42.

Osinski, Elsie. "Developing Patient Outcomes As a Quality Measure of Nursing Care." *Nursing Management* 18, no. 10 (October 1987): 28–29.

Phairas, Debra L., and Judith N. Peeples. "Advice on Informed Consent." *Patientvision Update* 3, no. 2 (Winter 1988): 8–9.

Pichert, J. W. *Effective Patient Teaching*. Pitman, N.J.: American Association of Diabetes Educators Continuing Education Self-Study Program (Module 3): 1984.

Pichert, J. W., S. L. Hanson, and C. A. Pechmann. "Modifying Dietitians' Use of Patient Time." *Diabetes Education* 10 (1984): 43.

Powers, Margaret A. *Handbook of Diabetes Nutritional Management*. Rockville, Md.: Aspen Publishers, Inc., 1987.

Pridham, Karen F., Freddi Adelson, and Marc F. Hansen. "Helping Children Deal with Procedures in a Clinic Setting: A Developmental Approach." *Journal of Pediatric Nursing* 2, no. 1 (February 1987): 13–22.

Pritchett, Sue. "Effectiveness of Educational Methods." *Patient Education Newsletter* 5, no. 5 (October 1982): 51–52.

Rankin, Jane A., and Mary B. Harris. "Using Self-Control Instructions To Change Oral Hygiene Habits." *New Mexico Dentistry Journal* 38, no. 1 (January 1987): 7–15.

Redman, Barbara Klug. *Issues and Concepts in Patient Care*. New York: Appleton-Century-Crofts, 1981.

———. *The Process of Patient Education*, 5th ed. St. Louis: C.V. Mosby Co., 1984.

Regner, Michael J., Freya Hermann, and L. Douglas Ried. "Effectiveness of a Printed Leaflet for Enabling Patients To Use Digoxin Side-Effect Information." *Drug Intelligence and Clinical Pharmacy* 21 (February 1987): 200–204.

Rendon, Diane C., Karl Davis, Evelynn C. Gioiella, and Mary Jane Tranzillo. "The Right To Know, The Right To Be Taught." *Journal of Gerontological Nursing* 12, no. 12 (December 1986): 33–38.

Rezler, Agnes G., and Victor Rezmovic. "The Learning Preference Inventory." *Journal of Allied Health* 10, no. 2 (February 1981): 28.

Riessman, F., et al., eds. *Mental Health of the Poor*. New York: Macmillan Publishing Co., 1961.

Rimer, Barbara. "Informed Consent Education: The Role for Patient Education." *Patient Education Newsletter* 8, no. 3 (June 1985): 1–3.

Rimer, Barbara, W. Jones, and Barbara Blumberg. "Challenges and Prospects in Cancer Patient Education." *Patient Education Newsletter* 6, no. 1 (February 1983): 1–3.

Ritter, Marilyn K. "Assessing Educational Needs of Ostomy Patients." *Ostomy/Wound Management* 16, (Fall 1987): 14–15.

Roberts, Cynthia. "Identifying the Real Patient Problems." *Nursing Clinics of North America* 17, no. 3 (September 1982): 481–90.

Robinson, Gary L., Alan D. Gilbertson, and Lawrence Litwack. "The Effects of a Psychiatric Patient

Education to Medication Program on Post-Discharge Compliance." *Psychiatric Quarterly* 58, no. 2 (Summer 1986–1987): 113–8.

Ross, Helen S. "Group Discussion Methods." *Patient Education Newsletter* 5, no. 1 (February 1982): 7–8.

Rothrock, Jane C. "Patient Education: A Cooperative Venture." *Perioperative Nursing Quarterly* 3, no. 1 (1987): 45–52.

Rowlands, Shirley. "Difficulties Facing the Nurse Educator." *National Association of Theatre News* 24, no. 2 (February 1987): 16–18.

Runkle, Cecilia. "Involving Patients in Decision-Making." *Patient Education Newsletter* 7, no. 4 (August 1984): 6–7.

Russell, Jan. "The Gray Zone." *Journal of Healthcare Education and Training* 3, no. 1 (1988): 7–8.

Rykwalder, Annette. "Productivity Management: An Essential Tool." *Patient Education Newsletter* 8, no. 4 (August 1985): 1–2.

Sana, Josephine M., and Richard D. Judge, eds. *Physical Appraisal Methods in Nursing Practice.* Boston: Little, Brown & Co., 1975.

Schroeder, Barbara. "Creating an Interesting Display." Resource sheet prepared for the American Hospital Association/American Society for Healthcare Education and Training Patient Education Liaison Program, 1987.

Segall, Ascher J., et al. *Systematic Course Design for the Health Care Fields.* New York: John Wiley & Sons, Inc., 1975.

Shaffer, Stuart M., Karen L. Indorato, and Janet A. Deneselya. *Teaching in Schools of Nursing.* St. Louis: C.V. Mosby Co., 1972.

Smith, C. J., M. J. Abrahmson, P. J. Henshilwood, and F. Bonnici. "The Effect of an Intensive Education Programme on the Glycaemic Control of Type I Diabetic Patients." *South African Medical Journal* 7 (February 7, 1987): 164–6.

Smith, Carol E. "Patient Teaching: It's the Law." *Nursing87* 17, no. 7 (July 1987): 67–68.

Steckel, Susan Boehm. "Predicting, Measuring, Implementing, and Following up on Patient Compliance." *Nursing Clinics of North America* 17, no. 3 (September 1982): 491–8.

Stine, Curtis C., and John P. Nagle. "Designing Patient Education in an Office Practice." *Patient Education Newsletter* 6, no. 5 (October 1983): 1–3.

Survey Report, *Blue Cross and Blue Shield Plan Support for Health Education.* Chicago: Blue Cross/Blue Shield, 1979.

Taggart, Virginia S., et al. "Adapting a Self Management Education Program for Asthma for Use in an Outpatient Clinic." *Annals of Allergy* 58, no. 3 (March 1987): 173–8.

Talkington, T. "Maximizing Patient Compliance by Shaping Attitudes of Self-Directed Health Care." *Journal of Family Practice* 6, no. 3 (1978): 591–5.

Tang, John C., et al. "Interactive Development and Evaluation of an Independently Accessible Video Education System for Rehabilitation." *Journal of the American Paraplegia Society* 8, no. 2 (April 1985): 38–41.

Taylor, Cynthia M., and Sheila S. Cress. *Nursing Diagnosis Cards.* Springhouse, Pa.: Nursing87, Springhouse Corporation, 1987.

Taylor, Pat. "Patient Teaching: Keys to More Success More Often." *Nursing Life* (November/December 1982): 25–30.

Taylor, Rosemarie Angela. "Making the Most of Your Time for Patient Teaching." *RN* (December 1987): 20–21.

Tobin, Helen M., Pat S. Yoder-Wise, and Peggy K. Hull. *The Process of Staff Development: Compo-*

nents for Change, 3rd ed. St. Louis: C.V. Mosby Co., 1979.

Vinicor, Frank, et al. "Diabeds: A Randomized Trial of the Effects of Physician and/or Patient Education on Diabetes Patient Outcomes." *Journal of Chronic Diseases* 40, no. 4 (1987): 345–56.

Walker, Annette. "Teaching the Illiterate Patient." *Journal of Enterostomal Therapy* 14, no. 2 (March–April 1987): 83–85.

Walker, Lou Ann. "What Comforts AIDS Families." *New York Times Magazine* (June 21, 1987): 18–63.

Walton, Barbara G. "Assessing the Benefits of Patient Education." *Patient Education Newsletter* 8, no. 4 (August 1985): 6–8.

Watts, F. N. "Behavioral Aspects of the Management of Diabetes Mellitus: Education, Self-Care, and Metabolic Control." *Behavior, Research, and Therapy* 18 (1980): 171–80.

Weisiger, Kathe E. "Making Your Patient Safe at Home." *RN* (February 1987): 59–60.

Wilson, Willetta, and Clara Pratt. "The Impact of Diabetes Education and Peer Support upon Weight and Glycemic Control of Elderly Persons with Noninsulin Dependent Diabetes Mellitus." *American Journal of Public Health* 77, no. 5 (May 1987): 634–5.

Woldrum, Karyl M., ed. *Patient Education: Tools for Practice.* Rockville, Md.: Aspen Publishers, Inc., 1985.

Wollert, W. M. "Achievement through Clinical Practice—A Practical Approach to Patient Care." *Exploring Progress in Nursing Practice.* New York: American Nurses' Association, 1965.

Young, Barbara. "Proposed Competencies for Patient Education Coordinators." *Patient Education Newsletter* 7, no. 1 (February 1984): 1–2.

Zander, K. "Second Generation Primary Nursing: A New Agenda." *Journal of Nursing Administration* (March 1985): 18–24.

Zufall, Dorothy L. "Testing: A Creative Experience for Learners and Educators." *Cross-Reference* 7, no. 2 (March–April 1977): 8.

Index

Page numbers in italics indicate figures and exhibits; those followed by "t" indicate tables.

About the Author

ANN HAGGARD, R.N., M.S., PH.D., is currently the coordinator of staff and patient education at Huntington Memorial Hospital in Pasadena, California. She was recently awarded a certificate of appreciation for her contributions to both the local and national American Society for Healthcare Education and Training (ASHET). She has served as secretary, program chair, nominating committee chair, and newsletter editor for the Southern California chapter. Dr. Haggard's publications concern education, staff development, and hospital management. She is the author of *Hospital Orientation Handbook* for Aspen Publishers, Inc. "Disaster!," a videotape that she wrote, acted in, and co-produced, recently won the International Television Association's Golden Angel Award and was the winning entry in the ASHET national audiovisual competition. Dr. Haggard has been a nursing instructor, inservice director, head nurse, and a staff nurse. Her educational background includes degrees from the Michael Reese Hospital and Medical Center School of Nursing (R.N.), Pittsburg State University (B.S.N.), California State University-Los Angeles (M.S.), and Columbia Pacific University (Ph.D.). She is a member of the Phi Kappa Phi Honor Society.